AQA English Language and Literature B

AS

Exclusively endorsed by AQA

Ron Norman

Marian Picton

Series editor
Chris Purple

 Nelson Thornes

Published in 2008 by:
Nelson Thornes Ltd
Delta Place
27 Bath Road
CHELTENHAM
GL53 7TH
United Kingdom

08 09 10 11 12 / 10 9 8 7 6 5 4 3 2

A catalogue record for this book is available from the British Library

ISBN 978 0 7487 9961 9

Cover photograph/illustration: Alamy/Photoalto

Page make-up by Pantek Arts Ltd, Maidstone

Printed and bound in Slovenia by Korotan-Ljubljana Ltd

Acknowledgements

The authors and publishers wish to thank the following for permission to use copyright material:

Carcanet Press Limited for the extract from *Welcome to the Caves of Arta* in *Complete Poems in One Volume* by Robert Graves (2000); Crown copyright © material is reproduced under Class Licence No. CO1 W 0000195 with the permission of the Controller of HMSO and the Queen's Printer for Scotland; David Higham Associates Limited on behalf of the estate of the author for the extract from *The BFG* by Roald Dahl. Jonathan Cape Ltd and Penguin Books Ltd (1982); Methuen Publishing Ltd for the extract from the 'Travel Agents sketch' in *Monty Python's Flying Circus: Just the Words Volume 1* by Cleese, Gilliam, Jones, Idle, Palin and Chapman (1999). Copyright © Python Productions 1989; Oxford University Press for definition of 'Travel' in the *Oxford English Dictionary*, eds J. Simpson & E. Weiner (1989); Penguin Books Ltd for extracts from *In Cold Blood* by Truman Capote (1967, 2000). Copyright © Truman Capote 1965; Jean Rhys, *Wide Sargasso Sea* (1968). Copyright © Jean Rhys 1966; Raymond Chandler Limited, a Chorion group company, for the extract from *The Big Sleep* Raymond Chandler. Copyright © 1939 Raymond Chandler Ltd, A Chorion Company; Rocky Mountaineer Vacations for the extract from its promotional DVD; Tripadvisor.com for the extract from a review on its website. Copyright © 2008, TripAdvisor, LLC.

Every effort has been made to contact the copyright holders and we apologise if any have been overlooked. Should copyright have been unwittingly infringed in this book, the owners should contact the publishers, who will make corrections at reprint.

Contents

AQA introduction

Nelson Thornes and AQA

Nelson Thornes has worked in collaboration with AQA to ensure that this book offers you the best support for your AS or A Level course and helps you to prepare for your exams. The partnership means that you can be confident that the range of learning, teaching and assessment practice materials has been checked by the senior examining team at AQA before formal approval, and is closely matched to the requirements of your specification.

Blended learning

Printed and electronic resources are blended: this means that links between topics and activities between the book and the electronic resources help you to work in the way that best suits you and enable extra support to be provided online.

Electronic resources are available in a simple-to-use online platform called Nelson Thornes learning space. If your school or college has a licence to use the service, you will be given a password through which you can access the materials through any internet connection.

Icons in this book indicate where there is material online related to that topic. The following icons are used:

🔮 Learning activity

These resources include a variety of interactive and non-interactive activities to support your learning.

✔️ Progress tracking

These resources enable you to analyse and understand examination questions (On your marks …).

🔎 Research support

These resources include WebQuests, in which you are assigned a task and provided with a range of web links to use as source material for research.

🔖 Study skills

These resources support you in developing a skill that is key for your course, for example planning essays.

🔍 Analysis tool

These resources help you to analyse key texts and images by providing questions and prompts to focus your response.

When you see an icon, go to Nelson Thornes learning space at **www.nelsonthornes.com/aqagce**, enter your access details and select your course. The materials are arranged in the same order as the topics in the book, so you can easily find the resources you need.

How to use this book

This book covers the specification for your course and is arranged in a sequence approved by AQA. The introduction to the book explains what will be required of you as an English Language and Literature student. The book is divided into two units and each unit into two sections. Each section will prepare you for a certain type of question in your examination.

Unit 1 Section A introduces you to the study of language and literature by taking you through many of the texts in the AQA English Language and Literature B *Anthology for Unit 1: 'Travel, Transport and Locomotion'*. Unit 1 Section B gives detailed guidance on responding to questions on the Anthology texts and practical advice on preparing for the unseen text question. Unit 2 focuses on the coursework assignment. Unit 2 Section A explores thematic links and stylistic differences between the paired set texts, focusing on preparing you for writing your analytical coursework piece (Part A). Unit 2 Section B provides additional guidance on your creative writing piece (Part B).

Definitions of all key terms and any words that appear in bold can be found in the glossary at the back of this book.

The features in this book include:

Learning objectives

At the beginning of each unit you will find a list of learning objectives that contain targets linked to the requirements of the specification.

Key terms

Terms that you will need to be able to define and understand. These terms are coloured blue in the textbook and their definitions also appear in the glossary at the end of this book.

Research point

Suggestions for further research to enhance your studies and develop the kind of thinking that will help you achieve the highest grades in your English Language and Literature B course.

Links

Links to other areas in the textbook, or in your experience from GCSE, which are relevant to what you are reading.

Further reading

Links to further sources of information, including websites and other publications.

Think about it

Short activities that encourage reflection.

Background information

In Unit 1, information that will inform your study of a particular Anthology text.

Practical activity

Activities to develop skills, knowledge and understanding that will prepare you for assessment in English Language and Literature B.

Critical response activity

Activities that focus on a specific extract to develop skills relevant to your assessment in the examination.

AQA Examiner's tip

Hints from AQA examiners to help you with your study and to prepare you for your exam and coursework.

Commentary

Examples of answers you might give to the activities. These are designed to help you to understand what type of response the examiner is looking for, not to tell you the answer. There are many equally valid responses, so you will find this book most helpful if you try the activity yourself first and then look at the commentary to read another opinion. Not all activities have a commentary.

AQA examination questions are reproduced by permission of the Assessment and Qualifications Alliance.

Web links for this book

Because Nelson Thornes is not responsible for third-party content online, there may be some changes to this material that are beyond our control. In order for us to ensure that the links referred to are as up-to-date and stable as possible, please let us know at **webadmin@nelsonthornes.com** if you find a link that doesn't work and we will do our best to redirect these, or to list an alternative site.

Introduction to this book

Integrated study of language and literature

The books in this series are designed to support you in your AS and A2 English Language and Literature studies. What is special about this subject is that it brings together aspects of two other kinds of A Level English course – the separate English Literature and English Language specifications – and there are real advantages in continuing your studies of English Language and Literature in an integrated course of this sort.

English at every level up to GCSE requires both language and literature to be studied as essential parts of the course. How can you study literature properly without being keenly interested in the medium of that literature – the ways in which words, sentences, paragraphs and chapters interrelate to create texts of various kinds? These texts may be novels, short stories, plays, documentary scripts, poems and non-fiction texts of a whole range of types and forms.

Being inquisitive about language in all of its forms and habitats is probably the most important quality that you can bring to your studies. We are immersed in language – it is our medium of communication with other people, it is the medium of entertainment (radio, television, comedy clubs, etc.) and a medium of instruction and information (how to … books, labels on medicines). More than that, my language and your language form essential parts of our identities, our individual personalities.

If you go on to study English at university, you will also encounter a subject which has largely abandoned sharp distinctions between 'literature' and 'language' study as unhelpful oversimplifications. You will inevitably be looking at how writers use language when you study a work of literature, and your knowledge about language and how it is used can help you to appreciate and understand how writers and speakers, readers and listeners can be creative and responsive in their experiences of language.

It is important not to think of A Level English Language and Literature as a mix-and-match course in which you 'do language' in one section of a unit and 'do literature' in another section. The point is that language study and literature study are integrated and you need to think about how your interest in language can extend and enhance your appreciation of literary texts. You also need to think about literary texts as examples of language being used in ways that repay close scrutiny, analysis and reflection. There are four main skills you need to develop during your AS and A2 course:

- You need to show that you are capable of reading texts closely and thoughtfully and writing about those texts in ways that show intelligent engagement and control.
- You need to show that you understand the characteristics of various kinds of spoken language, ranging from spontaneous exchanges between friends or strangers to carefully prepared speeches that are designed to persuade large numbers of people in live events or via television and radio.
- You need to show that you are capable of producing writing that is appropriate to the purpose and audience specified in the task, showing conscious control of your choices of vocabulary, grammar and structure.

Think about it

'Language most shows a man: speak that I may see thee.' *Ben Jonson*

- What do you think Jonson meant?
- Do you form an impression of a person from the way he speaks?
- Did Jonson intend his comment to apply to women, do you think? If so, why did he not refer to women as well as men?
- Does Jonson's comment also apply to the way men and women write?

You need to show that you are capable of writing in a focused and analytical way about your own writing – the processes you apply, the choices you make and the evaluation of whether the text works as well as you intended.

All of these activities build directly on the skills you have developed during your GCSE course and in your earlier secondary years, as well as in your primary school and during the pre-school years when you learned language skills by imitating adults and children with whom you grew up. These are skills that many of us continue to develop as the range of our experiences as readers, writers, speakers and listeners expands.

The units

This course focuses on a number of literary texts and on particular language topics. Here is a preview of each of the four units that make up the AS and A2 course.

Unit 1 (ELLB1): Introduction to language and literature study
Examination: 1 hour and 30 minutes

For this unit you will study an Anthology of thematically linked spoken and written texts. The Anthology covers the three main literary genres of prose fiction, poetry and drama as well as a range of non-literary texts. The theme for the first Anthology (covering examinations in 2009, 2010 and 2011 only) is travel, transport and locomotion. You will answer two questions, the first on an unseen text (or texts) which is thematically linked to the Anthology. The second question is set on the texts studied in the Anthology and will require you to comment on writers/speakers' uses of language and their attitudes towards a specified theme. This is an **open book examination**.

Unit 2 (ELLB2): Themes in language and literature
Coursework

The aim of this unit is develop your reading and writing skills through the study of one pair of texts, selected from the six pairs available. Assessment is by a two-part coursework:

- Part A requires you to apply principles of literary and linguistic study to your chosen texts in order to explore the theme specified annually by AQA for each pair of texts(1,200 to 1,500 words).

- Part B requires you to demonstrate your understanding of one or both of your chosen texts by producing a piece of creative writing which extends and enhances the thematic discussion you completed in Part A (500 to 800 words).

Units 1 and 2 comprise the first year or AS part of the course:

Unit 3 (ELLB3): Talk in life and literature and Unit 4
Examination: 2 hours

The emphasis in this unit is on the ways meanings are constructed and conveyed in spoken language. You are required to study one play from a choice of four set plays, including at least one by Shakespeare. You will also be required to apply your literary and linguistic understanding to the study of a variety of transcripts of real-life spoken situations. This is a **closed book examination**.

Unit 4 (ELLB4): Text transformation
Coursework

This unit requires you to choose two literary works from a selection of prescribed authors and use them as the basis for the creation of a new

Think about it

Think about how much of your ability in the subject we call English is derived from your experiences in school and how much is derived from ordinary everyday contacts within your network of friends and family.

For example, if you focus on spoken language for the moment, have you considered how you acquired your accent? Have you ever consciously modified the way you speak or been told to by someone else? If so, what does this suggest about the range of attitudes to spoken language?

Key terms

Open book examination: an examination in which you are allowed to take unmarked copies of the books you have studied into the examination room and refer to them if you wish as you write your answers.

Closed book examination: an examination in which you are not allowed to take copies of the books you have studied into the examination room.

text or texts. The new text or texts must be of a different genre from the original and must be between 1,500 and 2,500 words. You also need to write a commentary or commentaries (1,000 to 2,000 words) in which you reflect on the transformation task in order to demonstrate understanding of the creative process.

Units 3 and 4 comprise the second year of the A Level course.

Preparation

How should you prepare for approaching your studies in this way? The essential points are that you need to:

- approach your reading and writing in an integrated way, building on both linguistic and literary understanding and methods
- develop your creativity and independence as you encounter both spoken and written language
- think about texts and the relationships between texts, which also requires that you think about the social, cultural and historical contexts of these texts
- develop independent ways of working so that your individual skills as a producer of spoken and written language are extended, and you also become increasingly thoughtful and responsive in your judgements and evaluations of the language you encounter as reader and as listener.

Assessment Objectives

You also need to be clear about the Assessment Objectives (AOs) that underpin all of your studies within this subject. Although the term Assessment Objective may sound a little remote and forbidding, you do need to understand their importance in order to study effectively and give yourself the best possible chance of achieving high grades. The AOs are set by the Qualifications and Curriculum Authority (QCA), the agency responsible for overseeing the examination system, and they apply to all specifications in this subject (Table 1).

Table 1 *Assessment Objectives*

Assessment Objectives	Questions to ask yourself
AO1 Select and apply relevant concepts and approaches from integrated linguistic and literary study, using appropriate terminology and accurate, coherent written expression	Can I write accurately and coherently about a range of texts of various sorts, using specialist linguistic and literary terms and concepts that will help me to be clear and precise?
AO2 Demonstrate detailed critical understanding in analysing the ways in which structure, form and language shape meanings in a range of spoken and written texts	Can I discuss and write about structure, form and language of spoken and written texts in ways that reveal my critical and analytical understanding?
AO3 Use integrated approaches to explore relationships between texts, analysing the significance of contextual factors in their production and reception	Can I use my linguistic and literary understanding to interpret and evaluate texts and to compare different texts and their social, cultural and historical contexts?
AO4 Demonstrate expertise and creativity in using language appropriately for a variety of purposes and audiences, drawing on insights from literary and linguistic studies	Can I use my linguistic and literary understanding to produce written and spoken language appropriately to communicate effectively with a range of audiences and for a range of purposes?

You will have noticed that running through the questions in Table 1 is an insistence on the need to apply your knowledge and understanding of both language and literature, and this is the key to success on this course of study.

How to read

In 2007 John Sutherland, a professor of English, published *How to Read a Novel*, subtitled 'A User's Guide'. This book, which is accessible and well worth reading, raises many issues relevant to your studies at AS and A2 Level in its 28 short chapters. Sutherland shows us the importance of developing autonomy as a reader – that is, approaching our reading thoughtfully and evaluating what we encounter for ourselves, and not uncritically accepting the opinions of others. In his final chapter, for example, Sutherland explains why, for him, Thackeray's *Vanity Fair* is one of the greatest English novels. He also quotes the philosopher Alain de Botton, who describes the book as 'the most overrated ever'. There could hardly be a sharper contrast between their opinions, yet each man is capable of developing a cogent and persuasive case in support of his judgement. You as a reader need to work towards developing your critical and thinking skills so that you can form judgements, advance them and defend them in discussion and writing. It is also important to take your time and hold back from making judgements about texts that you might find unusual or difficult to get to grips with. As far as your examination texts are concerned, you need to persevere especially with works that you find difficult on a first reading, and you need to be receptive to a range of critical and explanatory comment from your teachers, books or web sources. If you eventually judge a book to be flawed in some way and you can establish a clearly argued and well supported case, you will be demonstrating exactly the kinds of skills and understanding that will entitle you to high marks in the examinations or in your coursework. Look again at AO3 and the corresponding third question in Table 1.

Before you begin to think in detail about how to read a novel (or a play, poem or non-fiction text), you need to ask an even more fundamental question: Why am I reading this book? More specifically, what exactly is my purpose as a reader? At different times in your reading lives you will doubtless have a wide range of justifications or reasons for reading. Because you are following a course in English Language and Literature, it is a safe bet that you enjoy reading as a leisure activity and you value the contacts you have via the printed page with the thoughts, ideas, stories and experiences of others.

Of the myriad possible answers to the question 'Why am I reading this book?', perhaps the most likely is that you derive some kind of pleasure or satisfaction from doing so. However, for the reading you do as part of the English Language and Literature course, you will almost certainly have an additional reason, a pragmatic or utilitarian one; to achieve the highest possible grades as a passport to a university place or a career.

Different kinds of reading can fit into three main categories:

- *Reading the lines:* reading for surface meanings. Much of our day-to-day reading takes place at this level: skimming a newspaper for details of what is on television, checking how long the ready meal needs in the microwave or reading a gossip column in a magazine, for example.
- *Reading between the lines:* this requires the reader to be alert to what a text hints at or implies, as well as what is stated explicitly. This is the kind of careful 'reading in low gear' that you must engage

Think about it

Think about the different types of reading in relation to the following quotations about how we read and what the effects of reading can be.

'Some books are to be tasted, others to be swallowed, and some few are to be chewed and digested.' *Francis Bacon (1561–1626)*

'A conventional good read is usually a bad read, a relaxing bath in what we know already. A true good read is surely an act of innovative creation in which we, the readers, become conspirators.' *Malcolm Bradbury (b. 1932)*

'Reading a book is like re-writing it for yourself … You bring to a novel, anything you read, all your experience of the world. You bring your history and you read it in your own terms.' *Angela Carter (1940–92)*

'There is creative reading as well as creative writing.' *Ralph Waldo Emerson (1803–82)*

'Books give not wisdom where none was before. But where some is, there reading makes it more.' *John Harington (1561–1612)*

'What is reading, but silent conversation.' *Walter Savage Landor (1775–1864)*

in as you study your examination texts; they have been selected for study because they offer richness and complexity of various sorts. They are not so much puzzles to be solved as creations of the writers' imaginations and they offer language and ideas which you, as a reader, need to interpret and enjoy on a number of levels, including the intellectual and the imaginative. You cannot study them adequately if you simply skim-read them and students who do not apply their skills of inference, evaluation and judgement will not be working in the ways necessary for success at AS, let alone A2, level.

- *Reading beyond the lines:* this refers to the ability of readers to extend their thinking so that their understanding of a particular book is related to their experience of life, their knowledge of other books, their attitudes to moral issues, their judgements about artistic values – indeed, the whole of a reader's awareness of his or her world. Some books can affect us so much that we are forced to take stock of what we really believe and what we really feel; reading beyond the lines enables us to develop as individuals. We engage so closely with a book that we allow it to expand our awareness, our understanding, our values: it can help to make us, in some small way, a different person after we have read the book than we were before.

Developing your skills

How can you best develop the skills and understanding necessary for success in your English Language and Literature B course? The obvious answer to that question is, of course, to study your set texts and language topics carefully, but that on its own is not enough. You also need to develop your ability to talk and write about books effectively, and that takes practice and a willingness to learn from others.

An excellent starting point is to listen to or watch radio or television programmes about books and reading. Here are some suggestions of programmes that will widen your knowledge:

- *Bookclub* (Radio 4) brings a small panel of readers face to face with a writer to discuss one of his or her books. It is available in the BBC Radio website using the 'Listen Again' feature and gives an excellent insight into different readers' responses to the novel and the writer's approaches to writing.

- *A Good Read* (Radio 4) involves discussion between three readers of a chosen book. Sometimes they agree about the merits of a particular book, but often they disagree. Listening to a discussion in which three intelligent readers express different views about the same book conveys a powerful message: what matters most is your personal response to books and your ability to explain and, where necessary, defend your position.

- The Richard and Judy Book Club has been an annual feature of their Channel 4 programme. As of 2008, Richard and Judy will feature on the pay-TV channel UKTV, along with their book club feature, so keep your eyes out for them. There is also a useful Richard and Judy Book Club website that includes reviews and other features on books and authors.

- *World Book Club* and *The Word* on the BBC Radio World Service – programmes can be listened to again via the website.

- *Emagazine* is a subscription magazine and website aimed specifically at all English A Level students with articles on a wide variety of authors and topics.

Try reading book reviews in the Saturday editions of newspapers such as the *Guardian*, the *Independent*, *The Times* and the *Daily Telegraph* and their Sunday editions. These reviews will help to familiarise you with the process of evaluating and conveying to others your judgements and responses to your reading.

Remember, though, that the AS and A2 course is designed to develop your personal responses, and not to turn you into an obedient mouthpiece for the views of this critic or that critic. If you enter the examination room having acquired detailed knowledge of your set texts and topics, as well as independent judgement, you are well prepared for success in the exam, and the benefits that come from a lifetime experience of being a good reader and a thoughtful writer.

This unit covers:

- studying a range of extracts related to the theme of 'travel, transport and locomotion' from the Anthology provided by AQA

- developing your understanding of a wide variety of forms and uses of English

- using a variety of critical approaches and to build up your vocabulary of terms for describing language

- finding connections between texts and developing the skills of comparison and contrast

- learning how to discuss the meanings, language and significant contexts of extracts.

Introduction

The purpose of this introductory unit is to provide a map of the themes, issues and areas for future exploration. It should serve as both a guidebook and a compass for the journeys ahead. You will encounter a wide variety of literary and non-literary writing, spoken and written language, and a range of texts from the distant past to the present day.

This unit will also introduce you to the kinds of ideas, approaches and terminology you will need when you extend your explorations of English Language and Literature in subsequent units. In particular, the Unit 1 examination will assess your learning with a 1½ hour examination paper. This consists of two questions: Question 1 is worth one-third (32 marks) and Question 2 two-thirds (64 marks) of the total marks for this unit.

- Question 1: you will be presented with unseen texts on the theme of travel to discuss and analyse.

- Question 2: you will be required to carry out a detailed comparison of any two of the extracts in the Anthology.

In total, the Unit 1 examination is worth 60 per cent of the total AS marks.

In this paper, your work will be assessed according to three Assessment Objectives. Think of these as questions that the examiner will be asking you.

AO1	Can you discuss a range of different texts using a range of suitable terminology, reflecting the combined study of language and literature?
AO2	Can you produce detailed, accurate and clearly expressed analyses of texts, both unseen and previously studied?
AO3	Can you make relevant and productive comparisons between different texts and their contexts, bringing out their most significant similarities and differences?

In order for you to be able to answer these questions with a resounding 'Yes!', this book will:

- focus strongly on the texts in the Anthology to develop the skills and knowledge you need for Question 2 of the Unit 1 examination
- plot a course through the texts that allows you to explore systematically some of the key linguistic and literary concepts that you need to learn – this means that important concepts and terminology are introduced early. However, you may prefer to use the index of texts (p83) to study the texts in a different sequence
- encourage you to develop a glossary of useful terms as you go along
- develop your skills of comparison and contrast
- suggest ways of applying your skills and knowledge to the analysis of unseen texts, as required by Question 1.

The Anthology is a vital part of this unit. The texts within it are not only the focus of Question 2 (which is worth two-thirds of the marks), they can also be used to develop the skills you need to deal with the unseen texts in Question 1. Section A of this unit uses texts from the Anthology to explore ways of analysing texts. Section B provides practice in applying these to each question in the examination.

Your personal glossary

At the end of this book you will find a glossary of useful terms that you will need to master for your examination. You will also need to build up your own collection of technical terms to enable you to discuss specific features of the texts you study and to communicate your understanding to other specialists, such as the examiner. Remember that for AO1 the examiner will be asking:

AO1	Can you discuss a range of different texts **using a range of suitable terminology,** reflecting the combined study of language and literature?

Link

An index of texts from the Anthology showing where they are covered in this book can be found on p83.

AQA Examiner's tip

Remember that you will be able to take a copy of the Anthology into the examination, but it must be a clean copy, that is, free of any notes or annotations.

Practical activity

Take a clean exercise book and dedicate a couple of pages to each letter of the alphabet. Get your glossary started by listing the terms you know already (from your GCSE course or elsewhere) that define features of language and literature. For example, under 'A' you may already be able to list adjective, alliteration, assonance, and so on.

As you encounter new terms, add them to your glossary together with the definition and an example.

The Anthology: introducing the theme of 'travel, transport and locomotion'

Wherever we look, people are on the move. It seems that, for humans, staying put is not an option. Odd, then, that the English language has had to borrow a word from German – *wanderlust* – to describe the restless compulsion to travel.

As all of the extracts in the Anthology you will study for Unit 1 are based on the theme of 'travel, transport and locomotion', we will start by exploring some basic ideas relating to the apparently irresistible impulse to travel.

Travel: why bother?

In the past, most travel would have been for business rather than pleasure, with a few intrepid explorers daring to boldly go where no one had gone before. The phenomenon of travel for pleasure and recreation is a relatively recent one. Although a small social elite may have been able to take something like what we would now call a holiday, it is only the development of cheap mass transport (starting with the railways in the 19th century, followed by the expansion of air travel in the 20th) that has opened up the possibility of travel for most people. Nowadays there are many more travel options available to most of us.

People do of course vary hugely in what they want from their experiences: some are motivated by the pure pleasure-seeking escapism of two weeks in the sun, and some by the gruelling challenges of activity holidays or the intellectual satisfactions of cultural and historical tours.

Whatever our reasons for travel, it would be foolish to expect the experience to be one of unbroken pleasure and satisfaction. Many of the extracts in the Anthology explore the possible benefits and problems of travelling, and express a range of attitudes towards these.

Critical response activity

In this activity we will consider some of the pros and cons of packing our bags and hitting the road. For each of the quotations below, write:

- an explanation of the point(s) you think is being made about travel

- your own response in agreement or disagreement.

1. 'Travel broadens the mind.' Popular proverb

2. 'To travel hopefully is a better thing than to arrive.' Robert Louis Stevenson, 1881

3. 'Travel is the most private of pleasures. There is no greater bore than the travel bore. We do not in the least want to hear what he has seen in Hong Kong.' Vita Sackville-West, 1926

4. 'One of the pleasantest things in the world is going on a journey; but I like to go by myself.' William Hazlitt, 1822

5 'Two roads diverged in a wood, and I –
I took the one less travelled by,
And that has made all the difference.'
Extract from '*The Road Not Taken*', Robert Frost, 1916

6 '*Jaques*: It is a melancholy of mine own, compounded of many simples, extracted from many objects and indeed the sundry contemplation of my travels, in which my often rumination wraps me in a most humorous sadness.

Rosalind: A traveller! By my faith, you have great reason to be sad. I fear you have sold your own lands to see other men's. Then to have seen much and to have gained nothing is to have rich eyes and poor hands.

Jaques: Yes, I have gained my experience.'
Extract from *As You Like It*, William Shakespeare, *c.*1599

7 'I'm fed up going abroad and being treated like sheep. What's the point of being carted around in buses, surrounded by sweaty mindless oafs from Kettering and Coventry in their cloth caps and their cardigans and their transistor radios and their *Sunday Mirrors*, complaining about the tea, "Oh, they don't make it properly here, do they, not like at home."' From *Monty Python's Flying Circus*, 1969

Commentary

Does travel truly 'broaden the mind', making us more informed about and tolerant of different countries and their customs and cultures? Or can it simply reinforce prejudices and stereotypes or damage relationships, particularly if tourists behave insensitively and without due regard for local traditions and culture? It is certainly debatable, and Shakespeare's Rosalind and the character in the *Monty Python* sketch both find good reasons to question the received wisdom that travel for its own sake is necessarily a good thing. Indeed, many travellers would recognise the truth of Robert Louis Stevenson's observation that the anticipation and the journey can be more exciting than the experience of the destination itself.

However, the popularity of both travel writing and travel programmes on television and radio suggests that, unlike Vita Sackville-West, we do not find other people's travels boring at all, although nothing can substitute for our own first-hand experience. Perhaps Robert Frost's decision to take the 'road less travelled' might inspire us to leave the beaten track and explore less 'touristy' destinations. However, some will question whether it is best to do so alone, as suggested by William Hazlitt – making friends along the way and meeting the challenges and risks of travelling independently.

Practical activity

1 Read and study examples of travel journalism in the travel supplements of a weekend newspaper.

2 Attempt your own piece of travel writing based on your experience of a place you have visited. It need not be somewhere exotic, but you should aim to create a vivid impression of the sights, sounds, smells and atmosphere of the place for an audience your own age.

2 Exploring lexis and semantics

🔍 💡 Lexical choices

Owing to its long and complicated history, the English language has developed a vast treasury of words, which we usually refer to as the **lexis** of the language. As a result of invasions, travel, translation and many other forms of influence, we have acquired from other languages numerous alternative words for similar concepts. The result is that we can make very precise and subtle distinctions between closely related ideas. If we take the idea of travel, for example, we may (especially with the aid of a thesaurus) think of a group of closely related words. We call this a **lexical field**, so these words belong to the lexical field of travel:

travel	adventure	trek
quest	outing	voyage
trip	tour	excursion
roam	wander	journey
tourism	expedition	holiday.

When we think carefully about the meanings of words and how words within a particular lexical field relate to one another, we are engaged in **semantics**. A useful distinction to make is the difference between the primary, basic sense of a word, which is called its **denotation**, and its secondary associations or implications, which we call its **connotations**. So we could argue that most of the words in our lexical field share very similar denotations, as they all denote different sorts of travel, but that their connotations are different.

Practical activity

1. Look at the list of words above, which are in the lexical field of travel. Make connections between any sets of two or more words that you can link together, labelling the links to show what the connection is. For example, if you think that 'holiday' and 'tourism' are linked, draw a line between them and label it 'travel for fun'.

2. Consider the following sets of words and try to explain the precise difference between them:
   - traveller/tourist
   - expedition/excursion
   - journey/voyage/trip/quest

3. Sort all the words from the lexical field of travel into a table like the one below according to the kinds of connotations they have. For example, if you think 'trek' implies a journey that is probably quite long and possibly on foot, you might write it under Duration and Form of transport.

Duration	Purpose	Form of transport	Level of challenge	Positive connotations (implies favourable attitude)	Pejorative connotations (implies unfavourable attitude)

Link

For more information on the history of the English language, see the Background information box, Milestones in English, on pp65–6.

Key terms

Lexis: the total stock of words in a language.

Lexical field: a group of words within a text relating to the same topic.

Semantics: the study of the meanings of words.

Denotation: the primary, literal meaning of a word or phrase.

Connotations: the associations and feelings that words evoke in addition to their basic meanings, for example, although 'smile' and 'grin' refer to similar facial expressions, the word 'smile' has connotations of warmth and friendship, whereas the word 'grin' may have connotations of falseness, malice or stupidity about it.

Commentary

1   Some possible links include 'expedition', 'adventure' and 'trek', all of which imply a journey of some length and physical hardship, with some connotations of danger and the unknown (especially 'adventure'). 'Adventure' might also be linked to 'quest' with its connotations of danger, although a quest implies a very clear, possibly unattainable, goal. By contrast, 'roam' and 'wander' share connotations of idle aimlessness, and 'outing' and 'excursion' are limited to short, return journeys made for recreational purposes.

2   Whereas the word 'tourist' has increasingly pejorative connotations, implying a superficial, gullible and fairly mindless attitude towards sightseeing and local culture, 'traveller' may imply a more independent, responsible and intellectual approach. 'Expedition' and 'excursion' share the Latin-derived **prefix** 'ex-', meaning 'going out', but while the latter suggests both a short duration and an inevitable return, the former strongly implies adventure and challenge. 'Journey' is an almost neutral term, with a very wide and non-specific application, but 'voyage' implies a mode of transport (by sea), 'trip' a slightly more casually undertaken and probably shorter journey, and 'quest' the extremely challenging and possibly futile pursuit of a goal, with connotations of medieval legends, holy grails, etc.

3   ▪ Duration: shorter journeys probably include 'trip', 'outing' and 'excursion', but an 'expedition', 'trek' or 'quest' will be much longer.

    ▪ Purpose: 'tourism' and 'holiday' will be recreational, 'adventure' and 'expedition' may imply challenge or thrill-seeking, but a 'quest' will be in pursuit of a hard-to-achieve goal.

    ▪ Form of transport: the most specific are 'trek' (on foot) and 'voyage' (by sea).

    ▪ Level of challenge: these range from the undemanding 'outing' and 'holiday' to the slightly more taxing 'tour' or 'voyage', and then to the extremes of 'adventure', 'trek' and 'expedition'.

    ▪ Positive and pejorative connotations: 'adventure' or even 'journey' can sound exciting, although a 'trek' may imply a weary distance and 'tourism' superficial sight-seeing.

▪ **Key terms**

Prefix: an element placed at the beginning of a word to adjust or qualify its meaning.

▪ **Practical activity**

Use a thesaurus to compile more sets of words within different lexical fields – try kill, love and fear – and define the subtle differences between the words in terms of both denotations and connotations.

▪ Text 16: *Oxford English Dictionary Online*

If 'travel, transport and locomotion' are the defining terms for this collection of extracts, it is probably a good idea to confirm your understanding of their meaning by checking them in a dictionary. Text 16 in the Anthology provides the definition of the word 'travel' offered by the *Oxford English Dictionary Online* (www.oed.com).

You may be familiar with various versions of the *Oxford English Dictionary* ('Shorter', Concise', etc.) but you may well not have encountered the full-length version. Its printed edition extends to 20 large volumes and is usually only found in reference and university libraries. However, since 2000 the online version has been available and your school or college may have an institutional subscription that allows you to access this fantastic resource.

Aims of the *Oxford English Dictionary* (OED)

The *OED* aims to do a great deal more than the average dictionary. For example, it aims to:

■ Key terms

Etymology: the study of the origin and development of words.

Archaic: language that is characteristic of an earlier period or has fallen into disuse.

■ provide a comprehensive record of the vocabulary of English

■ record the dates of the earliest recorded use of every word in written English

■ document the different forms of spelling a word has had over its history

■ record the pronunciation of each word

■ suggest the origins, or **etymology** (if known), of each word

■ define the different meanings a word may have had

■ include entries for as many regional (dialectal), **archaic** and obsolete words as possible.

Some facts about the *OED*

In view of these extremely ambitious aims, you may not be too surprised by these facts about the *OED*:

■ It contains over 60 million words of text.

■ It includes entries for over 750,000 different words.

■ Approximately 4,000 new words are added to the dictionary each year.

Reading the *OED*

To make use of the *OED*, you need to understand how its entries are organised and how the information is presented. The following is an extract from the *Oxford English Dictionary Online* (2nd edition).

'Travel' is the **head word** of the entry

The **pronunciation** of the word is recorded using a set of symbols called the International Phonetic Alphabet

Different **spellings** the word has had in the past are recorded

Meanings the word has had in the past are listed, with the oldest first. When a word's meaning changes over time, it is called semantic change

Dated **citations** provide written examples of the word in use throughout its history. Lists α and β show parallel examples of travail and travel.

The **class of word** (noun, adjective, verb, adverb, preposition, conjunction, etc.) is defined

travel, v.

('træv(ə)l] **Forms:** see prec. [orig. the same word as TRAVAIL *v.*; cf. prec. Derivatives, as *travelled, -er, -ing,* etc. are usually spelt with *ll* in Gr. Britain, with single *l* in America.]

1. To torment, distress; to suffer affliction; to labour, toil; to suffer the pains of parturition; etc.: see TRAVAIL *v.* 1–4.

2. a. *intr.* To make a journey; to go from one place to another; to journey. Also *fig.*

α *c*1290 *S. Eng. Leg.* I. 25/61 For ʒe Þus i-trauailede beoth fram so ferre londe..Ich eov nelle greui nouʒt. *c*1330 R. BRUNNE *Chron.* (1810) 3 He was of grete elde, & myght not trauaile. **1413** *Pilgr. Sowle* (Caxton) I. i. (1859) 1, I had longe tyme trauayled toward the holy Cyte of Ierusalem. **1548–9** (Mar.) *Bk. Com. Prayer, Litany,* To preserue all that trauayle by lande or by water. **1590** SPENSER *F.Q.* I. ii. 28 Long time they thus together traveiled. **1603** SHAKES. *Meas. for M.* I. iii. 14 He supposes me trauaild to Poland. **1691** NORRIS *Pract. Disc.* 94 Why should we..quit the Road.., if we may safely trauail in it? **1714** GAY *Sheph. Week* Proeme, Other Poet travailing in this plain Highway of Pastoral.

β *c*1375 *Sc. Leg. Saints* xxxi. (*Eugenia*) 326 Sen scho mycht nocht trawel hym til. *c*1410 *Sir Cleges* 16 To men, that traveld in londe of ware. **1483** *Cath. Angl.* 391/2 To Travelle, *itinerare.* *a*1550 *Freiris of Berwik* 39 in *Dunbar's Poems* (S.T.S.) 286 For he wes awld, and micht nocht wele travell. **1594** NASHE *Unfort. Trav.* 68 He is no bodie that hath not traueld. **1600**

Abbreviations provide more information about the way the word was or is used: here, *intr.* = intransitive; *fig.* = figurative

SHAKES. *A.Y.L.* I. iii. 111 What danger will it be to vs,..to trauell forth so farre? **1697** DRYDEN *Virg. Georg.* IV. 147 A thirsty Train That long have travell'd thro' a Desart Plain. **1768** STERNE *Sent. Journ.* (1775) I. 15 (*Desobligeant*) An Englishman does not travel to see Englishmen. **1855** PALEY *Æschylus* Pref. (1861) 28 They have..pointed out the path in which succeeding editors should travel. **1901** W. R. H. TROWBRIDGE *Lett. Mother to Eliz.* iv. 13 [They] travelled down from London in a special Pullman attached to the Bristol express.

b. *to travel it*: to make a journey; *esp.* to go on foot.

Critical response activity

1 Use the above explanations and these prompt questions to extract the key information from the *OED* entry for 'travel'.

  a The *OED* entry tells us about change in language over time – something linguists call **diachronic variation**. What do you find interesting about the connection between the words 'travel' and 'travail' and the way in which the meaning and spelling of 'travel' has developed?

  b The *OED* records many variations in spelling, some of them at more or less the same time. Linguists call this **synchronic variation**. List the different spellings cited, merging the examples from both lists of citations (α) and (β). Try to explain the many variations in the spelling of the word and the eventual development of the modern spelling.

2 Identify one citation that shows the word being used in a metaphorical (figurative) sense. Explain how the word is being used metaphorically.

Key terms

Diachronic variation: the changes in language over time.

Synchronic variation: the variation in language use at any given point in time.

Commentary

1 a The *OED* tells us that the modern word 'travel' derives from 'travail', the earliest meanings of which are related to suffering and hard work. Although the *OED* elsewhere defines the word 'travail' as archaic, it still has the sense of extreme hardship. Perhaps the conditions for any kind of travel in the 13th and 14th centuries were so grim that 'travel' inevitably entailed 'travail'. Over time, the many variations in spellings settled down, allowing the two different meanings to emerge and separate. As travelling gradually became easier, so the modern word 'travel' lost its associations with hardship.

  b Synchronic variation is given in the table opposite.

Early variations in spelling probably reflected the lack of any agreed standard, and variations in both pronunciation and spelling practices among writers and (after the arrival of William Caxton's printing press in 1472) printers. The modern use of *v* and *u* did not really become fixed until the 18th century, and until then *u* tended to be used in the middle of a word whether the sound was */v/* or */u/*. The second vowel sound in the word 'travel' was presumably much closer to an */ay/* sound in the past, and the different spellings may reflect wide variations in the way this vowel was pronounced.

Spelling	Date
Trauailede	c.1290
Trauaile	c.1330
Trawel	c.1375
Traveld	1410
Trauayled	1413
To travell	1483
Trauayle	1548–9
Travel	1550
Traveiled	1590
Traueld	1594
Trauell	1600
Trauail	1603
Travail	1691
Travell'd	1697
Travailing	1714
Travel	1768
Travel	1855
Travelled	1901

The fact that the same writer (Shakespeare) used two different spellings ('trauell' and 'trauail') just three years apart (1600 and 1603) reveals the lack of an agreed standard for spelling, and the inevitable degree of uncertainty that arose when the phonetic sound of the word was translated into letters. However, we see that the modern form of 'travel' appears for the first time in 1768 and all other forms have apparently been banished. The 18th century was the period in which scholars and academic writers tried hard to define a standard version of English and several dictionaries and grammar books were published. It would seem that both the pronunciation and the spelling of the word were fixed at this time.

This might all appear to show that synchronic variation has eventually disappeared and that there is now one universally accepted way of spelling. However, even in the 21st century, alternative spellings of words are recognised within the same language. The *OED* entry points out the US English forms 'traveled' and 'traveler' along with the UK English forms of 'travelled' and 'traveller'. So, as the *OED* itself suggests, the question of whether or not to 'double consonant' (and the influence of America over UK spellings) remains an issue both for children learning to spell and for lexicographers (writers of dictionaries).

3   One obvious example of a figurative use is from 1855: 'They have pointed out the path in which succeeding editors should travel.' In this case, the metaphor is a common one, comparing life itself (or an aspect of it, such as your career) to a journey.

■ Practical activity

Note down as many phrases as you can think of that use the basic metaphor of comparing life to a journey. To get you started, perhaps include 'the next step' and 'is your life at a crossroads?'

■ Key terms

Standard English: the vocabulary and grammar of English generally regarded as 'correct'.

■ Research point

If your school or college has a subscription to the *OED* Online, access it at www.oed.com and investigate the history of other words in our lexical field. Begin with 'transport' and 'locomotion' and go on to 'voyage' and 'journey'. Alternatively, log onto the BBC website and join in the Wordhunt organised by the programme *Balderdash & Piffle*, in association with the *OED* (www.bbc.co.uk/balderdash).

■ Background information

A short history of dictionaries

Although we take the existence of dictionaries for granted, they have not always been around. Shakespeare, for example, would not have had access to anything like a modern dictionary. The development of lexicography (the business of dictionary writing) was itself a long journey of discovery into the heart of the English language and an important aspect of the emergence of what we now call '**Standard English**'. Here are some of its milestones:

1604 Robert Cawdrey's *A Table Alphabeticall* published, offering 'the true writing and understanding of hard usual English words' for 'the benefit & help of Ladies, Gentlewomen and any other unskillful persons'.

1656 Thomas Blount's *Glossographia.*

1658 John Phillips's *Universal English Dictionary.*

1755 Dr Samuel Johnson's *Dictionary of the English Language.*

1828 Noah Webster's *American Dictionary of the English Language.*

1860 Work begins on the *Oxford English Dictionary* (*OED*).

1928 Publication of the first complete edition of the *OED*.

3 Text, language and context

Key terms

Context: the social situation, including audience and purpose, in which language is used; this situation is an important influence of the language choices made by speakers and writers.

Audience: the readers of or listeners to a text.

Text 1: Pages from an EC passport

As we study Text 1 from the Anthology, the approaches and terminology used in our analysis will provide you with a model that you can apply to your own exploration of texts.

Even if you have a passport and are a regular traveller, it is unlikely that you will have paid much attention to the words it contains. Your passport has a specific job to do – to provide proof of your nationality and identity to immigration and customs officials in countries throughout the world – and even the most beady-eyed official is unlikely to scrutinise the opening sentence:

> Her Britannic Majesty's Secretary of State requests and requires in the name of Her Majesty all those whom it may concern to allow the bearer to pass freely without let or hindrance and to afford the bearer such assistance and protection as may be necessary.

Nevertheless, we will pause to consider what is one of the most owned but least read texts in English.

Contexts of production and reception

Whether looking at a literary text such as a poem, a non-literary text such as a passport or even an example of everyday speech, you are likely to be able to understand its meanings fully and grasp its significance only if you also know something about its **context**. This means thinking about how the use of language is affected by the situation in which the language was produced and received – the contexts of production and reception.

Production	Reception
Who has produced it? (= author)	**Who** is reading or hearing it? (= reader)
When was it produced?	**When** is it being read or heard?
Where was it produced?	**Where** is it being read or heard?
Why was it produced? (= purpose)	**Why** is it being read or listened to?
For whom was it intended? (= implied **audience**)	**Who** is reading or hearing it? (= actual audience)

Critical response activity

1 Look at the table above and answer the questions in the production column for the passport text.

2 Explain how these factors might influence the way language is used in a passport.

3 What different meanings and functions might the passport have in the following contexts of reception?

- at the immigration desk of an airport

- at the counter of the post office where you have used it as proof of identity to collect a parcel

- at a hotel where you have been asked to submit your passport on arrival.

Commentary

1 The passport is issued by a government department (the Home Office) on behalf of the Secretary of State (a government minister), who in turn claims to be acting on behalf of the Queen. Valid passports must have been issued within the last 10 years, although the actual text of the document goes back much further (see the Background information box). The text is issued to provide citizens of the UK with proof of their nationality and identity, and all the entitlements that entails – not just to travel, but to claim the rights of a British citizen.

2 As it is an official and legal document, we would expect a high level of formality, but the somewhat pompous tone of the text ('requests and requires …') seems to claim for the British government a level of authority it enjoyed during the days of the British Empire. You might also consider whether its intended audience is the owner of the passport or officials throughout the world who may not necessarily know English – in which case, should the style, and indeed the language itself, reflect this?

3 Clearly, the text takes on different meanings in different contexts, and its 'end users' may infer different things. At the immigration desk, the passport says 'This person is who she says she is. She comes from the UK. She has the right to come into this country.' At the post office, it simply means 'This person has the right to collect this parcel.' At the hotel, it means security for the proprietor – passports are held so that you cannot leave the country without paying the bill. The study of the different meanings and functions that texts take on in different contexts is called **pragmatics**.

■ Key terms

Pragmatics: the study of what is implied and understood by language use in context.

■ Background information

A brief history of the UK passport

1414 An act of parliament refers to 'Safe Conducts' (the earliest passports).

1641 Earliest example of a surviving passport signed by King Charles I.

1772 Until this date, passports were written in Latin or English. From this date until 1858, they are written in French.

1794 From this date, all passports are issued by the Secretary of State and their issue is recorded. (Before this date, some passports were issued and signed by the king or queen.)

1858 Passports start to be written in English again.

1915 The first modern UK passport is issued. It is a folded one-page document.

1920 A new book format for passports is introduced.

1961 The British visitor's passport is introduced. It is available from Crown Post Offices and can be used for visiting western Europe.

1968 The first 10-year UK passports are issued.

1988 A common format is introduced for member states of the European Community.

1997 The first UK passports with references to the European Union are issued.

(Source: *Home Office Passport and Identity Service*, www.ips.gov.uk/passport)

■ **Think about it**

Consider why, at certain periods in the past, Latin and French were used as the language of the British passport.

Describing style using linguistic frameworks

When we start to ask what is distinctive about the way language is used in this text, it is helpful to think about several aspects or levels of language. In each case, analysis starts by defining *what* is distinctive in a text and then trying to explain *why*. The framework in the table below shows how you could analyse different aspects of the passport text.

Key terms

Declarative sentence: one that makes a statement.

Interrogative sentence: one that asks a question.

Imperative sentence: one that gives a command.

Level of analysis	Explanation	Questions to apply to the passport
Graphology and typography	The graphology of a text includes aspects of its visual presentation on the page – its design and layout and the use of graphics or images. Typography refers specifically to the variations in font, typeface and size	*What:* describe the distinctive features of the layout and font styles used in the text *Why:* suggest why these features have been chosen
Phonology	This is the aspect of language concerned with the actual sounds of words and the effects they produce. This may sometimes be significant even in written texts (as with alliteration, assonance, onomatopoeia, etc.) and will always be vital when we look at spoken language (see Chapter 5)	*Not really relevant to the passport*
Lexis	This is the choice of vocabulary in a text, such as the level of formality/informality, the degree of technicality of any of the vocabulary or the frequency of use of different classes of words (such as adjectives, verbs)	*What:* what degree of formality is there in the lexical choices? Are there any examples of archaic words? Is there any form of repetition or patterning in the lexis? *Why:* why do you think these patterns are used and what is their effect?
Grammar	This is the set of underlying rules that we follow when we combine and arrange words to form phrases and sentences. This applies just as much to spoken language as to written texts. It has two branches: *Syntax:* the order in which we arrange words and phrases to construct sentences, e.g. 'I left our passports at home', not 'Home at left I passports our' *Morphology:* the changes we make to words in a sentence according to the job they do, e.g. we change 'leave' to 'left' in the past tense, and add 's' to passport to make it plural Issues of punctuation may also be discussed under the heading of grammar	*What:* how long and complicated are the sentences in the text? Is the opening sentence: a statement (**declarative sentence**) a question (**interrogative sentence**) a command (**imperative sentence**)? Is the sentence in the first, second or third person? *Why:* why is 'whom' used rather than 'who' in the phrase 'all those whom it may concern'?
Semantics and pragmatics	We know that semantics is about the meanings of words and phrases; pragmatics is about the interpretations people place on language. For example, on the road, semantically an amber traffic light means 'get ready to stop'. In practice, however, its pragmatic impact seems to be 'speed up to get through before it changes to red'	*What:* what is the literal meaning of the first long sentence? *What:* what does it imply about the power of our own Queen and government in the world? *Why:* how relevant to the actual use of the passport today is the wording of this text?
Text structure and discourse	This concerns the organisation of the ideas and language in a text – how it begins, the sequence of points and how one leads to another, and how it ends – and how these may reflect features of different genres of text	*What:* how would you describe the functions of the two parts of the passport text? *Why:* why do you think these opening pages have been arranged in this way?

Graphology and typography

There is a noticeable contrast between the two pages: the first is presented in a cursive font suggestive of handwriting, endorsed by a rather special kind of logo – the royal coat of arms – whereas the second simply consists of a three sets of multilingual lists in a more conventional, neutral typeface. The style of the frontispiece possibly harks back to the earliest passports (see the Background information box on p12), which would have consisted of little more than a handwritten letter issued and signed by the Secretary of State or the monarch. The coat of arms and the watermarked paper lend authority and protect against forgery.

Lexis

The use of the adjective 'Britannic' to describe the Queen may seem formal or even archaic, as it is possibly used in no other context in modern English. Most of the vocabulary here is fairly formal, and there are three examples of paired near-**synonyms**: the verbs 'requests' and 'requires', the nouns 'let' and 'hindrance' (the former being somewhat archaic in this sense) and the nouns 'assistance' and 'protection'. The archaic elements arguably reinforce the sense of authority by appealing to history and tradition, whereas the pairing of similar words is a common rhetorical device that has the effect of reinforcement and power.

Grammar

We can describe sentences in terms of their length, function and structure. At 55 words, the opening sentence is certainly unusually long; it is technically a third person statement (i.e. a declarative) as it says that the 'Secretary of State requests and requires …', although the verbs 'requests and requires' almost give it the force of a command or imperative.

Syntax

Sentence structures can be of one of four types:

- Minor: common in speech, a 'complete' utterance that lacks one or more elements of a whole sentence, e.g. 'No passport, no entry!' (meaning, if you have no passport you will not be allowed entry).
- Simple: consisting of a single **clause** with a single verb, e.g. 'I left my passport at home.'
- Compound: consisting of more than one clause joined by the conjunctions 'and', 'but' or 'or', e.g. (clauses are numbered) '[1] I left my passport at home and [2] now I've ruined the holiday.'
- Complex: consisting of more than one clause joined by other means, e.g. '[1] Having left my passport at home, [2] I was unable to board the plane, [3] which left me no alternative [4] but to rearrange my holiday.'

To analyse the complexity of the opening sentence of the passport fully, you need to become quite technical. If you break down the sentence into its main constituent parts, or clauses, you can begin to see how it works. The table overleaf introduces some grammatical terms that we will explore more fully later in this book.

Key terms

Synonym: a word that has the same or similar meaning to another word; for example, 'smile' and 'grin' are synonyms, as they mean more or less the same thing, but carry different connotations.

Clause: a construction that contains, as a minimum, both a subject and a verb. It can stand alone as a sentence, as in 'I bought a book' (main or independent clause) but may be part of a larger construction, as in 'when I went out' (subordinate or dependent clause).

Clause	Analysis
Her Britannic Majesty's Secretary of State requests and requires in the name of Her Majesty all those whom it may concern …	Introduces main **subject** of sentence ('Her Britannic Majesty's Secretary of State') and the paired main verbs ('requests and requires'). Inserted adverbial phrase ('in the name of Her Majesty') separates these verbs from the **object** ('all those whom it may concern'). **Subordinating conjunction** ('whom') introduces the next **subordinate clause** ('it may concern')
… to allow the bearer to pass freely without let or hindrance …	This then leads to the third, **infinitive clause**, including another adverbial phrase ('without let or hindrance')
… and to afford the bearer such assistance and protection…	The next clause is introduced by the **coordinating conjunction** 'and' and includes both a direct object ('such assistance and protection') and an indirect object ('the bearer')
… as may be necessary	A final subordinate clause is introduced by the subordinating conjunction 'as'

Morphology

In traditional English grammar, 'who' is used as the subject and whom as the object of a sentence. This means that traditionally we would say 'Who is going on holiday with you?' but 'With whom are you travelling?' In modern English, however, 'whom' tends to be used only in more formal styles and already has a whiff of the archaic about it. Therefore, once again the passport opts for a style that is rather formal to achieve its desired gravitas.

Semantics and pragmatics

The sense of the sentence seems to be that it gives passport holders the right to go anywhere they please and to expect foreigners to give them any help they may require, at the command of the Queen and her representative. In practice, of course, it means no such thing. Countries may reserve the right not to admit passport bearers and the amount of 'assistance and protection' offered may be fairly limited. The text seems to invoke a bygone era when Britain 'ruled the waves' (or thought it did) and had the power to guarantee the safety and free movement of all its citizens. The second page, which subordinates the United Kingdom to the European Community, is a more realistic recognition of modern reality.

Text structure and discourse

In a way the purpose of both of these pages is to establish the nature of the document but in two distinct ways: the first is in traditional style whereas the second identifies itself in a more practical (and multilingual) fashion. It is unlikely they are ever read sequentially; the vital facts (country of origin, passport number) are presented much more accessibly on the right-hand page.

 Key terms

Subject: the person or thing acting on the verb.

Object: the person or thing being affected by the action.

Subordinating conjunction: words such as 'although', 'because' or 'unless', which are used to link a main clause to a subsidiary or dependent one.

Subordinate clause: this depends on the main clause, e.g. in the sentence 'I went to a salesroom where I saw a great sports car', the clause 'where I saw a great sports car' cannot stand alone.

Infinitive clause: the part of a verb usually preceded by 'to'; a clause containing such a verb.

Coordinating conjunction: words such as 'and', 'but' and 'or', which are used to link together independent clauses; for example, in the sentence 'he likes swimming but he hates shopping' each clause could stand independently.

Link

Extend your knowledge and understanding of grammar by studying the relevant sections from one of the texts listed in the Further reading box on p66, such as David Crystal's *Rediscover Grammar*.

Practical activity

1 Re-write the text of the passport in a much more informal style, using colloquial language.

2 Comment on the different impression this creates, and on whether or not this new version of the passport would still be fit for purpose.

Once you have decided you need to travel, there are many more decisions to be made. For example, what will be your preferred mode of transport?

Text 25: A leaflet for a Young Persons Railcard

Text 25 in the Anthology is part of recently issued leaflet about a Young Persons Railcard, which is distributed at railway stations and elsewhere, and how to apply for one. It is a fairly typical example of an informative leaflet, and we will try to answer the question 'How does it present and organise its information?' using some of the ideas and terms introduced in the previous topic.

Critical response activity

1. As with any text, you should first try to establish an overview – this means writing two or three sentences that define what you see as the main ideas, meanings and attitudes expressed. Have a go at writing an overview of Text 25. Try to comment on the general style of language used and the significance of any contextual factors.

2. Write two or three sentences in response to each of the questions in the table below.

Level of analysis	Questions
Graphology and typography	How does the layout and use of various fonts/typefaces contribute to the effectiveness of the text?
Lexis	■ The text addresses the audience directly as 'you' (using the second person pronoun) and uses contractions such as 'you'll' and 'you're'. What do these features contribute to the overall style of the text? ■ The text uses many **modal verbs** – a small group of verbs including 'can', 'could', 'may', 'might', 'will', 'would', 'shall', 'should', 'must' and 'need'. They usually indicate different degrees of certainty about an event. Highlight these and comment on how they are used in the text.
Grammar	■ One sentence begins 'And you can look forward to dramatic savings …' – apparently contrary to some traditional ideas about English grammar. Why do you think this sentence begins with the conjunction 'and'? ■ What proportion of the sentences are declaratives, imperatives or interrogatives? Comment on the significance of this.
Semantics and pragmatics	Comment on how and why the word 'please' (called a politeness marker) is used in the text.
Text structure and discourse	The text begins by stressing the potential savings of the card and moves on to 'Additional benefits' before including a list of exclusions ('Tickets you cannot get with a Young Persons Railcard'). How does this structure reflect the purpose of the text?

3. Identify any aspects of the text designed to encourage people to purchase as opposed to just informing them about it.

Key terms

Modal verb: an auxiliary verb expressing necessity or possibility.

Commentary

1   Example of an overview:

Text 25 provides **potential purchasers** (i.e. students) with information about the conditions and benefits of a Young Persons Railcard, with a variety of facts broken down into sections and bullet points. As the text is designed to encourage (mainly) young people to apply for the card, it stresses the benefits in a **friendly, accessible style** (although it avoids being too colloquial) and also points out the conditions and limitations of the card.

refers to audience and purpose

links general point about style to context (purpose and audience)

2   The graphology of the text is designed to make the information accessible by signposting different aspects and itemising factual content in vertical lists. Variations in typography (font, size and style, such as italic or bold type) help highlight key information (such as phone numbers and website addresses) and draw attention to some important conditions of use. The consistent use of the second person throughout (there are seven uses of 'you' in the first section alone) is designed to engage the intended audience directly from the start, and together with the use of contractions establishes a tone that is personal as well as mildly informal.

Different modal verbs imply different levels of certainty or confidence. Here are some examples from the text:

- 'You can save'
- 'If you'd (= you would) like'
- 'You may wish to make'
- 'It might save you'
- 'You must always show'
- 'We need to see'
- 'NUS cards will not be accepted'.

The promise that 'you can save' sounds pretty definite, more so than 'it might even save you more money', but is less strong than the conditions attached – 'you'll (= you will) need to provide proof' and 'you must always show your Railcard'.

The use of 'and' at the start of a sentence seems to break one of the rules of English written grammar but, as the use of 'and' in this way is a common feature of spoken, colloquial English, it reinforces this sense of informality. The sentences mainly alternate between informative declaratives with advisory imperatives (such as 'you must always show your Railcard …'), although these are often softened with politeness markers ('please note …') which seem to warn customers very delicately about potential limitations and problems if they ignore one or other of the conditions of use.

There are also many **conditional** sentences ('If … then …') that try to answer the questions the potential purchaser may be raising about the card. The overall structure of the text seems designed to convince customers of the potential benefits before making them aware of its limitations, reflecting a persuasive as well as informative intent.

3   Although the text is, for the most part, supplying factual information, the structure of the text implies a persuasive agenda that is reinforced by the use of the **pre-modifiers** 'just' and 'dramatic' in:

- 'the card costs just £20'
- 'you can look forward to dramatic savings'.

Key terms

Conditional: a clause that qualifies a statement, usually introduced by 'if', 'provided that' or similar conjunctions.

Pre-modifier: a modifying word or phrase placed before the subject of the modification.

Text 26: An 'Airmiles' letter

If your travel plans extend beyond the UK rail network, you may be more interested in Text 26 in the Anthology. This was received through the post by a member of an Airmiles scheme and has a more obviously persuasive intention. It is actually one genre of text (an advertisement) masquerading as another (a personal letter). First we will consider how persuasion works in general and then we will look at some specific persuasive tactics.

Practical activity

1. Listed below are some suggested tactics that are often used when speaking or writing persuasively. Choose any two of the following tactics and use each one as the basis for a short piece of writing designed to persuade a friend or teacher (your audience) to visit a location you know well. For example, you might use appeal to pity/guilt to persuade your friend to go to Alton Towers with you, because if they do not you will have to go on the rides all by yourself!

   - Bribery and reward: stress the great financial or other benefits your audience will enjoy if they comply.
   - Appeal to pleasure: stress the sheer pleasure that will result if they do what you say.
   - Blackmail and threat/appeal to fear: stress the terrible things that might happen to them if they do not comply.
   - Appeal to pity/guilt: stress the bad things that might happen to other people (perhaps yourself) if they do not comply.
   - Flattery: make your audience feel good about themselves, especially if they comply.

2. Once you have written your two persuasive texts, write a short analysis of how you have used language to make your appeal effective. Think particularly in terms of:
   - your choice of lexis
   - grammatical aspects (such as the sentence types you have used)
   - the structure of your text (How did you start? How did you finish?)

Critical response activity

Look again at Text 26 in the Anthology. How does this text use language to persuade and influence its intended audience? The following prompts should help you to answer this question:

1. Which of the tactics of persuasion have been used? (pragmatics)

2. How is language used to do so? (lexis, grammar)

3. How has the company attempted to make the text look and read like a personal letter? (graphology, text structure, discourse, lexis)

4. Why do you think they have done so?

Commentary

The primary appeal of the text is financial – little mention is made of the potential pleasure value of the cruise holiday, merely the extent of the savings and monetary rewards to be gained. So the basic tactic is one of bribery, and much of the pre-modification in the text emphasises the savings involved: the logo's 'unbeatable cruise deals' is immediately echoed in the body text with 'exclusive deals', 'exceptional savings' and the compound pre-modification of 'almost-too-good-to-be-true £1946'. At the same time, another set of pre-modifiers emphasises the quality of the product: 'great choice, the best cruise brands'.

Although this is clearly a mass-produced text for widespread circulation, it is designed to appear to be a personal communication. The inclusion of a personalised address, the overall layout and the inclusion of the managing director's cursive signature all suggest that it is a letter written to the customer personally, presumably to convince him or her of a genuine interest in providing a good deal. This friendly tone is reinforced by the use of personal pronouns (the first person plural 'we' giving the company a friendly, collective identity, and the second person 'you' implying a familiar personal relationship with the customer), often within contracted forms such as 'we'd' and 'you'll'. Meanwhile, there is a mixture of mainly declarative and some imperative sentences, several of the former promising benefits using the future tense ('we'll give you … you'll have the same great choice …' etc.).

◼ Think about it

Check your knowledge of the use of pronouns using the table below.

	Singular	Plural
First	I (subject) me (object)	we (subject) us (object)
Second	You *In archaic and dialectal speech:* thou (subject) thee (object)	you
Third	she/he/it/one (subject) her/him (object)	they (subject) them (object)

Therefore, 'I' = 'first person singular subject pronoun' etc.

Practise using this terminology to describe pronouns.

🔍 Text 11: 'Booking conditions'

It is likely that, at some time or other, anyone could be seduced by a brochure or other advertisement into taking a dream holiday. However, tucked away at the back of any travel brochure there are usually several pages of very small print setting out the precise legal terms of the contract you enter into with your booking. Text 11 in the Anthology is an example of a set of booking conditions issued by a travel company that specialises in holidays with a wine theme. Many people may fail to 'read the small print' when embarking on a holiday, so let us have a closer look at what you might be letting yourself in for.

Critical response activity

1 Write an overview of Text 11 in which you explain its purpose and define the most significant features of its style, referring to any relevant language framework.

2 Which modal verbs (see p17) are used most frequently in the text? Suggest why.

Commentary

1   The purpose of this text is simply to define unambiguously the precise legal terms of the contract, so that if a dispute or complaint arises all eventualities are covered. This is the reason for most of the significant features of language used in this text.

   The discourse is systematically organised in terms of headed and numbered sections for ease of reference and includes numerous links to other sections of the text ('as set out in clause 17 below') and to other authorities and organisations with which the customer may not be familiar. The tone remains personal – frequent use is made of the second person pronoun – but it is a formal text with much use of field-specific lexis from a legal context (for example, clause, liability) alongside vocabulary from the lexical field of travel. The need to cover all possible circumstances also accounts for frequent use of conditional sentences (see p17) and some lengthy and complex sentences that try to cover every possible outcome of a situation. However, there are some ambiguous elements: the phrase 'reasonable skill and attention' is clearly open to interpretation; the customers and the company may well disagree about what is 'reasonable' if things go wrong.

2   As a legal document, the requirement is for certainty and a lack of ambiguity, so the use of modal verbs is generally limited to 'must' and 'will'.

Register

The term **register** is used to describe the style of language used in a particular spoken or written text. What creates register is a combination of:

- the degree of formality/informality in the text, as reflected both in its lexis and in its grammar
- the degree to which the text is personal/impersonal, as reflected in the extent to which it refers directly to its own author(s) (I, we) and the reader/listener (you)
- the degree to which it uses technical or field-specific lexis.

Therefore, when taking an overview of any spoken or written text, we can speak of it 'belonging to a scientific register' or having a 'fairly informal register' or, even, and more commonly, 'a rather mixed register, including some personal and some field-specific elements'. In the case of Text 11, we could describe the register as formal/legal with field-specific lexis related to both the law and the travel industry.

Key terms

Register: a type of language defined in terms of its appropriateness for the type of activity or context in which the language is used, including the purpose, audience and situation of a piece of speech or writing.

Critical response activity

The same method can be applied when you make comparisons between texts. Compare and contrast the ways in which any two of Texts 11, 25 and 26 present information to their readers. Follow these steps to create an effective, well-written comparison.

1 Look at your two chosen texts in turn and use the vertical columns in the following table to compile your initial ideas.

	Text A	Text B
Overview of text: genre, purpose, audience, other relevant contexts, main ideas and attitudes		
Significant stylistic features: e.g. physical presentation of information; text structure/ discourse features; register; lexical/grammatical features; other significant details		

2 Write your comparisons and contrasts, working horizontally across the grid.

Comparing texts

In your Unit 1 examination you will be required to make productive comparisons between different texts. This requires a specific approach and technique. Let us say you have been asked to compare an apple and an orange: you might discuss the apple first, then the orange, making comparisons as you go along:

> An apple is an edible fruit and is round. The taste can be sweet or quite sharp, depending on the variety. It has a skin, although many people eat it with its skin on. It grows on trees and can be eaten raw or baked in pies. It can be made into juice or cider.

> An orange is also an edible fruit and is also round. It is about the same size as an apple. It is a citrus fruit and can have a sharp, refreshing, acid flavour but also comes in varieties with different tastes. It has a peel that should be removed before the fruit is eaten. It is mainly eaten raw. It grows on trees, in countries with warmer climates than that of the UK. Like apples, oranges are often turned into fruit juice.

However, there is a better way of bringing together your comparisons and contrasts. Once you have looked closely at both items, you should be able to organise your analysis in terms of things in common and things in contrast. Note the way words and phrases of comparison and contrast (underlined) are used to highlight these similarities and differences:

> Apples and oranges have several things in common. They are both round, edible fruits and come in different varieties with different degrees of sharpness and sweetness. Furthermore, they are both often turned into fruit juice.

> However, there are differences too. Whereas an apple is often eaten with the skin on, an orange has to be peeled first. Unlike apples, which are commonly grown in the UK, the orange is a member of the citrus family and is only found in warmer climates.

Commentary

Overview – states the main features in common

Distinguishes the contexts of reception

Makes a distinction between purposes of the texts

Makes the distinction between style/ register of the texts

New paragraph, announces basis for comparison

Linking phrase flags up contrast

New paragraph, announces point to be compared

Link announces new theme/contrast

A comparison like the one you have just written might begin something like this (for reference, all three texts are included in this example):

The three texts present their intended audiences with detailed information relating to different kinds of travel. **However, whereas Texts 25 and 26 are providing information needed before the decision to travel is made, Text 11 is more likely to be used to help resolve problems after an arrangement has been entered into.** All three are informative, but Texts 25 and 26 also have a persuasive element (Text 26 more so than Text 25), which is reflected in their enthusiastic tone. The information in Text 11 is more comprehensive and precise and is also devoid of emotional content, belonging to a more **formal and legalistic register.**

The texts use different methods to present information visually. Text 26 uses the conventional layout of a letter and a range of font styles to engage the reader with its key ideas ('get more for your money') and Text 25 exploits the typical features of a leaflet to break down and list details. Text 11, **on the other hand,** is not designed to attract attention nor, it seems, to make itself especially accessible, and its contract-like format and small print may intimidate some readers.

One factor common to all three texts is the **use of second person pronouns** to address the reader directly. For example, Text 11 tells its readers 'you must pay all costs', Text 26 begins 'we'd like to welcome you aboard' and Text 25 promises 'you can save $\frac{1}{3}$ on most rail fares'. However, Text 11 also refers to the reader in the third person as 'the Client'.

The tone of the texts differs considerably, **however**. The formal, legal and distant style of Text 11 is partly created by the use of field-specific lexis such as 'convention', 'regulation' and 'liability', whereas the informal contractions ('we'd', 'you're', 'now's the time') and hyphenated compound 'almost-too-good-to-be-true' gives Text 26 the air of a jaunty sales patter.

5 Studying spoken language

Key terms

Transcript: an exact written representation of speech.

Prosodic features: the vocal aspects of speech (volume, stress, intonation, speed) that contribute meaning.

Paralinguistic features: non-verbal aspects of communication such as intonation or pausing, which work alongside language to help speakers to convey meaning effectively.

So far, all the extracts from the Anthology that we have considered have been examples of written, non-literary and (mainly) modern texts. In each case, they are the result of the carefully made choices of the writer, who has been able to plan, draft and amend the text until it is as intended. However, on this course you are also interested in many other kinds of text and will encounter examples of spoken language, produced naturally and spontaneously, recorded and subsequently written down so that it can be studied. Such texts are called **transcripts**.

Text 17: 'Planning a family holiday'

Text 17 in the Anthology is the transcript of a conversation between three members of a family as they plan their holiday. (It is usual in transcripts for the speakers to remain anonymous, so they are represented here as S01, S02, etc.)

Critical response activity

1. Try to reconstruct the original conversation by reading the transcript aloud. Consider carefully the decisions you are making and what you are doing. Then write a paragraph about what you had to add to the words or how you used your imagination to make the transcript come to life.

2. Write an overview of the text. Explain what are the main ideas being discussed, the nature of any significant disagreements, the kinds of language being used and what seem to be the roles of each of the participants.

3. Make a list of the ways in which the language in the transcript is different from what you would expect to find in a written text.

Commentary

1. There is much more to speech than the words alone, as you will have discovered. Context is very important, so you would ideally need to know something about where and when the conversation was taking place and who, exactly, the participants were (and their relationships to one another). You would have to guess exactly how the words were spoken – which words were stressed, how loudly each person spoke and how their voices rose or fell with each phrase. These vocal aspects of speech are known as **prosodic features**. Then you would also be interested in what the body language of the speakers revealed – their gestures, how they looked at one another or even where they were positioned – all of which aspects are collectively referred to as **paralinguistic features**.

Key terms

Context-dependent: those aspects of a text whose meanings depend on an understanding of the circumstances in which it has been produced.

Ellipsis/elliptical: the omission of part of a sentence. 'Hope you get well soon' is an example of ellipsis, as the pronoun 'I' has been left out. Ellipsis can also be represented by three dots (…) to indicate the missing part of the sentence.

Non-fluency features: the natural 'mistakes' of speech which include hesitations, self-corrections and repetition.

Discourse markers: words or phrases that give structure to speech or writing, enabling a writer or speaker to develop ideas, relate points to each other or move from one idea to the next, e.g. however, likewise, in addition, in contrast, nevertheless, furthermore, therefore.

Question tag: short question frequently tagged on to the end of spoken utterances.

2 In the conversation three participants are discussing travel arrangements for a forthcoming journey to Europe, focusing on the pros and cons of going by car or using a combination of train and ferry. Of the three speakers, S01 possibly seems to be the most assertive; S02 offers some alternative suggestions (a railcard; taking the car; going for a city break), while S03 takes a less forceful role in the discussion. Although the discussion is reasonably informal, there is a significant element of field-specific lexis (travel) and only occasional uses of highly colloquial forms of speech. Perhaps the most interesting aspect of the transcript is the way in which potential conflicts of opinion are negotiated and developed as the group move towards some kind of agreement.

3 Spoken language tends to be more **context-dependent** than equivalent written texts: that is, it is harder to understand fully if we do not share the circumstances in which the conversation was taking place. Apart from suggesting the extent to which spoken language depends on prosodic, paralinguistic and other contextual features, this transcript exhibits the following features of spoken language:

- some use of casual, colloquial language (e.g. 'Yeah', 'ruckie', 'it's a wee bit', 'it's dead expensive')
- some use of grammatically incomplete (minor) sentences (e.g. 'Delft Holland', 'The ferry', 'Must be'). The omission of parts of a sentence is known as **ellipsis**
- other sentences may continue in a less clearly structured way than in writing, with repeated use of conjunctions such as 'and', 'but' and 'so'
- some hesitation, repetition and use of fillers, e.g. (underlined) 'It costs <u>erm</u> (6 secs) <u>hmm</u> (6 secs) 80 quid', 'If you go for <u>like</u> 17 days', '<u>I mean</u> that would give you loads …', '<u>We're not we're not</u>'. These are collectively known as **non-fluency features**
- in conversation, those listening indicate their attention/agreement/ sympathy using feedback, e.g. 'Yeah', 'mm'
- use of relatively empty words such as 'well' at the beginning of some utterances (**discourse markers**), e.g. 'Well what we need …', 'Well you've done inter-railing'
- some use of short **question tags**, especially at the end of utterances, e.g. 'That's quite a lot <u>isn't it</u>?'
- some imprecision of expression, e.g. 'Trying to find things'.

Think about it

At first, you may think the idea that the participants in an unscripted, unrehearsed conversation might be following rules is somewhat unlikely – after all, isn't talking something we learn to do naturally and without having to think about it too much?

However, the more closely you look, the more it may seem that for much of the time conversations do depend on everyone playing by the rules. Look again at Text 17 and note down what you consider to be the main rules that all three speakers are following before you compare your ideas with the suggestions in the Spoken language section on p27.

Critical response activity

It can be very revealing to look closely at how a conversation develops. Who is in charge? Does one speaker emerge as dominant? What happens to the various ideas that are introduced and discussed? A systematic approach to the analysis of conversation (usually referred to as **discourse analysis**) can help you to answer these questions.

1 Who speaks most often? Who speaks longest? A fairly simple way of assessing the contribution of each speaker to the discussion is to answer these two questions by counting the number of turns each speaker has and the total length of these turns (in numbers of words), noting also any unusually long turns taken by a speaker. Once you have carried out your calculations, suggest what this reveals.

2 How are ideas and opinions introduced? It is also interesting to look at the ways in which the three speakers introduce ideas and opinions. Note down in three columns examples of each speaker doing so and then write a brief analysis of any interesting trends this reveals.

3 Agree to disagree? You might also consider how the speakers express disagreement, how often they do so and with what degree of tact. Again in three columns, note down any such expressions of disagreement and write a brief analysis of your findings.

4 Question tags and feedback. Finally, you could focus on two revealing details of any discourse analysis: the use of question tags (e.g. 'isn't it?', 'hasn't it?') and simultaneous feedback during speech.

Key terms

Discourse analysis: systematic study of a text, often applied specifically to spoken language.

Commentary

1 The results of the statistical analysis are as follows:

Criteria	S01	S02	S03
Number of turns	23	14	15
Total number of words	285 (includes two turns of 89 and 44 words)	167 (includes one turn of 33 words)	143 (includes one turn of 29 words)
Average words per turn	12+	11.9	9.5

This might suggest that, as the most frequent contributor, S01 is the dominant speaker. She or he also has the two longest turns in the discussion (of 89 words and 44 words); the fact that no one has attempted to interrupt this speaker might suggest that he or she has the most influence or status in the group. However, the average number of words per turn does not vary hugely, especially when the exceptional longer turns are taken out of the analysis.

2 Here are some examples of new ideas being introduced:

S01	S02	S03
■ We'll just leave the car behind ■ Yeah I won't take any ■ Yeah just take one ■ Well what we need to take is ■ You know like if you got the earliest train	■ It might be worthwhile taking the car you know ■ I'll do the driving I like driving ■ Are you sure you want to go, I mean we can go for a city break?	■ But they do a Benelux tour rail card ■ But it does I mean that would give you loads ■ Did you know British Rail operate services to Amsterdam?

On the whole, S01 introduces ideas quite bluntly – for example, 'what we need is …' – whereas S02 is a good deal more tentative, using the weak modal verb 'might' in 'it might be worthwhile' and posing a question ('are you sure you want …') rather than a more direct form. S03 twice employs the tactic 'but …' and phrases his or her suggestion as a question.

3   Some disagreements:

S01	S02	S03
■ Nah … it'll be fine ■ That's a lot … each ■ That's a lot ■ Mm ■ It's dead expensive it's dear ■ Oh I don't know I can't be bothered with the hassle ■ It's not that it's the parking and ■ Yeah but then you're talking about	■ The only problem I suppose ■ Because originally when we thought ■ But then you've got to add ■ But if you don't	■ If you go to Amsterdam, it would be a nightmare

Revealingly, S01 raises many more objections and disagreements than either of the other two speakers, and often does so quite directly ('Nah …', 'It's dead expensive', 'I can't be bothered with the hassle'). This speaker's objection to the cost of a Benelux railcard is more subtle, or at least depends more on prosodic or paralinguistic features that can easily be imagined as accompanying the turn 'that's a lot … each', its subsequent repetition and the non-verbal response ('Mm') that follows.

4   There are three examples of question tags in the transcript:

■ S03: Well you've done inter-railing haven't you?

■ S03: That's a lot isn't it?

■ S02: It's all inclusive isn't it?

Question tags may have several functions in speech. They can simply act as a **turn-taking cue**, for example inviting the next speaker to join in. However, they can also indicate a degree of uncertainty or tentativeness in the speaker, and it is interesting that S01 does not use any.

Clear examples of simultaneous feedback are limited to S01 at line 2 ('Yeah') and line 35 ('Mm'). Feedback can be a sign of sympathetic listening, but here the first seems to be a premature attempt to reclaim his or her turn and the second an early non-verbal indication of disagreement about the value of the railcard that is to follow.

Therefore, many of these indicators seem to indicate that S01 is adopting a more assertive role throughout the conversation, with S02 and S03 behaving more tentatively.

Key terms

Turn-taking cue: conversational signal consciously or unconsciously given by a speaker indicating their 'turn' is coming to an end.

Practical activity

This task aims to generate a sample of spontaneous spoken language for analysis. You need to recruit three or four volunteers to take part in a discussion activity. Suggest half a dozen possible holiday types/destinations and ask them to agree, as a group, a rank order of preference (1 = high). Record the discussion and select about a minute's worth of it to transcribe. Go on to carry out your own analysis of the transcript, using the approaches we have used in this topic.

There are practical and ethical issues involved in this kind of field work; you must obtain the consent of anyone you wish to record and make sure any references to people and places are removed when you transcribe the recordings. It is not acceptable to make secret recordings or use material without the participants' consent.

Spoken language

When writing about spoken language, you may find it useful to refer to the concepts and terminology listed in the tables below.

Feature	Definition
Prosodic features	
Tempo	The variations in speed in an utterance
Dynamics	The variations in volume
Pitch	The level of the voice (high or low)
Intonation	The movement of the voice up and down in pitch across a phrase or sentence
Stress	The use of increased volume and pitch on a single word for emphasis
Paralinguistic features	
Body language	The behaviour of our bodies
Gestures	The use of hand, arm and other movements to accompany speech
Eye contact	The degree and intensity of direct eye contact between speakers
Proxemics	The physical relationship between speakers in terms of proximity and position
Non-fluency features	
Repetition	Repeated words or phrases (perhaps unconsciously)
Self-correction	The correction of an error mid-flow by a speaker
Fillers or filled pauses	The use of either verbal ('you know', 'like', 'sort of') or non-verbal ('er', 'um') empty utterances

Some rules or 'maxims' that have been proposed for 'normal' conversational behaviour	
Do	**Don't**
Allow others to take turns	Monopolise the conversation
Join in and make a contribution	Remain silent throughout
Give feedback when others are talking	Interrupt
Recognise 'turn-taking cues', e.g. sentences reaching an end (falling pitch is a clue), question tags, pauses, body language and eye contact	Change the subject abruptly
Use a style of language appropriate for the context	Use words that are likely to be considered offensive by other participants
Express disagreements with some tact – keep face and allow others to keep theirs	Be offensive

6 Audience, arguments and literary language

The ability to travel far beyond the place of your birth, and the ability to do so for pleasure as much as from necessity, owes much to the coming of the railways. The rapid development of a national rail network in the 19th century transformed Britain, and trains came to exercise a particular grip on the popular imagination. Steam trains, in particular, have often figured prominently in literature, films, children's toys and books, and even today many grown men (it does seem to be largely men!) devote themselves to model railways, train-spotting or even helping to run one of the many heritage lines staffed by volunteers.

Text 15: *Thomas and Friends Annual 2008*

In the 1940s, the Reverend W. V. Awdry first dreamt up his imaginary island of Sodor and its railway network masterminded by the Fat Controller. He can scarcely have imagined that the characters he created would live on in children's imaginations 60 years later. Thanks to the success of the original books and, more recently, cartoons, films and DVDs, Thomas the Tank Engine and his friends remain as popular as ever, as shown by Text 15 which is taken from the *Thomas and Friends Annual 2008*.

Critical response activity

1 This is clearly a text written for a much younger audience than any of the other texts in the Anthology.

   a How does it accommodate the needs of its young readers in terms of its graphology/typography and lexical choices?

   b List all the words in a particular word class that occur in the text (such as adjectives or verbs) and comment on what you find.

2 With children's books, there is often the question of whether they are designed to be read by or to the child. Note any evidence from the text that suggests how it is intended to be read. You might consider:

   - the visual appeal of the text

   - how easy the vocabulary is to recognise

   - how the text addresses the implied reader.

3 Studying the pragmatics of texts means looking a little beneath the surface.

   a What ulterior motives might the authors have in presenting the text to children as part of the annual?

   b What sort of values does the text imply, for example in terms of gender or 'good' behaviour?

Commentary

1   The graphology and typography of the text are attractively accessible. There is a relatively high proportion of images to text, and the size and font of the type are designed for ease of reading.

The lexical range of the text is relatively narrow. Here, for example, are the adjectives used to define the characters and the verbs used in the passage:

Adjectives	Verbs
gold	is (×16)
little green	are
kind blue	work(s) (×4)
real	take
fastest	loading
big	unloading
	pulls

This shows that most of the words are high frequency and monosyllabic, with adjectives limited largely to colours and size. The verbs are limited to the stative verb 'to be' and just five others, which are **dynamic** and again mainly monosyllabic. The world of Thomas and his friends seems simple and benign: characters are defined by a single feature, usually positive ('kind' Edward, 'fastest' Gordon), though with a hint of the kinds of naughtiness to be found in a school playground (Cranky the crane) and linguistic playfulness (Sir Topham Hatt).

 Key terms

Dynamic verbs: verbs that describe physical actions, such as 'to jump'.

2   If it is intended to be read by the child, possibly with an adult alongside, the text itself must be visually appealing (as it is) and not include too many words that are either uncommon or the spelling of which makes them difficult for a young reader to recognise. In this text, relatively few words would pose a huge challenge to very young readers. 'Gauge' and 'quarry' might be both unfamiliar concepts and awkward spellings (although even a young child could have encountered the *qu* sound in words such as 'queen'). Otherwise the vocabulary is not only high frequency but also phonetically predictable, except for those words with a silent final 'e' such as 'crane' (where the so-called magic 'e' has an effect on the central vowel, turning 'cran' into 'crane') and engine (where it softens the consonant 'g', making it 'engine' rather than 'engin'). The text even attempts its own kind of interactivity with the child by posing the direct question about the Fat Controller: 'Do you know his real name?'

3   The text seems to be designed to have an educational as well as an entertaining function. Not only does it provide an introduction (for new readers) to the characters to be found in the stories in the annual, therefore encouraging children to read the stories, but the A–Z format mirrors that of an alphabet book and may also be designed to develop children's literacy.

In gender terms, females seem underrepresented – only three out of the thirteen characters listed so far, and of those two are coaches as opposed to locomotives. A feminist analysis of this text might suggest that this unconsciously implies to children that women lack independent power (they need the male engines to pull them) and are less actively involved in the world of work and industry. What is more, their job is to take 'workmen' to work – there do not seem to be any females employed at the quarry. The introduction of Emily, 'the little green engine' (not one of the original 1940s characters), may be a modern attempt to redress the balance in the interests of political correctness. As for the Fat Controller, such direct reference to an apparent weight issue in a children's book might offend some sensitivities if it were published for the first time today.

Text 14: 'The Future is Rail'

In the real, if less colourful, world beyond the Reverend Awdry's island of Sodor, the business of running our railways has always been a little more complicated and problematic, as Text 14 illustrates. The main issues it addresses are:

- Should the railway be owned by the government or by private companies (such as the Fat Controller's)?
- Should taxpayers' money be used to keep railways going even if they do not make a profit?

This is very much an extract with a more mature audience in mind. This audience not only has a reasonably educated and literary lexical range and some relevant and historical knowledge, it also has an interest in the issues surrounding the future of rail travel in the UK. Unlike Text 15, the text is not particularly intended to entertain its readers. So what exactly *is* it trying to do?

Critical response activity

Which of the following options do you consider to be the main purpose of the article? Choose one before reading the commentary that follows.

1 To inform readers about the history of the railways.

2 To argue in favour of more public money being spent on the railways.

3 To inform readers about government transport policy.

4 To argue that the government should not interfere with the railways.

Key terms

Argument: a connected series of ideas, backed up by relevant facts, that tries to make a case and convince us of its truth and validity.

Discursive writing: exploring and discussing a topic or issue, usually non-fiction.

Commentary

Although there is a certain amount of information here (about both the history of railways and government policy), it is being used to support an underlying **argument**. Although it is critical of the attitude of government towards the railways, it is certainly not suggesting there should be no interference. On the contrary, at the end it argues strongly that the government should invest more money in the railways, following the example of other countries. This is the conclusion to which the whole text has been leading.

This text is an example of what is sometimes called **discursive writing** – a detailed exploration of a topic that works its way towards some kind of point or conclusion.

As the ability to construct an argument in this way is an important skill, we will look more closely at how this text is constructed and organised.

Critical response activity

The **coherence** of the text is the way in which ideas are sequenced logically so that one point leads naturally to the next. The following list shows the main points in the argument in the text, but not in the right order. Rearrange or number them to match the sequence of ideas introduced in the text.

1 The relationship between the railways and government has always been difficult and inconsistent.

2 The UK is out of line with other countries when it comes to new investment in rail travel.

3 In the past, the coming of the railways changed the country in many ways.

4 History shows that the way in which the railways are organised has always been the subject of change.

5 We do not fully appreciate the value of the railways.

6 Surprisingly, railways are currently enjoying a successful period but their future in the UK is still in doubt.

Commentary

In Text 14, the points appear in this order: 4, 6, 1, 3, 2, 5.

To help you learn a little more about the history of Britain's railways to fully catch the drift of the argument, read the Background information box below.

Coherence: the continuity of organisation and meaning that unifies a spoken or written text.

Background information

Milestones for Britain's railways

1825 Stockton and Darlington Railway is opened.

1829 Liverpool and Manchester Railway is opened to passenger traffic. Government minister William Huskisson is knocked down by train and killed.

1850 London to Edinburgh East Coast main line is opened.

1923 The many private railway companies that had sprung up all over the country merged to form four larger companies: London, Midland and Scottish (LMS), London and North Eastern (LNER), Great Western (GWR) and Southern.

1938 The steam locomotive *Mallard* achieves the world speed record of 126 mph.

1948 The four private rail companies are taken under government ownership and British Railways is created.

1963 The Beeching Report leads to the closure of hundreds of loss-making lines and stations (about a third of the entire network).

1968 The last steam engine is taken out of service.

1994 The railways are privatised, with several private companies (such as Virgin and First Great Western) buying parts of the network from the government.

2007 The new St Pancras terminal for cross-channel rail services is opened.

Critical response activity

In any argument, it is not enough simply to assert a point. Like a lawyer presenting evidence to a jury, a writer needs to present evidence to support each major reason that leads to the final conclusion. This activity asks you to look at how the writer of Text 14 does so.

Listed in the table below are the main points and some of the supporting evidence used, but not necessarily in the right order. Allocate each piece of evidence to the point it is being used to support in the passage.

	Statement		Evidence
1	The railways changed the country in many ways	A	New high-speed lines are being built in Spain, Italy, Taiwan and Korea but Britain only has 100 km of high-speed line
2	Sometimes the government should have got more involved in the running of the railways	B	In the 19th century, many people were killed in rail accidents
3	History shows that the way in which the railways are organised has always been subject to change	C	Railways are carrying more people now than at any time in the past
4	Surprisingly, railways are currently enjoying a successful period but their future in the UK is still in doubt	D	Railways boosted trade, led to social changes and helped Britain in war time
5	The UK is out of line with other countries when it comes to new investment in rail travel	E	The railways have moved from private ownership to nationalised and back to private again

Commentary

The points and evidence are matched as follows: 1D, 2B, 3E, 4C, 5A.

 Bias, attitude and authority

The writer of Text 14 has a particularly sympathetic attitude towards the railways in general. You may also feel that the writer succeeds in giving an impression of authority and knows what he or she is talking about and therefore deserves to be taken notice of. Here we will consider how these impressions are achieved.

 Critical response activity

One way of pursuing an initial hunch you may have about bias in a text is to investigate the way the main subjects of the text are referred to. Here, this means (a) the railways, and (b) the government.

1 The table below gives a list of phrases used to describe what has happened to the railways at different times. Write a paragraph describing what this investigation reveals about how the attitude of the writer has been conveyed to the reader.

Railways described as...	Things railways did or which happened to them
■ A special invention ■ It has ... heroes	They: ■ boosted trade ■ stimulated development ■ brought in changes ■ played a vital part ■ have been poorly treated ■ have undergone upheaval ■ can never be allowed to stand still

2 Carry out a similar investigation for yourself by collecting all the phrases used in the text to describe the actions taken by governments in relation to the railways. Write about your findings.

Commentary

The lexis associated with the railways is almost entirely favourable with positive connotations. If we consider the verbs listed above, four of them ('boosted', 'stimulated', 'brought in' [changes] and 'played' [a vital part]) all suggest an active, even dynamic, and beneficial role. By contrast, the two verbs that describe the effect on the railways of the actions of the government ('have been poorly treated' and 'have undergone upheaval') imply that the railways have been undeserving victims. Therefore, our sympathies are engaged on the side of the railways and against the government.

This feeling is confirmed by the list of the actions attributed to the government:

■ constant tinkering at the margins

■ politically inspired reorganisations

■ cannot stop meddling

■ hand-wringing and parsimony which accompanies investment.

Here, it is the verbs and nouns that are the locomotives doing the work, hauling the semantic train of disapproval behind them. 'Tinkering' and 'meddling' are practically synonyms, with their shared connotations of unhelpful, petty interference, whereas the nouns 'hand-wringing' and 'parsimony' both imply meanness and lack of generosity.

Therefore, virtually all of the key lexical features associated with the railways have overwhelmingly positive connotations, while the reverse is true for those associated with the government.

The right connections: conjunctions and cohesion

When constructing a logical argument, a vital group of words and phrases help lock the different ideas together and signal the direction of an argument. These are conjunctions (or connectives). Some of the key conjunctions used in Text 14 are:

■ 'yet' – a contrasting point is coming next (it may surprise you!)

■ 'but' – here is a contrasting point to consider

■ 'moreover' – here is another similar point to consider

■ 'not just ... but' – here are two related and similar points for you to consider

■ 'because' – here is the evidence or the explanation for the previous point.

Other examples include:

- words or phrases that announce 'Here is another thing':
  - and
  - in addition
  - furthermore
- words or phrases that announce 'Here is a different thing':
  - however
  - on the other hand
  - by contrast
- words or phrases that announce 'Here is something that follows on logically or as a necessary consequence':
  - so
  - therefore
  - as a result
  - inevitably.

Looking out for these logical 'signals' can be useful in two ways:

- When analysing a text that is making a case and putting forward an argument, this can help you identify the structure of the text and follow the author's train of thought.
- When writing an essay of your own, use these connectives to create a clear argument of your own, showing the logic of your own ideas.

🔍 The language of authority

If arguments are to make us take notice, we need to believe that the authors know what they are talking about – that they truly have authority. This is partly achieved by the nature of what they say (Is it coherent and are points supported with convincing evidence? Is the underlying logic signalled by appropriately cohesive connections?) but also by how they say it. In the context of Text 14, which is an extract from a non-fiction history book, this means sustaining an educated, authoritative and sophisticated style. There may be some lessons from this that you can apply to your own essay writing to ensure that you convince an examiner that you, too, have authority.

■ Critical response activity

1 How personal or impersonal is the style?

    a How often does the writer use the first person singular (I, me, etc.)?

    b What about the first person plural (we, us) – and who does it include?

    c How often is the audience addressed directly in the second person (you)?

2 What use does the author make of strong declaratives? For much of the time, the author makes direct and assertive statements (in the form of declarative sentences) that imply he or she is making judgements on the basis of considerable knowledge. Here are a couple of examples:

- 'As ... this book demonstrates, the railways transformed Britain'
- 'Across the world the railways are expanding'.

Look for more phrases that have a similar effect.

3 What use does the author make of tentative phrasing? There are occasional phrases that slightly soften or hedge these assertions, making a statement seem a little more tentative, as with the phrase: 'it could be argued that there should have been more …' What other examples of tentative phrasing can you find?

4 What grammatical choices has the author made which relate to the register? As we have seen on p20, the register of a text is a combination of grammatical and lexical aspects – the kinds of sentence structures being used and the vocabulary used. In this case the writer uses Standard English grammar throughout (it is unlikely that a text written in a local dialect would be taken as seriously) and employs a range of sentence types, including some reasonably long and complex ones. Some forms of sentence construction work particularly well and strike readers as especially effective – the art of effective writing (or speaking) is called **rhetoric**. The table below shows some examples of effective sentence types.

Sentence type	Examples from the text
A list of three items grouped together (**triplet**)	They generate economic growth, enable people … to travel comfortably, and cause less environmental damage
Extended lists	Not in the lands of Stephenson, Hudson, Watkin, Gresley, Sir Bob Reid and so many other heroes
Paired phrases that reinforce each other by saying the same thing in two different ways (**synonymy**)	[1] we have taken the railways for granted and [2] failed to realise what a very special invention they are
A clear pair of contrasts setting up an **antithesis** (a pair of opposites) – always a strong ending	The railways may be flourishing … But … their development is … constrained

Try to find other examples of each type of sentence in the text.

The right register: field-specific lexis

The choice of lexis in any text must, of course, depend on the context of production – its subject matter and the time, place and purpose. The choice of lexis will also imply the kinds of readers that the text is designed for and the level of specialist knowledge it takes for granted. We can call this field-specific lexis. It may include abbreviations, such as SRA, which are known as **initialisms**.

The right register: your lexical choice

The other key to the right register – at least in more formal, academic contexts – is to access the wide range of vocabulary available. Thanks to our history, with its series of invasions and conquests, the English lexicon is particularly rich, and we can think of it as having a number of 'layers' deposited at different times in the past:

- The layer at the bottom includes the oldest words in the language from Anglo-Saxon, or Old English, brought to England by Germanic tribes from AD449. These include the basic, down-to-earth vocabulary of everyday English like 'man', 'earth', 'hill', 'the', 'that', 'was' and 'him'.

Key terms

Rhetoric: the technique of using language persuasively in order to influence the opinions and behaviour of an audience.

Triplet: a pattern of three repeated words or phrases.

Synonym: a word that has the same or similar meaning to another word; for example, 'smile' and 'grin' are synonyms, as they mean more or less the same thing, but carry different connotations.

Antithesis: the juxtaposition of contrasting words or phrases to create a sense of balance or opposition between conflicting ideas.

Initialism: an abbreviation formed by a set of initials standing for a longer phrase.

Think about it

The following words from the lexical field of economics and business are all used in the text:

- privatisation
- economic growth
- the SRA
- booming
- capital
- amalgamation
- individualism.

What does this imply about the author's expectation of the audience?

- The next layer includes words brought to England by the Vikings (from their own Norse tongue) from AD787, such as 'score', 'fellow' and 'sky'.

- Some Latin words also came into English before AD1000 and as it was the language of the Christian Church, religious terms like 'altar' date from this period.

- The <u>invasion</u> of the Normans in 1066 started a long <u>revolution</u> in the <u>language</u> which <u>introduced</u> a thick new layer of French and Latin-based words, often <u>associated</u> with <u>legality</u>, <u>government</u>, <u>fashion</u> and <u>sophistication</u>. All the underlined words in the previous sentence are of Latinate origin.

- Many more words from Latin, Italian, Greek and other sources came into use with the great expansion in learning and culture during the Renaissance period (from 1500) and the process continues today. This 'top layer' includes the specialised, literary and technical vocabulary that we associate with an authoritative 'academic' style, and tends to be **polysyllabic**.

Key terms

Polysyllabic words: words with more than one syllable.

Critical response activity

The more formal and academic the register, the more words from the 'top layer' (or the more specialised, literary and technical words) there are likely to be.

Consider the sentences in the table below, which are taken from 'The Future is Rail' and then rewritten using lower-level lexis. How does this affect the impression of authority created?

Original	Re-write
It was rather <u>inauspicious</u> that at the opening of the first railway a government minister was killed	It was <u>bad luck</u> that a government minister was killed at the opening of the first railway
The railways were a <u>quintessential</u> 19th century invention	Trains were <u>pretty typical</u> of their time, really
without any of the <u>hand-wringing</u> and <u>parsimony</u> that accompanies any investment in the railways	without the usual <u>worrying</u> and <u>meanness</u> that goes on when considering spending money on trains

Think about it

Look back at *Thomas and Friends Annual 2008* (Text 15) and consider how the contrasting lexical ranges of the two texts reflect their very different implied audiences.

Practical activity

Compose your own argument either in response to Text 14 (perhaps making the case against the railways) or on a topic of your own choice about which you have strong feelings. Try to employ some of the techniques explored in this topic to make your text coherent, cohesive and convincing.

7　A journey into the language of literature

Text 31: *Dombey and Son* and Text 32: 'Adlestrop'

In their different ways, these two texts reflect the importance of railways in our culture, history and imagination, although the contrast in style with the previous texts could hardly be greater. These texts also introduce two literary genres (the novel and the lyric poem) so that you will be able to develop further the skills required to make productive comparisons between texts.

Some contexts of production

Charles Dickens, the author of *Dombey and Son*, was one of the great popular writers of his day. His novels were serialised sagas, comparable in their grip on the popular imagination to any television drama of our own time. By 1846, when he started writing *Dombey and Son*, Dickens was a highly successful author with a huge readership and the railways were spreading through the country like wildfire. The arrival of these huge iron monsters, roaring and bellowing, belching steam and smoke, and tearing across the countryside at previously unimaginable speeds, seems to have been met with a mixture of excitement and terror. In this extract, Dickens uses the description of a train journey to reflect the dark mood of his central character, young Mr Dombey.

However, by the time that Edward Thomas wrote 'Adlestrop' (the poem was first published in 1917, although the journey it refers to is thought to have taken place three years before, in June 1914), the railways were an established and essential part of life, and hundreds of branch lines had reached even the smallest and most isolated of villages. In this poem, the poet reflects on his memory of making an unscheduled stop at one of these places – Adlestrop in Gloucestershire.

As we explore both texts, we will be working towards answering the following question:

> How do the writers of these two texts convey their attitudes towards and ideas about their experiences of travel?

Critical response activity

A good overview captures the essence of a text and, in particular, identifies the kinds of ideas, feelings and attitudes it conveys. Read each text a couple of times and then decide which of the options in the table below seems to offer the best overview of each text.

Dombey and Son	'Adlestrop'
a A relatively unemotional account of a journey by train in which the writer uses a variety of metaphors to convey his relaxed enjoyment of the journey and which offers a gentle and peaceful description of the world that passes by his carriage window	**a** A celebration of the coming of the railways to the countryside and the travel that it has made possible

▶

b A powerful evocation of the almost destructive power, speed and rhythm of an express train, which reflects the despairing mood of the passenger and uses an extended metaphor that compares the train to a kind of monster and even to death itself	**b** A criticism of the impact of the railways on the countryside, especially the destruction of birdlife habitats
c A panoramic impression of the English countryside as it speeds by the window of a powerful express train, which conveys the author's resentment of the destruction caused by the coming of the railways	**c** A gently nostalgic reminiscence of a moment of natural tranquillity experienced, unexpectedly during a train journey one summer
d A celebration of the triumph of technology in general and steam locomotion in particular during the age of the Industrial Revolution, in which the writer is in awe of the power of the train	**d** A slightly melancholic reminiscence on which the poet uses his experience to convey a sense of loneliness and isolation

Commentary

Dombey and Son: as this is anything but 'uncmotional' and far from being a 'celebration', we can discount (a) and (d). There is some truth in (c): the effect of the long lists of sights from the window covering town, countryside, houses, roads, fields and buildings is certainly 'panoramic', and there is an emphasis on the train's destructive power. However, as the opening sentence of the extract establishes, the entire passage is conveying the point of view of a character that may or may not coincide with the author's personal views, so for this reason option (b) is preferred.

'Adlestrop'*:* after the two obviously inappropriate options – (a) and (b) – are eliminated, the remaining options both contain elements of truth. The tone of the poem is certainly nostalgic and could be described as melancholic, as the apparent absence of human activity does convey something of an isolated feeling. However, many readers might find a stronger sense of 'natural tranquillity' (c) emerging in the final two stanzas of the poem.

 ### Critical response activity

Write a short paragraph that sums up the significant similarities and differences between the two texts.

Commentary

Similarities: both texts are types of narrative that present us with personal responses to experiences of train journeys, and they describe both the train itself and its surroundings. Both texts use language to try to capture not just the experience of the journey but also the mood of the passenger.

Differences: the texts convey fundamentally different moods. The train in *Dombey and Son* is presented as a violent, destructive monster tearing through the land, whereas 'Adlestrop' captures a moment of silence, stillness and peace at a quiet country station. However, even 'Adlestrop' hints that this tranquillity is a short-lived interlude 'for that minute', before the train sets off again.

Critical response activity

A story or an anecdote can be narrated from a number of possible viewpoints, as summarised in the table below (using the story of *Goldilocks and the Three Bears* as an example). The particular point of view that a text adopts is sometimes called its **stance**.

Stance	Explanation	Example
First person: author	The author writes as himself or herself, using first person	I first encountered *Goldilocks and the Three Bears* as a small child, when my mother read me the story
First person: **persona**	The author creates a character (or persona) from whose first-person point of view the story is told	(Goldilocks) I decided to go for a walk in the woods one morning, so I set off in the direction of Mr and Mrs Bear's cottage
Third person: **omniscient**	An all-knowing author is not directly present in the story but simply relates it – and has access to the thoughts and feelings of all the main characters	When Goldilocks set off one morning little did she know what awaited her. Her heart was full of joy to be out in the woods. Meanwhile, Mr and Mrs Bear were preparing for breakfast
Third person: indirect/ restricted	The author uses the third person but only to express the inner feelings and point of view of some characters – perhaps even just one	Goldilocks set out into the woods with hope in her heart. She wondered whether she would meet anyone. After all, last week she had bumped into Mr Badger going about his business, which had been quite a surprise!

Which of these stances are adopted in each of the extracts from *Dombey and Son* and 'Adlestrop'?

Key terms

Stance: the position and attitude adopted by the narrator towards the events described or narrated.

Persona: a narrator or voice created by a writer (in prose or verse) who is different from the writer him/herself.

Omniscient narrator: an omniscient narrator has a complete overview of the story, and can move freely between different characters and scenes, with full knowledge of everything that happens.

Lyrical: associated with lyric poetry; highly emotional and full of feeling.

Commentary

In the case of Dombey and Son, which is clearly a third-person account, it is easy to overlook the fact that this is very much the point of view of the character, Mr Dombey, rather than that of the author. This is established in the opening sentence ('he found no pleasure or relief in the journey') and reiterated towards the end: 'As Mr Dombey looks out of his carriage window …' In 'Adlestrop', as with much **lyrical** verse, we often tend to identify the first person voice of the poem ('Yes, I remember') as that of the author, although we would be wrong to assume this always to be the case.

Form and structure

We have previously thought about some of our non-literary texts in terms of their genre and discourse structure. It is also helpful to consider the form and structure of literary texts. One way of understanding this is to think of an animal. Its form is its outside shape that makes it recognisable; we know a bear is a bear because of its fur, its size, its distinctive shape, its four legs and its characteristic way of moving. However, its structure is what lies beneath its skin – the arrangements of bones in its skeleton, the network of muscles that control the joints and the nature and position of its internal organs.

Although the two ideas of form and structure are closely linked, what is meant by the two terms is summarised in the table below.

Key terms

Metre: the rhythmic pattern in a line of verse. This depends on the pattern of stressed syllables in a line.

Form	Structure

In poetry:
■ What genre of poem is it? (sonnet, ode, ballad, lyric, epic, limerick, dramatic monologue, etc.)
■ How (if at all) is the poem broken down into verses/stanzas?
■ Is there a regular pattern (length, rhyme, **metre**) being followed?
	All kinds of literary texts:
	■ How does the text start?
	■ What kind of sequence does the text follow? Does it:
	  – develop an idea logically, like an argument?
	  – include any digressions or diversions?
	  If a narrative, does it:
	  – tell a story in chronological sequence?
	  – use flashbacks or other devices that break away from this order?

In prose narratives (novels, short stories): ■ What genre of prose is it? (science fiction, fantasy, thriller, etc.) ■ Was it written as a single text or produced in instalments as was *Dombey and Son*? ■ What is the narrative stance of the story? ■ How is the text broken down into chapters or other sections? ■ How are the three elements of narrative – narration, description and dialogue – employed?	■ How does each stage of the text relate to the previous one and lead on to what comes next? ■ Where are the points of real tension, crisis and climax, and how are they resolved? ■ How does the end conclude or resolve the previous ideas and problems?
In drama: ■ What genre of drama is it? (comedy, tragedy, mystery, pantomime, etc.) ■ How is it organised into acts and scenes? ■ What use is made of dialogue, monologue/soliloquy, physical action and other dramatic methods to tell the story?	

Critical response activity

Compare the form and structure of the two texts by following the prompt questions in the table below.

Dombey and Son	'Adlestrop'
How many paragraphs is the text divided into and how do they reflect different aspects or stages of the journey?	How many (and what kind of) stanzas is the poem divided into and what kinds of ideas are developed in each one?
What does each paragraph contain? Can you identify any patterns or repetitions being used?	What patterns of rhyme and rhythm (or metre) does each stanza follow?
The big question (try to think about this as you go along): how do these formal and structural aspects relate to any of the ideas, feelings and attitudes in the passage?	The big question (try to think about this as you go along): how do these formal and structural aspects relate to any of the ideas, feelings and attitudes in the passage?

Commentary

In *Dombey and Son*, each paragraph seems to represent a stage of the journey as the train leaves the town and then travels through a variety of landscapes before arriving at another town or city. Each paragraph consists of long lists of short phrases that capture the speed of the landscape passing the passenger's window. The many repeated patterns (in particular, the final phrase comparing the train to 'the … monster, Death', which acts in a similar way to a chorus or refrain in a poem) sets up a very distinct rhythm, possible imitating the regular rattling sound of a train speeding over the joints in the track.

In 'Adlestrop', Thomas uses a more or less regular verse form – three verses of four lines, or **quatrains**. The first stanza provides a 'frame' for the poem by introducing the reminiscence, the second describes the platform, and the third and fourth stanzas take the point of view to the surrounding countryside, the skies and the far distance.

A rhyme scheme operates on the second and fourth line of each verse and most of the lines consist of eight syllables (with several exceptions), although the pattern of **stresses** only really achieves a regular beat in the third verse, when the poet seems most at rest:

> And <u>will</u>ows, <u>will</u>ow-<u>herb</u>, and <u>grass</u>
> And <u>mead</u>ow <u>sweet</u> and <u>hay</u>cocks <u>dry</u>,
> No <u>whit</u> less <u>still</u> and <u>lonely</u> <u>fair</u>
> Than the <u>high</u> <u>cloud</u>lets <u>in</u> the <u>sky</u>

In the first two verses, Thomas disrupts the rhythm of several lines by a combination of **enjambement** and **caesuras**, as if to mimic the suddenness of the train's halt and to allow the very short sentences to suggest the stillness of the moment:

> **Yes. I remember** Adlestrop –   *Caesura*
> The name, because one **afternoon**   *Enjambement*
> Of heat the express-train drew up there
> **Unwontedly. It** was late June.   *Caesura*
> The steam hissed. Someone cleared his throat.
> No-one left and no-one **came**   *Enjambement*
> On the bare **platform. What** I saw
> Was Adlestrop – only the name.   *Caesura*

Key terms

Quatrain: verse of four lines.

Stresses: in spoken language, we stress some syllables and not others. In the phrase 'It's a nice day today', we probably stress three syllables: 'It's a <u>nice</u> <u>day</u> to<u>day</u>.'

Enjambement: continuity of the sense and rhythm from one line of verse to the next without end-stopping.

Caesura: a pause in the middle of a line of verse, usually indicated by a punctuation mark.

Background information

More poetry terms

You will already have a vocabulary for discussing poetic techniques from your GCSE English course. You can add to this by using these terms and concepts:

tetrameter: a line with four stressed syllables (see 'Adlestrop')

pentameter: a line with five stressed syllables

end-stopped line: a line of verse with a punctuation mark at the end of the line to indicate a pause.

Critical response activity

With your overview and some discussion of form and structure in place, the major part of your essay will consist of an in-depth examination of the details of the two texts.

In the examination you only have 45 minutes in which to discuss the texts you are comparing, so the question to ask here is: What are the most *significant* features of language and style that contribute most to the impact of the texts?

■ Note down your ideas about this on *Dombey and Son* and 'Adlestrop' before moving on to the tasks below.

1 For each of the texts, decide from the suggestions in the table below which language features are essential to be included in your discussion and which are less important. Do this by deciding on a rank order (1 = high) of the importance of the features for the overall impact of the text.

Dombey and Son		'Adlestrop'	
Feature	Rank order	Feature	Rank order
The use of exclamation marks		The use of onomatopoeia in the poem	
The use of long sentences consisting of lists of short phrases to convey the speed of the train and the passing landscape		The conversational tone established by the abrupt minor sentence containing the word 'Yes' at the start	
The use of a series of **adverbial phrases** in the third paragraph to convey the passing landscape		The use of some slightly archaic-sounding words, such as 'unwontedly', 'whit' and 'cloudlets'	
The use of many more or less onomatopoeic words to convey the sound of the train		The use of several short, simple and abrupt sentences	
The use of many verbs that convey speed and power		The use of lists of concrete nouns in the lexical field of plants in the third verse	
The repetition and variation of several key phrases throughout the passage		The use of **pastoral** imagery in the third and fourth verses	
The imagery of decay and dereliction in the final paragraph		The use of first person pronouns in the first and third verses	

2 Investigate and write a short paragraph to discuss some of what you have decided to be the most significant features, identifying examples from the text and explaining how they have contributed to the ideas, feelings and attitudes expressed.

Key terms

Adverbial phrase: phrase containing information about how, where or when an action takes place.

Pastoral: a list of words or phrases without the use of any conjunctions, portraying country life especially in an idealised or romanticised form.

Asyndetic list: a form of list, in which there is no conjunction (such as 'and' or 'but') separating the final two items. This can give an open-ended feel to the list, perhaps suggesting there is more that could be added. The opposite to this is a syndetic list, such as 'At the market I bought apples, oranges, pears *and* bananas'.

Commentary

Although there might be differences of emphasis, most readers of the texts would probably wish to discuss the following features.

Dombey and Son: the use of long **asyndetic lists** in each paragraph is perhaps the principal way in which Dickens conveys the speed of the train. There is a large number of verbs with violent connotations that suggest the train is committing some kind of assault on the landscape: these include 'whirled', 'forced', 'piercing', 'dragging', 'burrowing', 'flashing', 'mining', 'booming', 'bursting', 'tearing on' and 'plunging'. The lists of adverbial phrases help to convey speed: 'through the fields', 'through the corn', 'through the hay', 'through the chalk', 'through the mould', 'through the clay', 'through the rock', 'through the hollow', 'on the height', 'by the heath', by the orchard'. The various onomatopoeic terms ('shriek', 'cries', 'roar', 'rattle', 'yell') convey the sheer racket of the 'monster'. The text reiterates its central extended metaphor comparing the momentum of the train to the progress of death itself by its repeated, varied motif ('Triumphant monster ... Remorseless monster ... Indomitable monster') and by the nature of the imagery of the final paragraph with its references to 'ashes', 'everything around is blackened' and 'the end of everything'.

'Adlestrop': the abruptness of the opening minor sentence ('Yes') establishes a colloquial tone and a sense that we are arriving mid-conversation. The arrival of the train on the 'bare' platform suggests an absence of human activity (with the repetition of 'no-one left and no-one came'), and the evocation of nature is achieved mainly by the introduction of plentiful pastoral imagery (again, using a list of items although, unlike *Dombey and Son*, these are linked by the conjunction 'and').

Text 23: 'Zaire' and Text 24: *Heart of Darkness*

If you really want to find out about a place, what kinds of thing should you read? Perhaps an informative article from a well-respected magazine will tell you all you need to know. Or perhaps one of our great writers of literature may also have visited the place and chosen to use it as the setting for a novel.

These two texts will enable you to compare the results of a literary and a non-literary response to the same location: the river Zaire (also called the river Congo) in central Africa.

Background information

Contextual information for Texts 23 and 24

Zaire: the Republic of Zaire was formerly the Belgian Congo, but it gained its independence in 1960. It adopted the name of Zaire in 1971, then in 1997 the name was again changed to The Democratic Republic of Congo, which is the current name at the time of writing. The river running through it has also been known as the Congo and the Zaire at various times.

National Geographic magazine: a long-established and highly respected monthly magazine that is the official journal of the National Geographic Society. Its features cover a wide range of geographical, scientific, historical and other subjects, and are renowned not only for the quality and reliability of their reporting but also for outstanding photography.

Heart of Darkness: published in 1902, this short novel follows the journey taken by its narrator, Marlow, as he travels down the river Congo in what was then a Belgian colony in central Africa. He is appalled by what he finds in the so-called 'dark continent' and by its effect on other European settlers, one of whom, a character called Kurtz, has apparently abandoned all forms

Practical activity

You should now be ready to attempt as a full essay your answer to the question:

How do the writers of these two texts convey their attitudes towards and ideas about their experiences of travel?

AQA Examiner's tip

Remember that rather than write two separate essays, you should make comparisons throughout by using phrases such as 'Both Texts 30 and 31 ...' and 'However, whereas in Text 30 ... in Text 31 ...' (see Comparing texts on p21–22).

of 'civilised' values. In part, the title of the novel refers to the description of Africa that was common at the time. The whole novel is a kind of story within a story; Marlow is recounting his experiences to a group of companions who have gathered on a boat on the Thames in London.

Joseph Conrad: born in Poland and adopting English as his second language, Conrad was a well-travelled seaman before he embarked on his career as a writer. Many of his novels deal with the experience of foreign travel: *Heart of Darkness* is based on a journey he actually undertook as a captain of a river vessel. In the novel he explores the very idea of 'civilisation' and questions the way European countries had colonised and were attempting to govern many parts of Africa.

Key terms

Objective: a viewpoint that attempts to achieve neutrality.

Subjective: a personal, possibly biased, point of view.

AQA Examiner's tip

Make sure you do not confuse the words *objective* and *subjective* (which refer to points of view) with the words *object* and *subject* (which, in grammar, are the names of parts of speech). Check each of these terms in the glossary to make sure you understand the difference.

Critical response activity

In order to compare these two quite different responses to the river, you should ask yourself the same questions about both texts:

1 What factual information does the text present?

2 What impressions of the river does the text evoke and how are these impressions conveyed?

3 To what extent does the text present an **objective** or a **subjective** impression, and what attitude does the writer have towards the subject?

4 How do you think the contexts of production and reception are reflected in the texts themselves and the ways you respond to them?

5 What are the most significant differences between the literary language of National Geographic and that of *Heart of Darkness*?

6 Work through these questions for both texts before comparing your work with the commentary below.

Commentary

1 The *National Geographic* text seems to have been based on a real river journey undertaken by a reporter, and is peppered with facts and figures about the river that are supported by maps and photographic evidence. The report combines the first-hand observation and narration of the reporter with information and quotations provided by local people about the realities of life on the river. On the other hand, as a novel, *Heart of Darkness* may or may not be made up, and offers relatively few facts at all – it is a personal response, the factual content of which amounts to a description of the difficulties of navigating the river.

2 The impressions that emerge from the *National Geographic* text are of an increasingly chaotic, desperate and somewhat brutal trade being carried on amid the teeming wildlife, with little regard to animal welfare. The writer has tried to evoke the unpleasant sounds ('terrified screams') and smells ('stench of the latrines') as well as the sights of trading on the river. He has used asyndetic lists to convey the sheer quantity of goods being traded ('soap, salt, sugar, fishhooks, medicine') and wildlife being exploited ('tortoises, clawless otters, pangolins, monitor lizards'). Pre-modifying adjectives are used to create striking images ('murky river', 'bulbous lips', 'whiplike feelers', 'clamoring merchants') but it is perhaps the use of verbs that conveys most clearly both the noisy desperation of the activity ('the traders … yelling … hurled … clamouring') and the brutality with which the animals are handled ('crocodiles are trussed and dumped', 'game meat is stashed, and butchers' machetes are thumping').

In contrast, the focus in *Heart of Darkness* is more on the natural surroundings and the peculiar stillness that the narrator finds so unnerving. The initial description ('like travelling back to the earliest beginnings of the world') has a primeval quality, and there is a contrast between imagery of light ('the brilliance of sunshine … silvery sandbanks') and darkness ('the gloom of overshadowed distances') with even a hint of witchcraft ('you thought yourself bewitched'). The main theme of the description – the rather sinister stillness of the place – is reiterated several times and even personified ('brooding over an inscrutable intention. It looked at you with a vengeful aspect'). As Marlow continues, however, his words seem to hint at some deeper mystery or meaning. Explaining how the need for concentration on his job takes his mind off this sinister feeling, he adds 'The inner truth is hidden – luckily, luckily …' At this point a reader of literature may recognise this as a signal from the author that there are deeper thematic or philosophical ideas to be found here. Is Marlow saying that the routine but absorbing business of everyday life stops us from thinking too hard about the inner truth about life – and a good thing too?

3   Although the *National Geographic* article is written by a reporter, with occasional use of the first person, and is thus inevitably subjective to some extent, the inclusion of quotations from local people (the dialogue is reported without direct comment by the author) and photographic evidence helps to create the suggestion of objectivity. The reporter refers to himself in the singular ('I') only four times; this allows us to forget the subjectivity of the text some of the time and to accept his description and narration almost as if it were a camera directly recording the scene. Indeed, the magazine may pride itself on the 'objectivity' of its reporting. However, the captions provided for the photographs are emotive rather than objective ('crammed into every available space on the dilapidated government-operated riverboats') and are clearly designed to invite us to share the reporter's attitude – that is, to have sympathy for the local people on the boat and the conditions they have to endure – and there are also hints of criticism of the government. The descriptions of the treatment of animals may also be partly designed to shock by their brutality.

Heart of Darkness also offers a first person account, but in a literary work of fiction the 'I' of the text is rather less to be trusted than the 'I' of the *National Geographic*. Here, the 'reporter' (or narrator, as he would be described in a literary narrative) is himself a character (Marlow) created by the author, Joseph Conrad. As in *Dombey and Son* (Text 31), we are presented with a point of view and set of attitudes that may not be reliable and are certainly not intended to be objective. The interruption at the end of the extract by one of Marlow's listeners ('Try to be civil, Marlow') reminds us of this.

4   *National Geographic* has an international reputation for factual accuracy, so we are immediately inclined to treat its account as 'real' and reliable, whereas with *Heart of Darkness* we are much less certain how far the description is pure invention or how far it is based on Conrad's actual experience as a steamboat captain on the Congo in the 1890s.

As *National Geographic* has a generally well-informed and well-educated audience, the overall register of the text is relatively formal and specialised with a wide range of lexis from the appropriate lexical fields. Some quite field-specific geographical terms (such as 'navigable', 'tributaries', 'lianas') and some fairly unusual animal names ('sitatunga antelope', 'mangabey monkey') reflect expectations of the readership and their knowledge. However, most readers of the magazine will have very little experience of places and ways of life like the one described, and the detailed descriptions of sights and sounds – with the occasionally rather shocking details (such as the mangabey monkey) – seem designed both to create strong images and possibly to disturb its readers.

Similarly, Conrad's novel would originally have been read by people with very little chance of experiencing the realities of such a place for themselves, although they might have had fanciful, exotic or even glamorous ideas about the 'empire'. In 1902, many Europeans might have believed that Africa was 'less civilised' and might have found this view reflected in the text. However, the context of reception has changed and opinions are now divided about whether or not Conrad's novel is in some ways racist. His critics say that its description of Africa reflects 19th-century European views that few people now would support; his defenders point out that it is not Conrad's account but Marlow's and that Conrad is actually exposing such views, allowing readers to judge for themselves.

5 The first part of the *National Geographic* text relies on factual reporting and an interview, but even this non-literary piece actually uses a number of techniques which you might think of as 'literary'. It actually quotes Conrad's metaphorical description (taken from elsewhere in *Heart of Darkness*), which compares the river to a snake, and goes on to use a good deal of figurative language itself; think about the metaphors used as the river 'cuts an … arc', and 'countless tributaries lace the forest'. In the second part of the text, we have already seen that the reporter uses a wide range of colourful and multi-sensory language to describe life on the boat, with as much imagination as any novelist. Nevertheless, there is none of the symbolism or room for interpretation that began to emerge in *Heart of Darkness* – it makes its point directly and unmistakeably, and is unlikely to have students and tutors scratching their heads about any 'deeper meanings'. Conrad's text includes less specialised lexis from similar fields (vegetation, wildlife) but has more specialised lexis associated with navigation ('snag', 'channel', 'sandbank'), reflecting the expertise of the narrator. There is also a higher proportion of abstract noun phrases such as 'implacable force' and 'inscrutable intention', which makes the description seem less physical or earthy. However, although literary and non-literary are convenient labels we use to distinguish different kinds of writing, their language may not be as different as you imagined.

Practical activity

Take your exploration of these two texts further by answering this question:

Compare and contrast the ways these texts explore responses to the river Congo/Zaire.

Changing world, changing genres: language and context

Texts 2 and 3: Postcards and Text 12: A personal account from an internet travelblog

As long as people have set out to see the world and experience different cultures, they have sought to share their experiences with others. However, as the world and technology change, so do the means of communication available to people. Our next two texts illustrate the way different genres arise from developments in lifestyle and technology.

When travel of any kind was a novelty, and being able to take a holiday something of a major event, the need arose for a quick and easy way of keeping in touch with friends and family at home, giving them a snapshot of the exotic places (such as Blackpool) you were visiting. So, the humble postcard was born, in all its naughty and not-so-naughty varieties (see the Background information box below). As Texts 2 and 3 in the Anthology show, the postcard is still alive and well – even if you are only ever a text message away from someone just about anywhere in the world, you can usually squeeze rather more into a postcard than a text.

However, why limit yourself to the few lines a postcard allows when you can pop into an internet café on holiday and post your traveller's tales on a blog for all your friends at home (or anyone else who's interested) to access? Text 12 offers an example of such a blog that gives a fairly detailed account of the author's travels in Vietnam.

Texts 2 and 3: Postcards

Background information

A short history of postcards

1869 The first official postcard is created (by a Hungarian doctor)

1870 The Post Office introduces the first postcards in Britain. One side of the card is for the address and the other side for a very brief message. There are no pictures at this stage.

1894 Various companies start to make cards with pictures (by this time, mass travel by rail and increased annual leave allowed in mills and factories is encouraging holidays to fast-growing seaside resorts in Britain).

1899 A standard size of 4.75 inches by 3.5 inches is adopted in Britain. The address still has one side to itself; the other side contains the illustration and message.

1902 The British Post Office begins to allow pictures to appear on the front of postcards and the address to appear together with a message on the back. Postcard manufacturers start to produce cards with a line drawn down the middle of the back – this format is still used today.

1940s The 'photochrom' postcard makes it possible to use vivid colours.

Background information

Contextual information for Texts 2 and 3

Andechs: a town in Bavaria, Germany famous for its abbey and formerly a place of pilgrimage.

Klosterbräustüberl: the name of a hotel/restaurant in Andechs.

Hadj: the religious pilgrimage undertaken by Muslims.

Key terms

Genre conventions: the usual expectations or rules associated with a particular genre.

Ellipsis/elliptical: the omission of part of a sentence. Often part of a sentence is understood from the context e.g. 'See?' instead of 'Do you see?' Ellipsis can also be represented by three dots (…) to indicate the missing part of the sentence.

Homophones: words with the same sound but different meanings/ spellings.

Critical response activity

Some genres have a number of instantly recognisable features which have become standard ingredients – we might call these **genre conventions**.

Study Postcard 1. Try to identify and define some of the common features of the postcard genre. You might consider the:

- layout
- content and tone of the text
- kinds of sentences used
- lexis of the text.

Commentary

The first postcard (from R.B.) follows many typical postcard conventions – the date, the squeezing of writing into the space allowed, the slightly apologetic opening sentence and the obligatory semi-humorous ironic comparison with the weather at home ('Weather worse than in Bolton'). The very down-to-earth associations of Bolton create a humorous contrast with the rather glamorous-sounding Andechs Klosterbräustüberl. Perhaps you also noticed the use of shortened (**elliptical**) sentences with some key words omitted: 'Just to let you know' rather than 'I am just writing to let you know' and 'Am now in …' rather than 'I am now in …', which not only helps to create a chatty colloquial tone but also makes the most of the available space. The tenses used alternate between past ('there was even fresh snow …') and present ('am now in …'). The use of underlining representing the stress placed on the modal verb ('I <u>will</u> get in touch soon …'), thus strengthening the promise, and also gives the text the feel of spoken language, as does the exclamation mark at the end. The alphabetical **homophones** 'C U' (see you) at the end derive from the language of text messages. You might also have noted the use of non-English place names (complete with umlaut – ü and ä).

Critical response activity

Even if the genre of the postcard offers limited scope for originality and many of us stick pretty closely to the conventions when writing them, there is still variation in individual styles.

Let us continue to practise skills of comparative analysis by comparing Postcard 1 with Postcard 2, sent to the same recipient but by different authors. You might find it helpful first to organise your analysis using the headings and the structure provided in the table below, but remember to use connectives such as 'whereas', 'however', 'similarly' and 'on the other hand' (see pp33–4) when writing up your comparison in continuous prose.

Feature	Similarities	Differences
Layout		
Content and tone of the text		
Kinds of sentences used		
Lexis of the text		

Commentary

The layout and graphological organisation of both postcards is essentially similar as they follow the usual conventions (date, signatures) and constraints (only half a side of writing allowed) of the form. However, the author of Postcard 2 manages to squeeze in more neatly written text and more detail about their holiday. Like the first example, Postcard 2 refers by name to the place at which they are staying, although more detail is added about the accommodation and scenery. As with Postcard 1, but to a greater extent, the author has tried to achieve a colloquial tone and convey their enjoyment and enthusiasm by using three underlines to suggest the prosodic features of speech. Similarly, both postcards use exclamation marks to convey enthusiasm and humour at the end of the text, although Postcard 2 also does so elsewhere.

Both postcards make some reference to the place where the sender imagines the recipient to be, but in the case of Postcard 2 this means their own holiday destination (France). Both cards use ellipsis ('nice view though!', 'Hope France is going well!') and the sentences are mainly declaratives, although Postcard 2 includes interrogatives and a kind of filler ('you know') to create some kind of interactivity with the reader. In terms of lexis, the second card is noticeably more detailed though the adjectives used are basic enough ('good', 'narrow', 'quiet'). However, the use of the **intensifiers** ('very good', 'very quiet') and the much stronger adjective 'fantastic' make this seem a more enthusiastic account.

 Key terms

Intensifier: word or phrase (such as very, extremely) whose function is to intensify the meaning of the words to which it is attached.

Practical activity

Collect a selection of postcards that you or your family have received (or visit your local museum and archive to seek out older examples). Carry out your own independent analysis of two or three of them.

Text 12: A personal account from an internet travelblog

The original science fiction series *Star Trek* famously opened with Captain Kirk reading from his log, which recorded his reflections on all the significant events of the journey. Now, as cheap long-haul flights allow many of us to venture further afield, perhaps even taking a gap year to encounter new civilisations and boldly go where we have not gone before, the advance of internet technology can make us all Captain Kirks with our own blogs.

Text 12 is an example of this new genre – the travelblog – posted by an intrepid traveller during the Vietnamese leg of round-the-world gap-year tour.

Background information

Contextual information for Text 12

Before 1954, Vietnam was a French colony.

In 1954, the country was divided into North and South, which proceeded to fight each other with the non-communist south backed by the USA.

In 1973, the Americans withdrew, leading to the eventual reunion of the country in 1976 under the communist government in Hanoi, the capital city.

Ho Chi Minh was the leader of North Vietnam during the war, although he died in 1969. His body is still on display in the mausoleum in Hanoi.

Tuk-tuks are kinds of motorised tricycles used as taxis in South-east Asia, so called because of the sound made by their two-stroke engines.

Critical response activity

1 As you read the blog for the first time, try to define the kinds of attitudes and feelings the author conveys in her account of her experiences in Vietnam and how these are expressed. Overall, she talks about a 'mixed bag' of experiences so, for each of the topics described, collect evidence (in the form of quotations from the text) as suggested in the table below. Then try to comment on how these impressions have been created, using any appropriate terminology to describe the uses of language.

Topic	Favourable?		Unfavourable?		Comments
	Opinion	Evidence	Opinion	Evidence	
First impressions on entering the country					
The Ho Chi Minh mausoleum					
The Ho Chi Minh museum					
The behaviour of the other visitors					
The Museum of Ethnology					
The behaviour of the local people					
Lenin Park					

2 Consider the way the author of the blog represents herself and her travelling companions, and how she tries to engage the sympathy of her readers. Listed below is a list of references she makes to herself. Write a paragraph about the way she represents herself in the text and how this helps to engage our interest and sympathy:

- 'Ooo we were mad'
- 'We spit our dummies a bit'
- 'I can't explain how awful it was, but we were at breaking point'
- 'We left confused'
- 'prompting me to respond in the only way an Englishman can by speaking loudly about how rude it was … I'm well hard me'
- 'It was in Hanoi where I succumbed to tears … yes i miss dave, my family, my friends … soyeh, I had a little sob'
- 'Sofia is some kind of dancing queen … i however was AWFUL'

3 Consider the style of language adopted for this new genre. It is obviously in a fairly colloquial style – almost as if the writer wishes to create the impression that she is talking to us rather than writing. Think about how this impression of spoken language is achieved.

a Jot down your initial ideas about this before looking at the features of spoken language in the table below.

b Identify examples of each feature in the text.

c Write another paragraph to explain exactly what gives the text its colloquial, spoken language feel.

You may find it helpful to refer to the section on Spoken and written language on pp52–3.

Some features of spoken language	Evidence in Text 12
We often make minor errors in normal speech, such as slips of the tongue and other kinds of non-fluency	
We often supplement the words in speech with non-verbal sounds that also convey meaning	
We may tend to use more informal register in speech, according to context	
In speech we may blur or leave out some letter-sounds	
When telling a story we may tend to exaggerate (by using **hyperbole**)	
We may even resort to expletives and taboo language to make our point	

Key terms

Hyperbole: exaggeration used for impact and effect.

Phrasal verb: a phrase consisting of a verb and an adverb or preposition.

Commentary

1 The initial impression is of being somewhat overwhelmed and exploited, with the colloquial **phrasal verb** 'ripping off', the use of the pre-modifier 'unfortunate' to attract sympathy for the tourists' vulnerability and 'extortionate' to describe the extent of the intended exploitation. The metaphorical comparison through the verb 'swarmed' of the tuk-tuk drivers to angry bees is appropriate enough given the high-pitched buzz of their vehicles, but the writer then mistakes the sincerity of the couple who came to their aid. The writer uses irony on a couple of occasions, in her comment about the preserved body on display ('lovely'), which she subsequently clarifies as 'rather creepy actually', and the description of the sexual harassment of Sofia as 'nice'. The semantically connected words

■ Think about it

Like the author of Text 12, tourists often complain of being 'ripped off' by locals who inflate their prices and trick visitors with a variety of scams. Consider the other side of this coin: how can tourists sometimes be an unwelcome influence on the local community and culture?

■ Key terms

Phonetic spelling: the spelling of words to represent how they are pronounced (e.g. '...'elp me orf this 'orse').

Elision: the running together of words or the omission of parts of words, such as 'gonna' for 'going to' or 'y'know' for 'you know'.

Expletive: a swear word or phrase.

'bizarre' and 'confused' reinforce the somewhat puzzling experience of the Ho Chi Minh museum, but enthusiasm is conveyed by the adjective 'brilliant' applied to the Museum of Ethnology and the barbers in Hanoi. The writer's enjoyment of Hanoi street life is conveyed by a couple of uses of 'nice' and, more unusually, the use of 'mental' and 'craziness', which seem to take on positive connotations in this context. The adjectives 'angry' and 'aggressive' balance the impression, reminding us perhaps of those first impressions at the border town.

2   In many of these references the author seems almost to be making fun of herself and her emotional reactions, with relatively few 'straight' statements ('I can't explain how awful it was') untouched by irony. She implies she may have behaved rather childishly by using the idiomatic reference to the 'spitting out of dummies', and mocks her own lack of courage with the ironic 'I'm well hard, me.' She even distances herself from her attack of homesickness by describing it as 'succumbing' to tears and having a 'little sob', as if embarrassed by this. This self-mocking (self-deprecatory) tone is continued when she describes her dancing as 'AWFUL'. Perhaps we are more likely to find this engaging than if she had taken herself very seriously throughout.

3   In terms of 'normal' standards of 'correctness', the text contains many examples of what would usually be regarded as 'mistakes' in Standard English writing, such as the use of lower case 'i' and misspelled names, as well as lots of uncorrected typing errors (typos). It would seem that in genres such as this, and in e-communications generally, we seem to have fewer expectations of absolute 'correctness' and tolerate a higher proportion of such slips than in more traditional written genres. The writer also uses several examples of non-verbal utterances ('Hmmm', 'Ooo', 'tee hee', 'boo hoo'), which help to create the illusion of speech, and even inserts one mid-sentence to create an impression of the non-fluency of spontaneous talk – 'about mmmm 7 of your english pence'. There are lots of informal words and phrases (such as 'yeh' instead if 'yes') and some attempt to use **phonetic spelling** (as opposed to conventional spelling) to convey the usual pronunciation and **elision** of the phrases 'outta there' (out of) and 'gonna' (going to). Although most of the sentences are constructed and punctuated according to the usual conventions of written English, there are examples of one-word minor sentences ('Lovely') and the ellipsis of elements of a sentence ('Takes a bit of getting used to' instead of 'It takes a bit ...'). We sense the storyteller's hyperbole creeping in with 'There was a queue of approx 1 MILLION people' and, as with the spelling of 'AWFUL' later, the writer uses uppercase here to mimic the vocal stress which would be placed on the word if spoken. No doubt you also spotted the writer's use of an **expletive** which, although common enough in spoken English, occurs much less routinely in written genres.

Spoken and written language

When considering any text, especially those that represent or imitate speech in some way, it can be useful to bear in mind some of the differences between the spoken and written word:

■   *Writing* depends on letters, words and their presentation on the page. Pictures may also help; *speech* depends on the use of prosodic and paralinguistic features as much as the words themselves.

■   *Writing* (in most contexts) is usually in Standard English; *speech* may include non-Standard English such as dialect and slang.

- We usually expect *writing* to be planned and free of errors; as we usually make up *speech* as we go along, it includes all kinds of imperfections and non-fluency features.

- *Writing and speech* both depend on the grammar of the language to make sense; however, whereas sentences in *writing* usually have a clear construction, reflected in the way we punctuate them, sentences in *speech* may be more loosely constructed and omit words or phrases.

Speech in writing: we can represent spoken language on the page in several ways:

- make a transcript of what has been spoken which tries to record the conversation exactly see Text 17

- write a script with stage directions for actors, to help them interpret and speak the words correctly (see Text 28 on p58)

- in a narrative or report, present the words spoken in speech marks, using punctuation ('... !!', '... ??', etc.) and additional description ('he said hurriedly', 'she whispered', etc.) to convey the way they are spoken.

Nothing to write home about?

For many travellers, the experience of the journey itself – or just sending a postcard, even keeping a diary or blog – is not enough, and they try to share their impressions of the places they have visited with the wider reading public, either in the form of articles in the travel sections of newspapers, contributions to the numerous travel programmes on television or books which line the shelves of the travel sections of high-street book stores. Some fortunate people (such as Michael Palin, who has written and presented several popular travel series for the BBC) have even managed to become professional travel writers, being paid to see the world and write about it for the benefit of those of us unable to make the trip ourselves.

In this section we will consider some of this writing. We begin by asking, along with Text 13 in the Anthology, what is the point of it?

Text 13: 'Travel Writing: The Point of It'

The writer of Text 13 asks the question: 'What is travel writing for?' Before we look at the text itself, you might try to answer this question from two points of view – why should anyone want to write about a place they visit and why would anyone else want to read it?

Background information

Contextual information for Text 13

Paul Theroux: Theroux grew up in America. He has travelled widely and written several novels, but is best known for his travel writings. These include *The Great Railway Bazaar*, *The Kingdom By The Sea*, *Sailing Through China* and *The Imperial Way: By Rail from Peshwar to Chittagong*.

Vladimir Nabokov: a Russian writer/novelist who died in 1977.

Franco: a dictator who ruled in Spain as a republic from 1936 until his death in 1975, when the monarchy was restored.

Hindu castes: the system of social classes in Hindu society.

Tiananmen Square: the site of a famous mass protest in Beijing in 1989 which was strongly suppressed by the Chinese authorities with hundreds of casualties.

Critical response activity

1 The table below offers some suggestions from Text 13 which try to explain what the point of travel writing is, from the point of view of the writer and the reader. Place them in rank order (1 = high) according to the extent to which you rate their importance.

From the writer's point of view		From the reader's point of view	
Possible reason	Rank	Possible reason	Rank
a Provide a permanent record of your experiences		**a** Help decide where to go for your next holiday	
b Help advise other visitors about what to see and where to go		**b** Obtain information about what to see and do in a particular place	
c Entertain people who may never travel themselves by painting a vivid picture of life in other countries		**c** Enjoy learning about places you are never likely to visit yourself	
d Give an honest 'warts and all' description of the place, including the unpleasant as well as the enjoyable aspects		**d** Gain a really truthful picture of a place you are interested in finding out about	
e Interpret what is happening in different parts of the world and help predict major national and international events		**e** Understand more about what is happening in different parts of the world and be prepared for major events in the future	
f Contribute to international understanding and encourage tolerance and empathy between different cultures		**f** Learn more about and become more tolerant of other cultures in different parts of the world	
g Reassure potential tourists by giving a generally positive impression of a place so more people will be attracted to travel there		**g** Enjoy reading about what makes other places interesting and enjoyable for a foreign tourist to visit	

2 Look at the quotation from Vladimir Nabokov included in Text 13, in which he distinguishes two kinds of travel writing, only one of which he clearly approves. Put into your own words the difference you think he is trying to describe.

3 Say what you think is implied by Theroux's claim that 'I've taken people as I've found them.'

4 Look closely at the paragraph beginning 'Events ought to prove the worth of a travel book.' Put into your own words what Theroux is suggesting a good travel book should do.

5 Having answered these questions, return to 'writer's point of view' in the table above and complete the rank order exercise as if you were Paul Theroux. Go on to comment on how it differed from your own.

Commentary

There is, of course, no 'correct' solution to the first part of this exercise, but perhaps you considered whether or not travel writing has a practical purpose (to inform, instruct or even advise?) or whether it simply entertains as we sit reading (or watching the television) at home. Theroux's text makes his own position clear: he seems to endorse Nabokov's idea that good travel writing should not simply repackage the predictable clichés we tend to associate with different countries, but offer an authentically personal account whose attention to the everyday detail of life, such as the growth of fungus on the boots overnight, actually tells us more. He claims for his own writing a directness and honesty that has sometimes made him unpopular and goes on to suggest that travel writing should be as much about the way people in a particular place or culture think as a description of its physical landscape. If so, he argues, a travel writer may even be a kind of prophet, able to sense or even predict major events and upheavals such as the events of Tiananmen Square.

So, for Paul Theroux, the reasons that would top the list (not necessarily in this order) would probably be (d) and (e).

Text 4: *Italy* and Text 5: 'Walpole and Otranto'

Let us look at a couple of examples of the genre which show that travel writing comes in every shape and size. Text 4, a guide to the town of Otranto from the Lonely Planet guide to Italy, is possibly an example of what Theroux calls 'a bloodlessly factual' guide. We will compare it with a rather earlier account of the place (Text 5) written by H. V. Morton in 1969 in his book *A Traveller in Southern Italy*.

Background information

Otranto's place in literature

- Otranto: a small town in southern Italy famous for its medieval castle. The opening of a major road through the south of Italy made this previously remote area more accessible.

- Lonely Planet guides: a popular series of travel guides offering comprehensive information on a wide range of destinations throughout the world.

- H. V. Morton: a well-known journalist whose career and travels led him to write several notable travel books between the 1930s and the 1960s.

- Horace Walpole and the Castle of Otranto: the 18th-century writer Horace Walpole made Otranto famous when he set his early Gothic horror novel (*The Castle of Otranto*) there.

■ Critical response activity

Both texts offer a combination of subjective comment and factual information about the town of Otranto and its surroundings. Use the prompt questions below to build up a comprehensive comparison of the two texts.

1 Which of the suggested purposes of travel writing (see the table on p54 do you think each of the texts is designed to fulfil? Give your reasons.

2 Context of production: how is the 35 years that separates their publication reflected in the texts?

3 Context of reception: how does the different presentation and organisation of the texts suggest their authors intended them to be read and used?

4 Overall, to what extent does each text create a favourable impression of Otranto and how is this impression conveyed?

5 Is the Lonely Planet guide (Text 4) a more 'bloodlessly factual' treatment of its subject than Morton's text (Text 5)? To answer this question, you will need to investigate the way each text combines factual (objective) information and personal (subjective) impressions and opinions, and comment on significant aspects of the tone of each text. This might mean asking how personal the text is and noting any uses of humour.

Use a table like the one below to gather your evidence and note how both facts and opinions are presented.

Text	Facts included	Opinions/ impressions	Tone
Italy (Text 4)			
'Walpole and Otranto' (Text 5)			

Commentary

1 Both texts seem to share a wish to convey to their readers an enjoyment of the place, although Text 4 is designed to provide useful information and advice for people who have already decided to travel – the use of present tense ('the road south takes you …') helps to place the reader in the here-and-now of actually being there. On the other hand, Morton's text offers a more leisurely account, as much designed for an 'armchair' traveller as an actual one and, unlike Text 4, is a personal and emphatically past tense narrative ('I plunged into the sunlight …', 'it was the sirocco …') to be enjoyed almost for its own sake. Look, for example, at how the two texts deal with food: Text 4 recommends the food in a number of restaurants, whereas Text 5 provides a narrative of an actual meal. The typography and graphology of Text 4 implies a particular context of reception: the use of short, headed sections and bold font allows us to dip in and out of the text and probably assumes we are travelling ourselves – you would not just read a Lonely Planet guide for pleasure. The continuous narrative style of Text 5, on the other hand, more resembles a novel and is less likely to be of such practical 'use' to a traveller.

2 and 3 This may also reflect the contexts of production, as the relative remoteness of this part of Italy (until the construction of a major highway) and the comparatively exclusive nature of foreign travel until the 1960s made it unlikely that many of Morton's readers had, or would be able to, visit for themselves. His account almost has the feel of a pioneer discovering a previously unknown land. However, in the modern global village where we seem to be able to fly anywhere and see anything, which is what the Lonely Planet guide caters for, we can all expect to see such places for ourselves, with the aid of a few tips from our trusty guidebook about where to go, what to see and what to eat.

4   Text 4 uses a variety of adjectives to describe Otranto's attractions (the beaches are 'scenic', the cathedral is 'magnificent', the hotel rooms offer 'great views' and some of the food is 'delicious') but it is perhaps the inclusion of the various anecdotes and 'fanciful tales' and the detailed description of the mosaics in the cathedral that convey the writer's enthusiasm for the place. It is not a particularly personal response – there is no use of the first person pronoun in the text. By comparison, Morton's account is emphatically personal (the first person is used throughout) and more visually descriptive. This is shown by the inclusion of many visual details in the form of **noun phrases** so, in the first two or three paragraphs we have 'deep green sea', 'stony earth', 'ancient castle', 'old streets', 'circular bastions', 'large cathedral' and 'gentle waves'. Then, we have a number of verbs which also contribute to the visual imagery ('the olive trees shimmered', 'the old streets struggled up a hill', 'the gentle waves curled over'), often by using language figuratively, as here, personifying the streets.

5   So, is the Lonely Planet guide a more 'bloodlessly factual account' than Morton's? The two texts cover a good deal of common ground: the cathedral, its mosaics, aspects of the town's ancient past (including the 'Sack' in 1480), the landscape and the food. There are differences of emphasis: the Lonely Planet guide includes brief snippets of what it calls 'fanciful tales' whereas Morton is more interested in the literary associations of the castle, which merits only a brief mention in Text 4. There are clear contrasts in the way some of these subjects are treated: Text 4 refers briefly and unemotionally to the events of 1480 ('killed 800 Christians') and almost humorously to the 'blood and gore' involved, turning it into a joke with the reference to 'the only fright … is the number of people on Otranto's beaches'). The lexical content of Morton's account is more sensational and emotive, as he describes the event as a 'massacre', quotes a priest's reference to the victims as 'martyrs' and describes the 'headless bodies weltered in pools of blood' in an image depicting the event.

That is not to say Text 4 is devoid of colour. Although the author does not draw attention to him/herself in the first person (it is, after all, not intended to be a subjective account – this is a Lonely Planet guide, not the personal views of any one of its authors), the text uses the second person to address its readers personally on several occasions ('If you're ghoulish you can see …') and includes some wry humour. There is an occasional rhetorical question ('Who said all the best hotels were in the Valle d'Itria?'), which helps to sustain the tone of authority achieved by prefacing remarks with impersonal phrases such as 'the truth is …' and 'it is amazing that …'.

Morton's text is insistently personal, using 'I' but not 'you'. There are some very clear statements of personal opinion ('I thought Otranto one of the most beautiful little towns I had seen') and you might have noted a literary, almost poetic style in such phrases as 'vague outlines pencilled against the sky and tipped with snow' and the unusual syntax of the exclamatory sentence 'How beautiful are the colours in Southern Italy!' Two final distinguishing features of Text 5 are the inclusion of dialogue from 'locals' and the use of italicised **loan words** like *sandolino* and *feudo* to give his account authenticity, authority and local flavour.

Key terms

Noun phrase: a group of words consisting of a noun and the adjectives/articles that describe and define it.

Loan word: word adopted from a foreign language with little or no modification.

Think about it

Look closely at Texts 8 and 9 in the Anthology, which both offer information about the Lancashire town of Clitheroe and its surroundings. Compare and contrast the way these two texts inform their readers about the town.

The past is a foreign country

The author L. P. Hartley began his novel *The Go Between* with the words 'the past is a foreign country – they do things differently there'. So as we consider some of the less modern of the texts in the AQA Anthology, we may need to prepare for a culture clash. But do not be put off – although the language of the past may strike us an oddly old-fashioned, perhaps it is the fact that these texts give us a real glimpse of how things were in a bygone age that makes them all the more fascinating.

In this section we will consider three such texts: extracts from Oliver Goldsmith's play *She Stoops to Conquer* (Text 28), William Cobbett's 'Kensington to Uphusband' (Text 29) and Dorothy Wordsworth's 'The Grasmere Journals' (Text 22).

Text 28: *She Stoops to Conquer*

Background information

Contextual information for Text 28

- Oliver Goldsmith wrote *She Stoops to Conquer (Or the Mistakes of a Night)* in 1771 and it was performed for the first time in 1773.

- The characters in the play include:
  - Hastings: a sophisticated young man
  - Tony Lumpkin: the country-born and raised central character of the play who is largely responsible for the practical jokes which drive its plot forward
  - Miss Neville: a young lady with whom Hastings is in love.

- Synopsis: the comedy is based on a series of misunderstandings and practical jokes, the principal one being that a group of visitors to the country mistake the house of country squires Mr and Mrs Hardcastle for an inn, and its inhabitants for inn keepers and servants. The title refers to the character of Kate Hardcastle, who pretends to be a serving girl to help the young man she admires overcome his natural shyness.

- Themes of the play: although a farcical comedy of manners, the play also deals with some more serious themes such as social class, love, marriage and the contrast in values and lifestyle between town and country.

- This extract: the extract comes from Act 5, Scene 2, towards the end of the play. The previous evening, Mrs Hardcastle (Tony's mother and Miss Neville's aunt) has discovered Miss Neville's secret plans to elope with Hastings, of whom she disapproves. In order to prevent this, she has demanded to leave immediately with her niece and commands Tony to drive them 30 miles through the night.

Think about it

This extract offers a comical snapshot of the practicalities and hardships of travel in Britain in the 18th century. What does it reveal about the experience of travellers at the time the play was written and how this compares with modern times?

Commentary

As Tony says, any kind of travel, especially at night, was 'cursedly tiresome' and his reference to the shaking of 'the basket of a stage coach' and the 'poor beasts' reminds us that horse-drawn carriages over bumpy roads and tracks were the only means of passenger transport available. He also implies that an average speed of 10 miles an hour represented good going; perhaps we can begin to understand the excitement (and fear) that greeted the arrival of railways just 50 years later, and appreciate the power of steam as captured by Dickens in our extract from *Dombey and Son* (see Chapter 7).

However, some things have not changed so much. The trick being played on his passengers by the mischievous Tony Lumpkin – here, they are led to believe they have travelled 40 miles whereas in fact they have merely been driven round in a circle near their own house – is not very different from the experience of some travellers at the hands of unscrupulous taxi drivers and the 'ripping off' of tourists reported in the travelblog (Text 12).

Key terms

Collocation: an established phrase which places words in a fixed order.

Idiom: a commonly used phrase whose meaning is not related to the literal sense of its words.

 Critical response activity

A living language never stands still and is constantly changing in every way. The most obvious kind of change is lexical (with the constant stream of new words) and semantic (as words take on new meanings and uses). Even the phonology and grammar of language changes over time, and in a text written over 230 years ago we can expect to find many illustrations of these changes.

For each of the categories below, find the relevant examples from the text, suggest a modern English equivalent and comment on what has changed. If you have access to the *OED*, find out what you can about the history of unfamiliar words.

	Example in Text 28	Modern equivalent	Comment
Lexis			
a Adjective used to describe an unpleasant experience			
b Noun used as a term of abuse, derived from the word for an unpleasant animal or pest			
c Latin-derived term for a round-about way of doing something			
d Noun meaning bog or muddy hollow			
e Past participle meaning to make something wet and dirty by dragging			
Collocation			
Inverted word order used to express a number (e.g. 'five-and-twenty' rather than 'twenty-five')			
Idioms			
a Verb used to convey the exertion of the horses			
b Two phrases used at different points by Tony to express the strength of his feelings			
c A phrasal verb (consists of a verb and preposition) meaning to go away quickly			
Grammar			
Use of a past tense form of a verb where a past participle would be used in modern Standard English			

Commentary

Lexis

a Although 'tiresome' is still very much part of Standard English, we might now associate it more with a relatively high register rather than the colloquial context in which it is used here, and the pre-modifying 'cursedly' is much less likely to occur in modern English. There are many possible modern equivalents in different registers – 'annoying', 'a pain in the neck' (or elsewhere!); the pre-modifier is as likely to be 'bloody' or an even stronger expletive.

b The term 'varmint' may be a local (dialectal) variation on the word 'vermin' from which it derives – still used in modern English to describe unwanted animals such as rats, but less likely to be used as a term of abuse. We do, of course, still resort to the animal world to provide numerous other abusive terms, such as 'rats', 'pigs', 'dogs', 'bitches' and 'cows'.

c Although you could be forgiven for thinking that 'circumbendibus' has something to do with a new form of public transport, the suffix 'ibus' gives it away as a Latin-derived term for a long-winded way of doing something. The *OED* describes it as a 'humorous formation' first noted in 1682 but last cited in 1867, and thus more likely to be rendered in modern English by 'roundabout'.

d The inhabitants of the Berkshire town of the same name will not be pleased that 'slough' refers to a muddy bog or hollow in the road.

e According to the *OED*, to 'draggle' meant to make something wet or dirty by dragging it through the dirt – though with a latest citation of 1880. Oddly, it seems to have survived in the form 'bedraggled' but is unlikely to appear without its prefix 'be-'.

Collocation

The inversion of 'five-and-twenty' for 'twenty-five' used to be common enough in English, but now only really survives in archaic contexts such as 'four-and-twenty blackbirds baked in a pie'.

Idioms

It is in the colloquial registers of our language that change is likely to be most rapid and obvious, as each generation popularises its own vocabulary of slang and idiomatic expressions.

a When Tony says 'The poor beasts have smoked for it' he is using a colloquial, hyperbolical metaphor to describe the extreme exertion of the horses; we might equally well suggest they 'busted a gut' or even that were 'bursting a blood vessel'.

b 'Rabbit me' and 'by jingo' express the strength of his feelings, although a modern colloquial equivalent might be 'blow me' (or something considerably stronger).

c The phrasal verb 'whip off' may nowadays be rendered as 'run off', 'scoot' or even 'do one'.

Grammar

When Tony says of the journey that 'it has shook me …' he uses the past tense instead of the past participle 'shaken' which would be used in modern Standard English. However, as Tony is a relatively unsophisticated country character, Goldsmith is deliberately making him speak in his local dialect; the 18th century was the century in which a great deal of attention was being paid to the issue of what constituted 'good' or 'correct' English (see the Background information box Milestones in Modern English on p65–6).

■ Further reading

Bragg, Melvyn, *The Adventure of English*, Sceptre, 2004

Crystal, David, *The English Language*, Penguin, 2002

Leith, Dick, *A Social History of English*, Routledge, 1997

Talk in life and on the stage: scripted and unscripted speech

When studying transcripts of real talk (see Topic 5), we explored some of the distinctive features of modern, spontaneously spoken English. When a dramatist or screen writer sets out to write a 'realistic' script, she or he faces the challenge of convincing the audience or viewer that the dialogue is believable, but without including many of the features of real spontaneous speech that would actually make it difficult to listen to.

Let us first consider in general terms how dialogue on the screen or stage differs from talk in real life, and go on to consider *She Stoops to Conquer* in particular.

Critical response activity

1 **Scripted and unscripted talk**: Look again at some of the features of natural, spontaneous spoken language we noted earlier. For each of them, comment on the how far you think they also would occur in a modern television script that aims for realism (such as *EastEnders*). Comment on the reasons for any difference between scripted and unscripted talk.

Features of spontaneous talk	Used in television script?	Comment
Some use of casual, colloquial language, possibly including expletives and taboo language		
Some use of grammatically incomplete (minor) sentences. Other sentences may continue in a less clearly structured way than in writing, with repeated use of conjunctions such as 'and', 'but' and 'so'		
Some use of non-fluency features		
In conversation, those listening indicate their attention/agreement/sympathy using feedback		
There may occasionally be interruptions and overlapping, with two or more speakers speaking at once		

 Practical activity

After you've completed Critical response activity 1, check out your ideas and predictions by taping, transcribing and analysing a short piece of dialogue from your favourite realistic television drama.

2 **She, er, stoops to, um, conquer, innit?** We can now go on to ask the same questions about *She Stoops to Conquer*, allowing for the period when it was written. Write your own analysis of the ways that Goldsmith has tried to create an illusion of realistic spontaneous speech, commenting also on the features that mark it out as scripted, dramatic talk.

3 **Analysing talk**: We also developed earlier a Discourse Analysis approach to 'real' conversations that allowed us to make discoveries about individual participants and their relationships (see Chapter 5). This involved looking closely at the patterns of turn-taking and the language each character uses. We can now apply these same questions to discuss the traditionally 'literary' aspects of scripted speech – how a playwright uses dialogue to portray characters and their relationships. So, for Text 28, write answers to each of the following questions:

- Who speaks most often and for longest?
- Who seems to be in charge of the dialogue?
- How does each speaker introduce their thoughts, ideas and opinions?
- What are the distinguishing features of each speaker's contributions to the dialogue?
- How do the speakers address each other?

Critical response activity

Making use of the relevant contextual information in the Background information box on pp65–6, compare and contrast the way in which both texts present their experiences of the countryside to their readers. As usual, prepare to carry out a comparison by making plenty of notes first and organising your discussion in a well-structured essay according to appropriate paragraph-topics.

You should consider:

- the kinds of impressions and feelings expressed in both texts
- what the purpose of each text might have been, and how this is reflected in its content and style
- how the personality and gender of the writer is reflected in each text
- how we might guess that Wordsworth's text was a private diary and Cobbett's intended for a wider audience
- any evidence of language change to be found in the texts.

Commentary

Dorothy Wordsworth's 'The Grasmere Journals' mainly consists of the unremarkable stuff of everyday life in and around her Grasmere home, recorded with occasional metaphorical flourishes that reveal her respect for and enjoyment of the natural landscape: 'the river came galloping', 'the company of rivers came hurrying down', 'Wild scene of crag and mountain', 'Helm Crag – a being in itself'. Her diary records a number of casual social meetings and reflects her interest in the personal and domestic lives of the people she meets. By contrast, Cobbett begins with highly unflattering description of the area around Guildford ('the land is a rascally common … some of the worst lands … in the world!') before moving on to a complex and highly political discussion of some of the issues of the day (see the Background information box on p65). His interest in people is focused on economic and political rather than domestic detail, and his most striking use of metaphor is to make a political point ('it was the sheep surrendering up the dogs into the hands of the wolves').

From all of this we might conclude that Dorothy Wordsworth composed her journal largely to provide a personal record of everyday life, and in particular to record moments of pleasure and appreciation of the surroundings. Cobbett, however, seems always to be driving towards some kind of political point, and his observations seem calculated not to celebrate the power of nature but rather to highlight the political weakness of his fellow men. In terms of gender, in the context of the time it is not surprising that Wordsworth should focus on domesticity and nature, and Cobbett on the world of politics and power: a woman in the 19th century would not be expected to take any particular interest in the 'masculine' world of politics. Dorothy Wordsworth's personality emerges in the exuberance of her writing and the detail of her observation: the way she comments that her neighbour Aggy Fleming 'looked shockingly with her hair tyed up', her enjoyment of eating rosehips ('the hips very beautiful, and so good!!') and her evident energy ('I came home first – they walked too slow for me'). Cobbett immediately strikes us as more outspoken and opinionated, from his initial description of Guildford common to his insulting description of the 'knaves' at the Crown and Anchor, and his final direct appeal to Lord Onslow to 'acknowledge his errors'.

The journal has many of the characteristic features of a private diary; it refers routinely to local people (e.g. Aggy Fleming, Mr Clarkson, Mrs Luff) who would be completely unknown without explanation, and records a series of mundane events in short, simple sentences : 'We played at cards … baked pies and cakes … it was a stormy morning'. It also features the kinds of ellipsis we might expect in a diary. She writes 'Met Townley with his dogs', not 'We met Townley with his dogs', omitting the pronoun subject and 'The Birches on the crags beautiful', omitting the main verb 'were'.

Although, like Wordsworth, Cobbett generally uses the first person, it is obvious that he has written his text with publication in mind from the start. He introduces the local inhabitants fully ('Mr Webb Weston, whose mansion and park are a little further on towards London') and uses a range of persuasive, rhetorical techniques clearly designed to make his point to the readers of his *Political Register.*

There is less evidence of lexical and grammatical change in either of these texts than in Goldsmith's text, but some interesting details nevertheless. Dorothy Wordsworth affectionately addresses Coleridge as 'thee' – previously an informal, intimate form of the second person pronoun which was already in retreat from Standard English but which survived (as it does today) in some rural dialects. Both texts refer to a 'gig' – a simple type of horse-drawn vehicle – and Cobbett uses the word 'knaves' as an insult, common enough in Shakespeare but last cited in the *OED* in 1847 and nowadays replaced by any number of possible alternatives. Perhaps the most distasteful feature of Cobbett's text is less a matter of language than changing political sensitivities and ideas – his apparent objection to 'Jews' taking over the ownership of estates. Such overt anti-Semitism would not now be tolerated.

▪ Background information

Milestones in English

The texts in the AQA Anthology range from the 18th century to the present day. Here are some important milestones in the development of English language and culture before and during that period:

1066 The arrival of the Normans establishes Norman French as the language of government; Anglo Saxon (or Old English) continues to be spoken by the vast majority of the population. However, over time many French and Latin words are adopted.

1380s Geoffrey Chaucer writes his epic *Canterbury Tales* in what we now call Middle English. By now various forms of Middle English are spoken in different parts of the country.

1476 England's first printer, William Caxton, sets up shop in London. The first books to be printed in English (including Chaucer's *Canterbury Tales*) start to appear.

1590s–1616 Shakespeare's poems and plays are published and performed. By now it is usual to describe the language of the period as Early Modern English.

1755 Dr Samuel Johnson publishes his hugely influential *Dictionary* – not the first dictionary in English, but the most influential so far in pinning down the vocabulary, spelling and meanings of the language.

1785 The first edition of *The Times* is published (as *The Daily Universal Register*).

▶

Practical activity

Study Text 20, an extract from Isabella Bird's *A Lady's Life in the Rocky Mountains*, first published in the 1870s. Compare the way it presents the author's experiences with either Text 22 or 29.

■ Further reading

Bragg, Melvyn, *The Adventure of English*, Sceptre, 2004

Bryson, Bill, *Mother Tongue*, Penguin, 1991

Crystal, David, *The English Language*, Penguin 2002

Games, Alex, *Balderdash and Piffle*, BBC Books, 2006

Green, Jonathan, *Chasing the Sun: Dictionary Makers and the Dictionaries They Made*, Pimlico, 1997

Winchester, Simon, *The Meaning of Everything: The Story of the Oxford English Dictionary*, Oxford University Press, 2004

On grammar:

Crystal, David, *Rediscover Grammar*, Longman 2004

1795 Lindley Murray publishes his *English Grammar*, perhaps the most important of several attempts to define the 'rules' of good English during the 18th century and thus define what we mean by 'Standard English'.

1870 The Education Act makes education compulsory up to the age of 13 for all. For the first time, universal literacy becomes a reasonable aim.

1914–18 The consequences of the First World War provoke a number of longer-term social changes.

1918 Women gain the right to vote – a key milestone along the long road towards women achieving some sort of equality in society.

1922 The first broadcasts by BBC Radio help to establish Received Pronunciation as the 'official' accent of English.

1928 The first edition of the *Oxford English Dictionary* is completed.

1939–45 The Second World War boosts the importance of BBC Radio.

1953 The broadcast of Queen Elizabeth II's coronation boosts television ownership.

1960s The general relaxation of formality in dress and behaviour is accelerated by the availability of the contraceptive pill, new fashions and the youth culture associated with pop music.

1981 The first IBM personal computer is launched.

1992 The first SMS text message is sent via mobile phone.

10 The unseen extract question (Question 1)

■ In the examination

The Unit 1 examination is the end of your journey – and although, yes, to travel may be better than to arrive, in order to make the outcome successful you need to prepare yourself fully for this vital final leg of your trip.

Requirements and timing

When you turn over your Unit 1 paper at the start of the examination, the first thing you see will be one or more texts you have never encountered before. They will be connected, in some way, to the general theme of travel, and will have been chosen because they allow you to demonstrate some of the skills, knowledge and analytical approaches you have developed over the first term or so of your AS English Language and Literature course. The two texts will be designed to lend themselves to some productive comparisons and contrasts.

Your task is to take a close look at both texts and produce a comparison of them along the lines suggested by the question, all in about 30 minutes.

The question will also assess how far you have become an independent reader of texts and how successfully you have learned to think for yourself and organise your own response to unfamiliar material.

AQA / Examiner's tip

Your work will be assessed according to the relevant Assessment Objectives for this question:

AO1	Remember to start with an overview of the texts that show you understand the main ideas, attitudes and feelings they convey.
	Try to use plenty of relevant terminology in your answer – you need this to be precise and to show the examiner what you have learned about language and literature during the course
AO2	Remember that you are writing a relatively formal essay and your audience is the examiner. Therefore, organise your ideas into paragraphs, use a suitable register of Standard English and go into as much detail as you can, supporting each detailed point you make with short quotations from the texts
AO3	Remember to compare and contrast the texts *throughout*, using connecting phrases to move from one text to the other. Remember also to refer to what you are told about the context of each extract where this contributes to a full understanding of the text

---

So, your principal enemy is the clock. To allow yourself enough time to do justice on the Anthology-based question, you need to approach this question with brisk efficiency and a clear method. (There is, of course, nothing to stop you attempting the Anthology-based question first, but you should still not spend much more than 30 minutes or so on the unseen extract question.

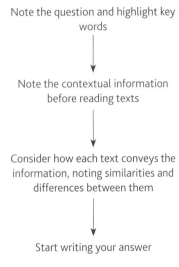

Note the question and highlight key words

↓

Note the contextual information before reading texts

↓

Consider how each text conveys the information, noting similarities and differences between them

↓

Start writing your answer

Fig. 1 *The four-stage approach*

Link

You will find an example of an approach to Question 1 on p75.

How to approach Question 1

Here is a four-stage approach that should enable you to meet the demands of this paper:

1   Note the question and highlight its key words first. This will provide you with a focus for your reading.

2   Make a point of noting the contextual information provided about the texts before reading them for the first time. Try to gain a clear overview of the main information, ideas, feelings and attitudes expressed. In other words, be clear about *what* the text is saying and doing.

3   Think about *how* each text conveys all of this, working quickly with your pencil and highlighters. Pick out the significant language features, noting similarities and differences between the texts.

4   Get busy and try to give your answer the same sort of structure as the essays you have been writing on the Anthology texts, with three or four well constructed and developed paragraphs each addressing a significant aspect of both texts.

Some pairs of unseen texts for practice

The following exercises illustrate the type of text pairings that you could encounter in your examination paper. There are four pairings, and it is for you and/or your teacher to decide what use you will make of them. You may, for example:

■   use a pair of texts to work through as a class, going through the stages listed above to create a list of points that could be used in an examination answer

■   work through a pair of texts as a group, discussing your ideas, then producing your own essay summarising your analysis

■   write a comparison of a pair of these texts as a homework activity, practising your analysis skills without worrying too much about the timing

■   write a comparison of a pair under examination conditions.

1 Impressions of Canada

Text A is the transcript of part of a recent promotional video for the Rocky Mountaineer train which runs from Vancouver through the Rocky Mountains to Calgary in Canada.

Text B is a posting from an internet travellers' forum.

Compare the ways the writers of the texts present their experiences of the journey.

You should write about:

■   how the purpose and context of each text has influenced the use of language

■   how language is used to convey impressions, feelings and attitudes.

Text A

Key
(.)   Short pause or micropause
(2)   Length of longer pause in seconds
<u>Underlining</u>   Stressed word or syllable

MALE VOICE. It was created over a <u>century</u> ago (.) a <u>road</u> of <u>steel</u> (.) that helped create the <u>nation</u> of <u>Canada</u> (.) <u>hewn</u> by <u>hand</u> (.) through some of the most <u>rugged</u> ter<u>rain</u> in the <u>world</u> (.) today (.) this historic route (.) is recognised as one of the world's <u>classic</u> rail journeys (3) <u>welcome</u> to the <u>Rocky</u> Mountain<u>eer</u> (.) <u>welcome</u> aboard (.) the <u>trip</u> of a <u>lifetime</u> (3) <u>join</u> us along this spec<u>tac</u>ular route for a taste of the <u>his</u>tory the breathtaking <u>scenery</u> the <u>places</u> and the <u>people</u> (.) come with <u>us</u> past the <u>coast</u>al forests (.) through the steep river <u>can</u>yons and into the <u>tower</u>ing Ca<u>na</u>dian <u>Rockies</u> come with <u>us</u> back in <u>time</u> and <u>for</u>ward to ad<u>ven</u>ture on the most spec<u>tac</u>ular <u>train</u> trip in the <u>world</u> …

… the <u>dawn</u> of our first day of travel finds us passing through the <u>Fraser Valley</u> (.) a <u>broad</u> alluvial plain (.) built up by the <u>mighty</u> and for<u>mid</u>able <u>Fraser River</u> (10) this <u>fertile valley</u> gradually closes in on us (.) until we enter (.) the <u>Fraser Canyon</u> (.) here we follow the <u>gold</u> rush trail of 1858 when <u>hope</u>ful pros<u>pec</u>tors clung to the <u>narrow</u> <u>twist</u>ing trail along the almost <u>vert</u>ical Fraser canyon <u>walls</u> (.) the Fraser river is almost 1300 kilometres in length from its headwaters in the Rockies to its release in the Straits of Georgia at Van<u>cou</u>ver (2) it was first <u>navi</u>gated in 1808 by Simon Fraser (.) an explorer seeking a trade route (.) to the Pacific Ocean (.) it is also home (.) to the largest salmon run in the <u>world</u> (15)

FEMALE VOICE. Our tracks cling to the sides of <u>sheer</u> cliffs much like that trail of old (.) building a railroad through this canyon is a story of hardship (.) courage (.) and perseverance (.) the Alexandra bridge named after Princess Alexandra of Wales was the first suspension bridge in the west initially built in 1863 (.) the original bridge washed away in a flood in 1894 (.) until the Alexandra was rebuilt in 1926 people would pay a dollar to pull themselves across in a bucket linked to a cable.

Text B

I went on the Rocky Mountaineer's winter train on December 20th, the journey got off to an eventful start with a slide on the Fraser Canyon which meant twice the usual rail traffic would be trying to get through the single line left open. What was scheduled to be a short day (8 hours) turned into 12 hours, much of it spent waiting for other trains. Dinner would normally be served at the Kamloops hotel, but due to our late arrival I skipped it. Who would want to eat a big meal at 9:30PM when the train leaves at 6AM the next day? Some people did eat at the hotel despite the late arrival and said it was rather disappointing and greasy. On board they served both breakfast and lunch, but instead of serving a real dinner instead provided various snacks which were good but hardly take the place of an actual dinner considering the price you pay. Due to the delays about 1/3 of the first day was in darkness. The food meals they did serve on board were nothing to brag about, one breakfast for example was cold. The next day we departed for Banff, we had an excellent clear day but were still plagued by delays. We ended off the day 3 hours late missing some of the best scenery from Field, BC to Banff, AB. I think Rocky Mountaineer is rather poorly organised, and should provide a little more considering the price of a ticket. It's not to say I didn't enjoy the trip, the actual attendants were very good and the scenery I did get to see was nice. How ever from what I've seen of there service, it simply doesn't justify the price they charge. If you really want a rail trip in the rockies you can take a

Via Rail trip in economy for a fraction of the price, in fact the price of a Red Leaf ticket in peak season will nearly pay for a first class Via Rail ticket. I would recommend renting a car and exploring the park that way, and using the money you save to either take a longer vacation or stay at nicer hotels.

2 Fantastic voyages

Text C is a passage from Roald Dahl's *The BFG*, first published in 1982. Here, the Big Friendly Giant (BFG) of the title is taking the book's child hero, Sophie, on a terrifying journey.

Text D is an extract from *Gulliver's Travels* by Jonathan Swift, first published in 1726. The novel describes the fictitious adventures of its narrator, Lemuel Gulliver. Here, Gulliver describes his arrival on the unknown island of Lilliput which is inhabited by extremely small human beings.

Compare the way the writers of these texts convey the experiences of their central characters.

You should write about:

- how the purpose and context of each text has influenced the use of language
- how language is used to convey impressions, feelings and attitudes.

Text C

Sophie crouched in the blanket, peering out. She was being bumped against the Giant's leg like a sack of potatoes. Over the fields and hedges and rivers they went, and after a while a frightening thought came into Sophie's head. *The Giant is running fast*, she told herself, *because he is hungry and wants to get home as quickly as possible, and then he'll have me for breakfast.*

The Giant ran on and on. But now a curious change took place in his way of running. He seemed suddenly to go into a higher gear. Faster and faster he went and soon he was travelling at such a speed that the landscape became blurred. The wind stung Sophie's cheeks. It made her eyes water. She could no longer feel the Giant's feet touching the ground. She had a weird sensation they were flying. It was impossible to tell whether they were over land or sea. This Giant had some sort of magic in his legs. The wind rushing against Sophie's face became so strong that she had to duck down again into the blanket to prevent her head from being blown away.

Was it really possible that they were crossing oceans? It certainly felt that way to Sophie. She crouched in the blanket and listened to the howling of the wind. It went on for what seemed like hours.

Then all at once the wind stopped its howling. The pace began to slow down. Sophie could feel the Giant's feet pounding once again over the earth. She poked her head out of the blanket to have a look. They were in a country of thick forests and rushing rivers. The Giant had definitely slowed down and was now running more normally, although normal was a silly word to use to describe a galloping giant. He leaped over a dozen rivers. He went rattling through a great forest, then down into a valley and up over a range of hills as bare as concrete, and soon he was galloping over a desolate wasteland that was not quite of this earth. The ground was flat and pale yellow. Great lumps of blue rock were scattered around and dead trees stood everywhere like skeletons. The moon had long since disappeared and now the dawn was breaking.

Sophie, still peering out from the blanket, saw suddenly ahead of her a great craggy mountain. The mountain was dark blue and all around it the sky was gushing and glistening with light. Bits of pale gold were flying among delicate frosty-white flakes of cloud, and over to one side the rim of the morning sun was coming up red as blood.

Text D

On the fifth of *November*, which was the beginning of Summer in those Parts, the Weather being very hazy, the Seamen spied a Rock, within half a Cable's length of the Ship; but the Wind was so strong, that we were driven directly upon it, and immediately split. Six of the Crew, of whom I was one, having let down the Boat into the Sea, made a Shift to get clear of the Ship, and the Rock. We rowed by my Computation about three Leagues, till we were able to work no longer, being already spent with Labour while we were in the Ship. We therefore trusted ourselves to the Mercy of the Waves, and in about half an Hour the Boat was overset by a sudden Flurry from the North. What became of my Companions in the Boat, as well as of those who escaped on the Rock, or were left in the Vessel, I cannot tell; but conclude they were all lost. For my own Part, I swam as Fortune directed me, and was pushed forward by Wind and Tide. I often let my Legs drop, and could feel no Bottom: but when I was almost gone, and able to struggle no longer, I found myself within my Depth; and by this Time the Storm was much abated. The Declivity was so small, that I walked near a Mile before I got to the Shore, which I conjectur'd was about eight a-clock in the Evening. I then advanced forward near half a Mile, but could not discover any sign of Houses or Inhabitants; at least I was in so weak a Condition, that I did not observe them. I was extremely tired, and with that, and the Heat of the Weather, and about half a Pint of Brandy that I drank as I left the Ship, I found myself much inclined to sleep. I lay down on the Grass, which was very short and soft, where I slept sounder than ever I remember to have done in my Life, and, as I reckoned, above Nine Hours; for when I awakened, it was just Day-light.

I attempted to rise, but was not able to stir: For as I happen'd to lye on my Back, I found my Arms and Legs were strongly fastened on each Side to the Ground; and my Hair, which was long and thick, tied down in the same Manner. I likewise felt several slender Ligatures across my Body, from my Armpits to my Thighs. I could only look upwards; the Sun began to grow hot, and the Light offended my Eyes. I heard a confused Noise about me, but in the Posture I lay, could see nothing except the Sky. In a little time I felt something alive moving on my left Leg, which advancing gently forward over my Breast, came almost up to my Chin; when bending my Eyes downwards as much as I could, I perceived it to be a human Creature not six Inches high, with a Bow and Arrow in his hands, and a Quiver at his Back. In the meantime, I felt at least Forty more of the same Kind (as I conjectured) following the first. I was in the utmost Astonishment, and roared so loud, that they all ran back in a Fright; and some of them, as I was afterwards told, were hurt with the Falls they got by leaping from my Sides upon the Ground. However, they soon returned, and one of them, who ventured so far as to get a full Sight of my Face, lifting up his Hands and Eyes by way of Admiration, cried out in a shrill but distinct

Voice, *Hekinah Degul*: the others repeated the same Words several times, but I then knew not what they meant. I lay all this while, as the Reader may believe, in great Uneasiness; At length, struggling to get loose, I had the Fortune to break the Strings, and wrench out the Pegs that fastened my left Arm to the Ground; for, by lifting it up to my Face, I discovered the Methods they had taken to bind me, and at the same time, with a violent Pull, which gave me excessive Pain, I a little loosened the Strings that tied down my Hair on the left Side, so that I was just able to turn my Head about two Inches. But the creatures ran off a second time, before I could seize them; Whereupon there was a great Shout in a very shrill Accent, and after it ceased, I heard one of them cry aloud, *Tolgo Phonac*; when in an Instant I felt above a Hundred Arrows discharged on my left Hand, which pricked me like so many Needles; and besides they shot another Flight into the Air, as we do Bombs in *Europe*, whereof many, I suppose, fell on my Body (though I felt them not) and some on my Face, which I immediately covered with my left Hand.

3 Poetry and prose

Text E is a poem written by the writer Thomas Hardy. It is thought to refer not to any actual castle, but to the village of Boscastle in Cornwall, which Hardy had visited with his wife.

Text F is taken from a current website providing tourist information about the village of Boscastle.

Compare the way the two texts present the location to their readers.

You should write about:

- how the purpose and context of each text has influenced the use of language
- how language, structure and form are used to convey impressions, feelings and attitudes.

Text E

As I drive to the junction of lane and highway,
And the drizzle bedrenches the waggonette,
I look behind at the fading byway,
And see on its slope, now glistening wet,
Distinctly yet.

Myself and a girlish form benighted
In dry March weather. We climb the road
Beside a chaise. We had just alighted
To ease the sturdy pony's load
When he sighed and slowed.

What we did as we climbed, and what we talked of
Matters not much, nor to what it led, –
Something that life will not be balked of
Without rude reason till hope is dead,
And feeling fled.

It filled but a minute. But was there ever
A time of such quality, since or before,
In that hill's story? To one mind never,
Though it has been climbed, foot-swift, foot-sore,
By thousands more.

Primaeval rocks form the road's steep border,
And much have they faced there, first and last,
Of the transitory in Earth's long order;
But what they record in colour and cast
Is – that we two passed.

And to me, though Time's unflinching rigour,
In mindless rote, has ruled from sight
The substance now, one phantom figure
Remains on the slope, as when that night
Saw us alight.

I look and see it there, shrinking, shrinking,
I look back at it amid the rain
For the very last time; for my sand is sinking,
And I shall traverse old love's domain
Never again.

Text F

Just 14 miles south from Bude and 5 miles from Tintagel, within an designated 'Area of Outstanding Beauty' lies this small village with one of the few remaining unspoilt harbours on the North Cornish Coast.

The small harbour now hosts a number of little fishing boats but was once a hive of activity with trade taking place between Wales, Bristol and the south of England.

The National Trust own and care for the beautiful medieval harbour and surrounding coastline and some of the most beautiful countryside within the British Isles.

An excellent base for touring the area, all of Cornwall or North Devon, including moorlands, sheltered wooden valleys and coastal footpaths offering magnificent views, are all on our doorstep.

Here too a lovely valley heads inland, a path follows a fast flowing burbling stream which leads to several hidden churches allowing you to discover the little known connection between North Cornwall and Thomas Hardy.

4 Travel and humour

Text G is an extract from a sketch which appeared on the television comedy programme *Monty Python's Flying Circus* in 1969. Text H is an extract from a Spanish tourist guide to a local attraction, the Caves of Arta, and a poem written by Robert Graves in the 1930s (*Welcome to the Caves of Arta!*) which it inspired.

This final pair of texts is designed to present a level of challenge somewhat greater than might usually be expected in an AS Level examination, and are included here to stimulate a range of possible explanations and discussions.

Compare the ways the writers of the two texts find humour in their subject.

You should write about:

- the ideas, attitudes and feelings expressed in the texts
- how the purpose and context of each text has influenced the use of language
- how language is used to create humorous effects.

Text G

Scene: A travel agent's shop. A tourist enters

Tourist: Good morning.

Secretary: Have you come to arrange a holiday? Now where were you thinking of going?

Tourist: India.

Secretary: Ah one of our adventure holidays.

Tourist: Yes.

Secretary: Well you'd better speaker to Mr Bounder about that. *(Calls out to Mr Bounder)* Mr Bounder, this gentleman is interested in the India Overland.

Bounder: Anyway you're interested in one of our adventure holidays?

Tourist: Well I saw your adverts in the paper and I've been on package tours several times you see, and I decided that this was for me.

Bounder: Ah good.

Tourist: Yes I quite agree I mean what's the point of being treated like sheep. What's the point of going abroad if you're just another tourist carted around in buses surrounded by sweaty mindless oafs [...] in their cloth caps and their cardigans and their transistor radios and their *Sunday Mirrors*, complaining about the tea – 'Oh they don't make it properly here, do they, not like at home' – and stopping at Majorcan bodegas selling fish and chips and Watney's Red Barrel and calamares and two veg and sitting in their cotton frocks squirting Timothy White's suncream all over their puffy raw swollen purulent flesh 'cos they 'overdid it on the first day'.

Bounder: (agreeing patiently) Yes absolutely, yes I quite agree …

Tourist: And being herded into endless Hotel Miramars and Bellvueses and Continentales with their modern international luxury roomettes and draught Red Barrel and swimming pools full of fat German businessmen pretending they're acrobats forming pyramids and frightening the children and barging into queues and if you're not at your table spot on seven you miss the bowl of Campbell's Cream of Mushroom soup, the first item on the menu of International Cuisine, and every Thursday night the hotel has a bloody cabaret in the bar presenting Flamenco for Foreigners.

Bounder: (beginning to get fed up) Yes, yes now …

Tourist: And once a week there's an excursion to the local Roman Remains to buy cherryade and melted ice cream and bleeding Watney's Red Barrel and one evening you visit the so called typical restaurant with local colour and atmosphere and you sit next to a party from Rhyl who keep singing 'Torremolinos, torremolinos' and complaining about the food – 'It's so greasy isn't it?' – and you get cornered by some drunken greengrocer from Luton with an Instamatic camera and Dr Scholl sandals and last Tuesday's *Daily Express* and he drones on and on. And sending tinted postcards of places they don't realise they haven't even visited to 'All at number 22, weather wonderful, our room is marked with an "X"'.

Text H

They are hollowed out in the see-coast at the muncipal terminal of Capdepera at nine kilometer from the town of Arta in the Island of Mallorca, with a stuporizing infinity of graceful colums of 21 meter and by downward, which prives the spectator of all animacion and plunges in dumbness. The way going is very picturesque, serpentine between style mountains, til the arrival at the esplanade of the vallee called «The Spiders». There are good enlacements of the railroad with autobuses of excursion, many days of the week, today actually Wednesday and Satturday. Since many centuries renown foreing visitors have explored them and wrote their elegy about, included North-American geoglogues.

(From a Spanish tourist guide)

Such subtile filigranity and nobless of construccion
Here fraternise in harmony, that respiracion stops.
While all admit thier impotence (though autors most formidable)
To sing in words the excellence of Nature's underprops,
Yet stalactite and stalagmite together with dumb language
Make hymns to God wich celebrate the stregnth of water drops.

¿You, also, are you capable to make precise in idiom
Consideracions magic of ilusions very wide?
Already in the Vestibule of these Grand Caves of Arta
The spirit of the human verb is darked and stupefied;
So humildy you trespass trough the forest of the colums
And listen to the grandess explicated by the guide.

From darkness into darkness, but at measure, now descending
You remark with what esxactitude he designates each bent;
«The Saloon of Thousand Banners», or «The Tumba of Napoleon»,
«The Grotto of the Rosary», «The Club», «The Camping Tent»,
And at «Cavern of the Organs» there are knocking strange formacions
Wich give a nois particular pervoking wonderment.

Too far do not adventure, sir! For, further as you wander,
The every of the stalactites will make you stop and stay.
Grand peril amenaces now, your nostrills aprehending
An odour least delicious of lamentable decay.
It is poor touristers, in the depth of obscure cristal,
Wich deceased of thier emocion on a past excursion day.

(Welcome to the Caves of Arta! by **Robert Graves**)

An approach to Question 1: Impressions of Canada

Following the suggested approach outlined on p68, what follows is an example of an approach to this question. Here is the question again:

Text A is the transcript of part of a recent promotional video for '*The Rocky Mountaineer*' train which runs from Vancouver through the Rocky Mountains to Calgary in Canada.

Text B is a posting from an internet travellers' forum.

Compare the ways the writers of the texts present their experiences of the journey.

Link

To remind yourself of the extracts for this question (Texts A and B), look back to pp68–70.

You should write about:

- how the purpose and context of each text has influenced the use of language
- how language is used to convey impressions, feelings and attitudes.

Before starting to write you should have noted (mentally, or otherwise) the following:

1 Keywords of the question

Compare: make connections between the two texts throughout

Experiences: discuss the reactions of the writers to their journey – their feelings and attitudes.

Present: don't just comment on what the writers say – analyse HOW they say it.

2 Purpose, context and language

As a promotional video created by a commercial company, *Text A* is clearly designed to persuade people to travel on the Rocky Mountaineer train, and would presumably be viewed prior to travel. As a result the language is enthusiastic, dramatic and enticing. In contrast, as a posting on a travellers' internet forum, the purpose of *Text B* is to share information about personal experiences and opinions with other travellers, and to offer advice. As a result, the language is less exuberant and includes more humdrum, even critical observations.

3 Similarities and differences

Here some basic points you may have thought of:

Similarities	Differences
Both describe experiences of train journey	Text A is highly enthusiastic, Text B is critical.
Both convey attitudes and impressions	Text A is focussed on scenery and history, Text B is focussed more on food and arrangements
Both are persuasive and designed to influence the reader/viewer, using rhetorical techniques	Text A uses first person plural to speak on behalf of the company: Text B is a first person singular account and addresses reader as 'you'.
Both use adjectives and other figurative language to convey attitudes	Text A is scripted speech – depends on timing of pauses, stress and other prosodic features for effect: Text B is a written internet posting
Both may use some exaggeration, or hyperbole	Text A may be more hyperbolic than Text B
	Text A: Gives direct commands (imperatives); Text B offers advice.

Sample answer for Question 1

  Practical activity

Now study the sample essay below, with examiner's comments alongside. There is, of course, no such thing as a perfect 'model' answer which examiners are waiting for; however, you can see from this example the kinds of skill, knowledge and understanding that are always going to be rewarded.

Both texts describe the same journey but present different experiences. Text A speaks invitingly and directly to the viewer, offering a spectacular, even awe-inspiring journey packed with historical and geographical wonders, whereas Text B is more like a catalogue of problems encountered with little enthusiasm for the experience. This reflects the purpose and contexts of the texts, as A is a kind of advertisement designed to persuade people to travel on the train, whereas B is part of a forum for travellers to share their actual, 'real-life' experiences.

Starts with sound overview comparing both texts with focus on keywords of question (AO1)

Clear sense of how contexts have shaped language (AO3)

Text A conveys an enthusiastic attitude and a feeling of awe by the use of many dramatic adjectives and metaphors which are almost hyperbolical. The landscape is described as 'rugged', breathtaking' and 'towering' and the railway is a 'road of steel', which 'clings' to the sides of the cliff. The verb 'cling' personifies the rails and creates a real sense of drama and danger for the viewer. There are several superlatives – 'the most rugged terrain... the most spectacular trip... the largest salmon run….' which also contribute to the hyperbole. In text B it is a different story; the only positive descriptions it includes are that the snacks were 'good', and the scenery 'nice', which are very weak adjectives compared to those in Text A. The writer focuses much more on the food than the scenery, and conveys his criticism with adjectives such as 'disappointing' and 'greasy' and the more colloquial 'nothing to brag about'. Text B does also use occasionally figurative, even hyperbolic language – the day was 'plagued' with delays.

Clear statement of attitudes (AO2) with sound terminology and examples (AO1).

Makes productive comparisons (AO3)

As it is a very colourful description, Text A uses some rhetorical techniques to impress its viewers, such as the repetition of 'come with us', and the use of antithesis in 'back in time and forward to adventure'. Text B is also persuasive, and uses a rhetorical question (Who would want to eat a big meal….?') as well as direct statements of opinion using the first person (I think… from what I've seen…).In fact it is interesting to compare the use of pronouns in the texts. A uses the 1st person plurals 'we' and 'us' several times to create a sense of group identity. The repeated imperatives 'come with us' and 'join us' try to persuade the viewers to become part of this happy group. As we hear 'The dawn of our first day of travel finds us passing through….' spoken in the present tense we are already imagining ourselves there. Text B uses the first person singular (I went on…) to record the writer's personal account, and uses the second person to offer advice directly: 'If you really want a rail trip….'

Compares in terms of purpose/ context (AO3)

Good range of language analysis (AO2) and terminology (AO1)

Perceptive critical understanding (AO2)

It is interesting to compare these texts as one is a transcript of scripted speech, whereas the other is a posting on a website. We can see that the use of vocal stress (and we guess other prosodic features) is important in Text A, as the speaker uses it to emphasis some of the most persuasive and spectacular descriptions like the 'vertical' canyon walls and the 'sheer' cliffs, The use of micro-pauses in Text A also helps punctuate the memorable phrases (often these are minor sentences) such as 'the trip of a lifetime', with longer sentences containing some of the more factual information about the length of the river or the history of a bridge. As it is a scripted speech, it is not surprising that there are no non-fluency features. If anything, the written text, Text B, is actually a little less formal in its register with lexis such as as 'nice' and the use of contractions such as 'it's, and 'doesn't.' This may be because postings online do tend to be more personal and informal and to have some of the characteristics of spoken language.

Well structured paragraph – coherent expression

Variety of approaches:– compares speech/writing (AO3)

Focus on context (AO3)

The Anthology question (Question 2)

AQA Examiner's tip

As with Question 1, the examiners will use their Assessment Objectives to assess your work. Here are the questions the examiners will be asking about your answer:

- Have you answered the question fully?

- How well have you understood the content of the texts and explained the attitudes they convey?

- Have you related the texts to their intended purpose and audience?

- Have you understood how other contextual factors have influenced the texts?

- Have you used terminology accurately to explain key features of the form, structure and language of the texts?

- Have you compared the texts effectively, using relevant examples?

In the examination

Requirements and timing

In your Unit 1 examination, you will be assessed on your responses to texts from the Anthology in Section B. You will be given just one question and, as it is worth two-thirds of the total marks, you need to spend about two-thirds of the time (about 1 hour) on planning and writing your response.

Types of question

The questions will invite you to choose two texts from the Anthology that are linked by a theme suggested in the question. The question will then ask you to write a detailed comparison and contrast of your chosen texts.

You can expect some limited guidance from bullet points which suggest a specific focus for your analysis.

Preparing for the examination

Aside from the preparation you have made by reading Section A of this unit and familiarising yourself with the texts in the Anthology, there are specific ways that you can prepare yourself for the examination itself.

When you have completed your study of all the texts in the Anthology, you need to revise the work you have done earlier in the course, and consider the variety of ways in which texts from the Anthology might be usefully linked and compared. The following exercises would provide the basis of a useful series of revision sessions.

Practical activity

1. Create a set of cards with each card representing one of the texts in the Anthology. Shuffle the set, placing them face down in a pile. Turn over the cards in turn, each time noting a comparison between the text you have just turned over and the one you revealed before.

2. Use the same cards to group together the texts in different categories. You can group texts in any way: by theme or topic, genre, audience, style, period or any other criterion. However, there are some rules:

   - all texts must be used
   - a 'category' must include at least two texts
   - each category must be named – you cannot have 'other' or 'miscellaneous'.

3. Find two texts that meet each of the following criteria, which means that they have something in common. These pairings can then be used to form a comparison of the two texts. What other criteria could you add to the list?

Criteria	Texts for possible comparison	
Aimed at a specific audience		
Illustrate the benefits of travel		
Illustrate change in travel, technology and language		
Use a colloquial style		
Adopt a sympathetic attitude towards the places they describe		
Use literary language		

Practical activity

Here are some examples of paired texts to explore. You might like to use these to help with your revision and practise your skills of analysis and comparison.

1. Look again at 'So near and yet so far' (Text 10) and 'Travel Writing: The Point of It' (Text 13). Compare Palin's ideas about travel writing – and the way he presents them to his readers – with those of Paul Theroux.

2. Compare the way Dorothy Wordsworth writes about Grasmere (and Helm Crag in particular) in Text 22 with the way it is presented by a more modern Lake District enthusiast, the walker Alfred Wainwright, in his 'Ascent from Grasmere' (Text 21).

3. Compare the way the writers' attitudes are expressed towards a foreign culture in *Carnet de Voyage* (Text 7) and 'Walpole and Otranto' (Text 5).

4. Compare the ways the experiences of travellers are presented in the travelblog (Text 12) and *She Stoops to Conquer* (Text 28).

Which texts to choose?

In preparing for the examination, you will have compared many of the texts and the question will allow you to choose the ones you wish to write about. However, you should not expect to be able to reproduce an essay you have already written in the examination. The question on the paper is unlikely to be exactly the same as the one you have already answered, and by trying to make 'one you did earlier' fit into a different question you may be using an inappropriate choice of texts. Therefore, be prepared to write about *any* of the texts and to compare any two of them that you may not previously have thought about comparing. The important thing is to choose the texts that best fit the requirements of the question.

Practical activity

Choosing texts

Whatever the question set in your exam, you are likely to be asked:

How do the writers and/or speakers convey their ideas? You may wish to consider some of the following:

- word choice
- figurative language
- grammar
- sound patterns
- form and structure
- contexts of production and reception.

▶

Not all of these aspects apply equally to all texts and you need not follow them slavishly – indeed, it would be unwise to do so. Which aspects you concentrate on will very much depend on the texts you choose.

However, the question will provide you with a *focus* for your comparison which may give you the job of choosing the best texts to discuss. It is important to make a sensible choice of texts that:

a   relate to the focus given

b   will suggest some interesting points of similarity and difference.

For example, it might be good to compare texts from different periods, or in different genres, or with different purposes and audiences.

Here are some examples of the kinds of question focus that you might encounter in the exam. For each of them, decide which texts you would choose as the basis of your answer, and why.

1   Choose any two texts which you think would prove most useful to someone planning a visit to one of the places described.

2   Choose any two texts that most vividly convey a traveller's impressions of a place they have visited.

3   Choose any two texts which present responses to rail travel.

4   Choose any texts that you think capture either the joys or the difficulties of travel.

Commentary: choice of texts

1   Key words: 'useful' and 'someone planning to visit'. 'Useful' could include anything from the pages from an EC passport (Text 1) and the extract from Manchester Metrolink Tramguide (Text 30) to the various guide-book extracts like Wainwright's walking guide 'Ascent from Grasmere' (Text 21) or the extract from *Great British Bus Journeys* (Text 9). Make sure you give yourself plenty to write about – choosing two short texts such as the Passport and the timetable may fulfil the focus of this question but leave you short of material to get your teeth into.

2   Key words: 'vividly' and 'impressions'. A short list of possibilities might include Postcard 1 and Postcard 2 (Texts 2 and 3), the descriptions of Otranto in *Italy* from the Lonely Planet Series (Text 4), 'Glenelg' (Text 18) or the extract from *A Ladies Life in the Rocky Mountains* (Text 20) which all show early travel writing, the personal account from an internet travel blog on Vietnam (Text 12) or 'Zaire' (Text 23). It would be good to compare a more modern with an older text, as this will give you chance to discuss some aspects of change in language and contexts.

3   Key words: 'Rail travel' and 'responses'. So, it's two from 'The Future is Rail' (Text 14), the extract from *Thomas and Friends Annual 2008* (Text 15) and 'Adlestrop' (Text 32) – the leaflet for a Young Person's Railcard (Text 25) is not really a 'response', so it doesn't fit with the key word. For this question there are fewer texts to choose from, but some potentially interesting comparisons of different genres, including poetry from an earlier period and writing for children.

4   Key words: 'joys or difficulties'. 'Joys' might bring in the descriptions of Otranto in *Italy* from the Lonely Planet Series (Text 4), the article by Michael Palin, 'So near and yet so far' (Text 10), the personal account from an internet travelblog on Vietnam (Text 12) or several others. 'Difficulties' might suggest the extract from Carnet de Voyage (Text 7), the transcript 'Planning a family holiday' (Text 17), the extract from *She Stoops to Conquer* (Text 28) or *Heart of Darkness* (Text 24). Stick to either 'joys' or 'difficulties'. Comparing the transcript with a written text opens up the chance to discuss written and spoken language, and it is often interesting to compare a literary with a non-literary text.

The importance of planning and timing

A comparison essay does *not* consist of two separate mini-essays about two texts with a few points of similarity and difference summed up at the end. Throughout this unit you have been practising the skills of comparison required and you would be wise to use a similar approach when writing under examination conditions.

Here is a recommended approach to choosing your texts, then planning and writing your answer, while keeping an eye on the clock.

Practical activity

Go back to any of the questions above that you have already considered, and practise your examination skills by developing your ideas into a full-length essay response.

Time spent on this activity	Overall time elapsed	Activity	Outcome
5 mins	5 mins	■ Read the question carefully and identify or highlight key words ■ Skim the Anthology and choose the two texts that are relevant to the question and which will lead to interesting comparisons	■ You are clear about the key words of the question ■ You have chosen the texts you are going to compare
5 mins	10 mins	■ Skim through your chosen texts, noting and mapping the major points of similarity and difference (using mind maps or tables) and picking out the details from each you will discuss and analyse in depth ■ Note any useful and relevant terminology as you do this	■ You have collected the main details of the ideas and examples that will be the basis of your essay ■ You have reminded yourself of the kinds of terminology you need to use
5 mins	15 mins	■ Organise your ideas into a clear sequence, paragraph by paragraph. There may be something like half a dozen well-developed paragraphs, each given over to a particular aspect of the texts or question	■ You have a well-organised blueprint for the essay you are going to write
40 mins	55 mins	■ Following your plan, write the essay ■ Each paragraph should begin with a clear statement of the main idea you will be comparing, followed by a discussion of the relevant aspects of both texts, including quotations, analysis using relevant terminology and explanation ■ Make sure you are using words and phrases like 'whereas', 'on the other hand,' 'similarly', etc. to flag up the similarities and differences between both your chosen texts	■ You complete a full and detailed essay
5 mins	60 mins	■ Try to allow time for a quick proofread to eliminate any basic errors of expression that may have crept into your work under the pressure of the examination	■ Essay complete

Sample question and answer for Question 2

Choose any two texts which you think would prove most useful to someone planning a visit to one of the places described.

Use the knowledge and skills you have acquired during your study of the Anthology to compare the attitudes of the writers/speakers of your chosen texts towards this subject

Practical activity

Now study the sample question and essay below, with examiner's comments alongside. There is, of course, no such thing as a perfect 'model' answer which examiners are waiting for; however, you can see from this example the kinds of skill, knowledge and understanding that are always going to be rewarded.

You may wish to consider where appropriate:

- word choice
- figurative language
- grammar
- sound patterns
- form & structure.

Overview of 2 texts. Focus on question. Compares and notes contexts (AO1,3)

Both Texts 8 (Enjoy a weekend in Lancashire) and 21 (Ascent from Grasmere) would be useful for visitors as they provide practical information and guide the visitor around the places they describe. Both use a combination of text and images/diagrams to assist the visitor and convey the writers' enjoyment of the place, though text 8 is a modern magazine article, aimed at attracting a wide range of possible readers, whereas Text 21 is an extract from a somewhat older and more specialised book aimed at keen walkers.

Organised response; coherent comparison (AO1). Compares graphology, lay-out, typography (AO2)

There are obvious similarities in lay-out and graphology between the two texts. Text 8 follows the conventions of a magazine article by using columns, pictures and diagrams. The left hand column acts as a kind of 'trailer' for the text as a whole, with bold text attracting the casual reader to the names of the main attractions of the area. A photograph adds to the attraction, and the guided walk around Clitheroe is helpfully broken down into 6 sections which correspond to places marked on a map. Although Text 21 also uses text and images, the effect is much more like a hand-drawn and hand-written notebook than a professional magazine, as it uses a script-like font and makes no use of photography. Neither does it use bold or italics to attract readers but as with Text 8, the instructions for the walk correspond to the place names on the map.

Understanding and contexts (AO2, 3)

Varied approaches – lexis (AO2)

Terminology (AO1)

Compares (AO3)

Contexts – period (AO3)

The lexis of both texts conveys affection and enthusiasm as well as mere information. In Text 8 there is lots of adjectival pre-modification: the terrain is amazingly varied, the countryside is 'most attractive', the uplands 'rugged', the shores of Morecambe are 'tree-fringed', and so on. This part of the text seems designed to persuade readers of the magazine ('people outside the county') that Lancashire is worth visiting. Wainwright's text is less like a travel brochure, but still uses some adjectives such as 'rugged'. Words like 'exquisite' and 'excellent, though, belong to a different register; the period of the text is reflected in the higher formality of 'an epitome of Lakeland….an excellent foretaste'…..and the old-fashioned sounding 'Tarry long….'

Compares (AO3)

Grammar/lexis understanding (AO2)

In a way, Text 8 includes two different styles of writing; the persuasive list of its attractions and the more factual guide around the town. Text 21, on the other hand, seems to combine personal comment and practical instruction as it goes along. The guided walk in Text 8 is written in a mixture of declarative and imperative sentences using the 2nd person pronoun. The imperatives give brief instructions for the walker to follow, and the declarative sentences include factual and historical information such as dates. Text 21 also uses one direct imperative ('tarry long!) but its 'instructions' are implied in the description and the map; more of Wainwright's text offers advice ('it is better reserved….' and personal comment. His use of exclamation marks in the text ('for the long winter of exile….!) and, unusually, on the diagram ('seat (perhaps!') convey his personal enjoyment and humour.

Coverage of Anthology texts and links to language study topics

You may find it useful to refer to this grid when revising the Anthology texts or if you study them in a different order than the one in this book.

Text	Title	Coverage	Language study topics
1	Pages from an EC passport	pp11–15	■ Linguistic frameworks ■ Describing style ■ Contexts of production and reception ■ Pragmatics
2	Postcard 1	pp47–49	■ Genre conventions ■ Spoken and written language
3	Postcard 2	pp47–49	■ Genre conventions ■ Spoken and written language
4	*Italy*, the Lonely Planet series	pp55–57	■ Contexts, purpose and attitudes
5	'Walpole and Otranto', *A Traveller in Southern Italy*	pp55–57	■ Contexts, purpose and attitudes
6	'Always our Likely Finale'	–	–
7	*Carnet de Voyage*	–	–
8	'Lancashire', *Country Walking* magazine	–	–
9	*Great British Bus Journeys*	–	–
10	'So near and yet so far', *Guardian*	–	–
11	'Booking Conditions'	pp19–22	■ Field-specific lexis ■ Register
12	A personal account from an Internet travelblog	pp47–53	■ Genre conventions ■ Spoken and written language
13	'Travel Writing: The Point of It', *Fresh-Air Fiend*	pp53–55	■ Contexts and attitudes
14	'The Future is Rail', *Fire and Steam*	pp30–36	■ Arguments, attitudes and authority
15	*Thomas and Friends Annual 2008*	pp28–30	■ Audience, context and pragmatics
16	*Oxford English Dictionary Online*	pp7–10	■ Lexis, semantics and language change
17	'Planning a family holiday', *Exploring English Language*	pp23–27	■ Spoken language ■ Analysing talk
18	'Glenelg', *A Journey to the Western Isles of Scotland*	–	–
19	'Travel Writing'	–	–
20	*A Lady's Life in the Rocky Mountains*	–	–
21	'Ascent from Grasmere', *The Central Fells*	–	–
22	'The Grasmere Journals', *Journals of Dorothy Wordsworth*	pp62–65	■ Language change ■ Audience, purpose and pragmatics
23	'Zaire', *National Geographic* magazine	pp43–46	■ Literary/non-literary language
24	*Heart of Darkness*	pp43–46	■ Literary language
25	Leaflet for a Young Persons Railcard	pp16–17, 22	■ Language frameworks and stylistic analysis ■ Modal verbs ■ Conditionals
26	'Airmiles' letter	pp18–19, 22	■ Persuasion and rhetoric ■ Personal pronouns
27	*The Innocents Abroad*	–	–
28	*She Stoops to Conquer*	pp58–62	■ Language change ■ Scripted and unscripted talk
29	'Kensington to Uphusband', *Rural Rides*	pp62–65	■ Language change ■ Audience, purpose and pragmatics
30	Manchester Metrolink Tramguide	–	–
31	*Dombey and Son*	pp37–43	■ Narrative stance ■ Form and structure
32	'Adlestrop'	pp37–43	■ Language and poetry

Themes in language and

This unit covers:

- exploring the relationships between texts, using integrated critical approaches to language and literature

- demonstrating detailed critical understanding, using appropriate terminology

- demonstrating expertise and creativity in using language appropriately for a variety of purposes.

AQA Examiner's tip

Read both books straight through as early in the course as you can, just to get an idea of what happens. Then when you come to study them in detail you will see more easily the coursework opportunities that are open to you.

Introduction

The coursework in English Language and Literature B is designed to help you to do two things:

- to deepen your knowledge and understanding of books that other people have written

- to show this understanding through creative work of your own.

The two are closely connected. As you read and comment on other people's writing, you will gain ideas that you can put into practice when you are the author yourself.

Your tasks

In this unit you will be studying two full-length books, written at different periods but with some connection between them. This connection could be the same genre (for example, detective stories), the same topic (for example, crime and punishment) or the same audience. One of the books might be a deliberate sequel or prequel to the other, or an adaptation of its ideas.

This unit, Themes in language and literature, discusses a range of ideas and approaches to help you consider how meanings are constructed and how you as a reader can engage with the meanings of these and other texts. At the end of Section A (analysis) there is a worked example to show how you might tackle the first part of the coursework. You can then build on this knowledge in Section B (creative writing), which gives suggestions for the kind of text you might write yourself, with examples of how both professional writers and students have approached the task.

Your candidate brief

This unit is assessed through two coursework tasks; there is no examination. As you begin to study the books you will be given a specific theme to consider, and both tasks will be related to this.

You are going to study in detail what each author has to say and the way in which he or she says it. You will then show your understanding as follows:

- Part A of the coursework you produce will analyse the way a particular theme appears in two short extracts from the set texts. You choose these extracts yourself. Your analysis should be 1,200 to 1,500 words long. This assignment carries 40 out of 64 marks.

- Part B will show your understanding of the material by asking you to adapt your set texts creatively. This second piece of coursework should be 500 to 850 words long. It carries 24 out of 64 marks.

The complete coursework unit carries 40 per cent of the total marks for AS English Language and Literature.

You are not required to submit drafts or commentaries for assessment, but you will need to show evidence of planning. You can do so in either a single document covering both tasks or two separate ones; this material does not contribute to the word count.

In this paper, your work will be assessed according to the Assessment Objectives. Think of these as questions that the examiner will be asking of you.

		Part A	Part B
AO1	Can you discuss a range of different texts using a range of suitable terminology, reflecting the combined study of language and literature?	✓	✓
AO2	Can you produce detailed, accurate and clearly expressed analyses of texts	✓	✓
AO3	Can you make relevant and productive comparisons between different texts and their contexts, bringing out their most significant similarities and differences?	✓	
AO4	Can you show expertise and creativity in using language appropriately for a variety of purposes and audiences, drawing on what you have seen in your study of language and literature?	✓	✓

This unit discusses as wide a range of texts and ideas as possible, covering all the set pairings. We shall also be referring to two specific themes and using two pairings of texts as worked examples. These are:

- the deceiving appearance – in Poe's *Selected Tales* and Chandler's *The Big Sleep*
- conflict – in *Jane Eyre* and *Wide Sargasso Sea*.

Practical activity

As you work through the set texts, keep a part of your file where you can note rough ideas for creative writing. These might be points where the set text could be expanded with new material, ideas for seeing plot developments from a different point of view, or notes on character.

Write down the number of the page in the book that gave you this idea, so that you can come back to it later.

Working with your set texts

Key terms

Narrative: an account of connected events.

Two set texts

The point of studying two books that are related is that by comparing them you gain a greater insight into what each author is doing. Comparing the similarities makes you notice the differences, too. For example, Robert Louis Stevenson's *Travels with a Donkey in the Cévennes* and Bill Bryson's *The Lost Continent* are both records of real journeys taken by the writer, but at even the simplest level of coverage there are obvious contrasts between them. It takes Stevenson 12 days to cover something over 120 miles; using a car, Bryson can do that in an afternoon, so there is a huge difference in pace and range, as you will notice immediately. The styles that the writers use are as different as their methods of transport.

Finding links between texts

The texts you will study are linked in some way by their subject matter, but the two are separated by a time gap. This means that there will usually be other significant differences. For example, there may be differences that relate to the social and historical context of the texts, as well as different features of language and style that are characteristic of the periods in which the texts were written. To bring out the significance of each text, you first of all need to be able to distinguish between what happens in the **narrative** and the way in which it happens. You also need some appropriate critical vocabulary to help you do this.

Although every text is different, they share common problems of how to shape the narrative and keep the reader's attention. All the texts here use speech, and they all introduce characters and place the action in appropriate settings, even though the ways in which these matters are presented differ greatly. Comparing the ways that authors shape their material helps you to appreciate the individual qualities of each narrative.

As you study the different topics, you will find examples from books other than the ones on which your own coursework will be based. This will widen your general background in literary criticism and help you to grasp some of the broader concepts of analysis. Applying your knowledge about techniques of writing to a range of literary prose will develop your understanding in ways that will help you to become a better writer yourself.

Approaching analysis

You have already learned a good deal about critical approaches in Unit 1 and you need to be able to apply that knowledge here. However, so far you will have studied short extracts or poems rather than full-length prose works. There are a few new critical terms for you to learn as you explore longer narratives.

This section is divided into different topics for convenience, but in the end it is never entirely possible to separate what writers say from the way in which they say it. Matters such as character description, speech and sentence length all contribute in different proportions to the overall meaning and they all shade into one another. You might think of it as being like a kaleidoscope, with each little bit contributing to a larger pattern.

A word of warning here: your work needs to focus on the actual written texts. Many novels and biographies have been adapted to make films. Some of these are excellent and you might even consider writing part of a film script yourself for the second part of your coursework. However, they are always different in some way from the original text, and it is the *original* texts that you are studying and writing about in your coursework.

 Practical activity

If there is a film versions of your set text, make a list of the differences between the two and consider why the alterations were made. Among other things, this activity often gives an insight into changes over time in such aspects as audience expectations, language style and narrative technique.

13 What do we mean by themes in language and literature?

This chapter covers:

- understanding the ways in which different aspects of narrative structure can be related
- distinguishing story from plot
- recognising the relationship between theme and genre.

AQA Examiner's tip

Do not worry if you know other people doing the same course, English Language and Literature B, who have been allocated different themes. This is because the theme is set for the specific time at which you enter for the coursework unit, and will change for each year and for each pair of texts (rather in the way that questions change from year to year and book to book in a formal examination).

Key terms

Plot: the main sequence of narrative events in a story, organised in such a way as to create links between them and maintain interest for the reader.

Narrative structures: the storyline and its development

Plot and theme

For each session, AQA will set different themes to be used as a focus for coursework analysis and creative writing.

Themes are related to ideas. They are what the book is about, rather than simply what happens in it. To understand how themes work, let us go back a little and talk first about story and **plot**.

When we start to read or tell stories, the first thing we notice is what happens – the simple sequence of events. At first children write 'and then and then and then …' when they make up stories, using just the simple order of time. However, mature writers soon see that it is the pattern of events that matters, so their stories have a more developed plot.

Consider this story: a poor girl meets a rich and desirable man; he falls for her, they are separated by difficulties, but are eventually reunited and enabled to marry. It is the story of *Cinderella*, of course, but it is also the story of *Jane Eyre*. The two narratives have the same underlying structure but they are widely different in context, setting and style.

Practical activity

Reduce the storyline of the books you are studying to no more than three sentences. Seeing how the skeleton of a story works may help you find ideas for creative work based on it.

Writers shape their narrative structures carefully even in non-fiction works, which you might at first think would be organised simply by time sequence. Stevenson's *Travels with a Donkey in the Cévennes* uses the idea of his attitude to the donkey, Modestine, as an organising structure for the narrative. He buys her as part of his preparations for the journey through the south of France. Along the road their relationship develops, and the narrative ends with his selling her to someone else and telling us about his feelings on doing so.

> I had lost Modestine. Up to that moment I had thought I hated her; but now she was gone,
>
> > 'And oh!
> >
> > The difference to me!'
>
> For twelve days we had been fast companions; we had travelled upwards of a hundred and twenty miles, crossed several respectable ridges, and jogged along with our six legs by many a rocky and many a boggy by-road. After the first day, although sometimes I was hurt and distant in manner, I still kept my patience; and as for her, poor soul! She had come to regard me as a god. She loved to eat out of my hand.

Stevenson returns to descriptions of his struggles with her over and over again in the progress of his journey. Finally, in the above example, he rounds off the narrative on an emotional note of nostalgia and regret that the reader will respond to. The animal even gets a place in the title of the book.

The writer E. M. Forster discusses the idea of sequence in *Aspects of the Novel*, where he explains it very succinctly. He says that 'The king died and then the queen died' is a story but 'The king died and then the queen died of grief' is a plot – one event depends on the other. Plot is important: it keeps us turning the pages. When you come to choose your extracts for analysis you might focus on a moment of discovery or an important event and explore how this contributes to the plot.

Theme is subtly different from plot. In the example of the king and queen, there might be two themes. One could be death, because this obviously happens more than once and so is a recurring idea in the narrative. The other possible theme is grief, which is not an event at all but an emotion. You can imagine other possible plots arising from the same story. Perhaps the queen murdered the king and then took her own life in a fit of remorse. If we investigated the queen's reactions, we might see another theme: guilt.

Themes are unifying ideas that the writer explores and develops in the course of a narrative.

Plot structures

The classic plot structure goes like this:

Situation ⟶ Complication ⟶ Resolution

In the beginning, the author has to set time and place, introduce the main characters and establish a point of view. At the end, he or she has to resolve the issues in some way satisfactory to the reader; otherwise, as Raymond Chandler once said, the story is 'an unresolved chord and leaves irritation behind it.'

Beginnings

The Big Sleep begins with a character: Philip Marlowe. *The Lost Continent* begins with a place: 'I come from Des Moines. Somebody had to.' *Wide Sargasso Sea* begins with a major theme: race.

They all do more than that. They have to give you a reason for reading on. Chandler and Bryson both do this with humour. Marlowe follows up the statement 'I was neat, clean, shaved and sober' – which already raises the question of whether this is unusual – with 'and I didn't care who knew it', deliberately twisting a cliché into an unexpected context.

Rhys begins *Wide Sargasso Sea* with something of a puzzle: 'They say when trouble comes close ranks, and so the white people did. But we were not in their ranks.' The explanation only gradually becomes clear over the next few pages, which establish the setting as the West Indies within a few years of the emancipation of the slaves.

All of these narratives have openings that are both economical and striking, rapidly conveying information and setting the tone. Novice writers may find openings difficult, and often begin too far back with something a little dull when they would be better to start further into the story and fill in the details later.

Key terms

Theme: themes are ideas in a piece of writing, often ideas that recur during the narrative.

AQA Examiner's tip

This is something you might bear in mind for your coursework. A striking opening creates momentum in a story. You might write the opening last or return to your first attempt at an opening and re-draft it in light of the way your narrative has developed.

Practical activity

List as many genres and sub-genres as you can. Browsing in a library or bookshop will help you to appreciate the range and diversity. You will probably be surprised by how many there are, and you may find some ideas for creative work in the second part of your coursework task.

In gothic horror, for example, we expect characters to feel threatened by mysterious events, in an atmosphere of gloom, the macabre and the supernatural.

Some genres may be written for particular audiences. Romances on the whole target a female audience, and war stories on the whole a male one. Some, such as science fiction, may have particular settings and subject matter. Some texts may have elements of different genres. *Frankenstein*, for example, belongs to the broad genre of the novel, but it also contains strong elements of horror story; it seems partly like science fiction, but some sections of it have detailed descriptions of travel, which add a realistic element to the novel.

Some genres have widely recognised rules of structure: the detective story is one of these. Raymond Chandler listed 'ten commandments for the detective novel', which are interesting to relate to *The Big Sleep*. They are as follows:

1   It must be credibly motivated, both as to the original situation and the denouement.

2   It must be technically sound as to the methods of murder and detection.

3   It must be realistic in character, setting and atmosphere. It must be about real people in a real world.

4   It must have a sound story value apart from the mystery element; i.e. the investigation itself must be an adventure worth reading.

5   It must have enough essential simplicity to be explained easily when the time comes.

6   It must baffle a reasonably intelligent reader.

7   The solution must seem inevitable once revealed.

8   It must not try to do everything at once. If it is a puzzle story operating in a rather cool, reasonable atmosphere, it cannot also be a violent adventure or passionate romance.

9   It must punish the criminal in one way or another, not necessarily by operation of the law … if the detective fails to resolve the consequences of the crime, the story is an unresolved chord and leaves irritation behind it.

10 It must be honest with the reader.

*(Quoted in **N. Parsons**, The Book of Literary Lists, **1986**)*

The mystery must be resolved; the crime must be punished. This list is unusually detailed, but Chandler is not simply writing to a formula in his novels. He is saying that readers will have expectations of the genre before they pick up the book and that structure, as well as setting and characterisation, must take these expectations into account.

14 How do writers explore themes in novels and literary non-fiction?

Key terms

Voice: the distinctive manner of expression that is characteristic of a particular writer or speaker, or of a created literary character.

First person narrative: a story that is narrated by a character from within the story itself using the pronoun 'I'.

Protagonist: the leading character, or one of the major characters, in a literary text.

Point of view: who tells the story?

Each narrative has a characteristic **voice**. The way the story is told will colour its whole meaning. In *Utopia*, for example, Thomas More invents a narrator, Raphael Hythloday, who tells the story of his travels. Everyone knows that Utopia does not exist (its name means 'no place') and neither does Raphael Hythloday, but using this voice conveniently makes the book seem like a real traveller's tale. Just as conveniently, it puts a little distance between the ideas expressed in the narrative and More himself. It makes it seem as though More is describing a system set up by someone else, not inventing one himself.

There is an important difference between a narrator who is part of the action and one who is an outside observer of it. There is a difference, too, between telling what happens through description and comment and showing it through dialogue.

Let us look at some different approaches to storytelling.

First person narrative

This is the way of telling a story that uses the pronoun 'I'. The **first person narrative** is, of course, the most intimate. We hear the voice of the character directly and share his or her experience. Take this moment from near the end of *The Big Sleep*, as Marlowe faces Carmen Sternwood:

> The gun pointed at my chest. Her hand seemed to be quite steady. The hissing sound grew louder and her face had a scraped bone look. Aged, deteriorated, become animal and not a nice animal.
>
> I laughed at her. I started to walk towards her. I saw her small finger tighten on the trigger and grow white at the tip.
>
> I was about six feet away when she started to shoot.

This is exciting stuff. The 'I' of the story is Philip Marlowe, who is right in the centre of the action. We watch him there as he faces danger. He can give us close detail as he observes it, with descriptions such as 'I saw her small finger tighten on the trigger and grow white at the tip.' The suspense is tremendous as we follow him step by step. There is a snag, though – he has to stay alive to tell the story, unless the writer can find some other exceptionally clever solution. After this point, Chandler has to resolve the plot quickly or risk an anticlimax.

In a first person narrative there are always limitations. We can see events only as the **protagonist** sees them. Inevitably, the point of view is biased; however, writers can use this bias creatively to their advantage. One way of inviting readers to reflect on the possibility that everything may not be quite as a first person narrator reports it is by using multiple narrators, so that different versions of reality coexist.

Using multiple narrators

Here is the central moment of *Frankenstein* – the vision that Mary Shelley had when she and her husband and friends started to tell ghost stories at Byron's house in Switzerland, one wet summer day in 1816. It is a first person narrative and the speaker is Victor Frankenstein, who has just given life to a creature he had made from stolen body parts. He has been having a nightmare when he wakes to see the creature.

Critical response activity

How does Shelley convey his reactions?

> I started from my sleep with horror; a cold dew covered my forehead, my teeth chattered, and every limb became convulsed: when by the dim and yellow light of the moon, as it forced its way through the window shutters, I beheld the wretch – the miserable monster whom I had created. He held up the curtain of the bed; and his eyes, if eyes they may be called, were fixed on me. His jaws opened, and he muttered some inarticulate sounds, while a grin wrinkled his cheeks. He might have spoken, but I did not hear; one hand stretched out, seemingly to detain me, but I escaped and rushed downstairs.

Critical response activity

Now compare Victor's version of these events with the way the creature reports them.

> It is with considerable difficulty that I remember the original era of my being: all the events of that period appear confused and indistinct. A strange multiplicity of sensations seized me, and I saw, felt, heard and smelt at the same time; and it was, indeed, a long time before I learned to distinguish between the operations of my various senses. By degrees, I remember, a stronger light pressed upon my nerves, so that I was obliged to shut my eyes. Darkness then came over me, and troubled me; but hardly had I felt this when, by opening my eyes, as I now suppose, the light poured in upon me again. I walked and, I believe, descended …

Commentary

Each of these narrators gives a first person account of the same events, and of his physical sensations during them. Victor's is all violent terror; his teeth 'chattered', his limbs 'convulsed', he 'rushed' downstairs, feeling threatened. Even the moonlight 'forced' its way through the window. He goes on to describe the creature as 'a thing such as even Dante could not have conceived' – in other words, something out of hell.

Victor becomes violently agitated, but the creature does not even recognise him. He is born completely innocent and has to learn about light and dark, heat and cold, before he ever begins to understand about humans and their reaction to physical ugliness. Notice how slow and measured his sentences are, using long words and rather abstract vocabulary, such as 'original era of my being' and 'multiplicity of sensations'. His account is much more reasonable than emotional.

All through the novel, Shelley is asking who was to blame for the crimes and disasters that occur in it: was it Victor or the creature? The reader's sympathy shifts between the two. This is largely because of the complex narrative method that contrasts different accounts and leaves us to judge between them. Letting characters speak in their own words is an important method of characterisation.

Using different formats

Another way of solving any problems that result from having a limited viewpoint is to bring in something like a letter or a diary. A letter can give information that the character reading it would not otherwise have known and add another voice to the narrative.

As a matter of fact, *Frankenstein* does not only have two first person narrators. The entire story of the conflict between Victor and the creature is enclosed within a framework of letters from the sea captain, Walton, to his sister. Walton gives yet another viewpoint, and incidentally solves the problem of both Victor and the creature being dead at the end of the novel and so unable to finish their own accounts of events.

Yet more letters give information at key points in the story. A letter from Elizabeth introduces the character of Justine, who is about to play a brief but important role in the plot. Then, shortly after this, one from Alphonse Frankenstein announces the creature's first murder (of which Justine is falsely accused). Shelley is not much interested in Elizabeth as a character, but feels obliged to make some sort of gesture towards individualising her and giving a realistic framework for the letter, so after its main business the letter goes on: 'Now, dear Victor, I dare say you wish to be indulged in a little gossip concerning the good people of Geneva.'

Twentieth-century narratives often include documents of various kinds as a way of suggesting realism. *In Cold Blood*, which is not a novel but an account of actual events, is able to quote some real documents. Perry Smith's statement in Chapter 4, complete with digressions and faulty grammar, is his authentic voice. Other documents, such as published newspaper reports, are technically written in the third person but can have similar effects.

The unreliable narrator

Usually, although not always, we can assume that first person narrators are telling the truth as they see it, but this does not mean that the reader necessarily has to believe everything the narrator says. For various reasons, a narrator may be unreliable.

Wide Sargasso Sea contains a whole series of unreliable narrators. In the first part Antoinette (the mad wife kept in the attic in *Jane Eyre*) is a child and so has only partial insight into events. Later, she becomes mentally unstable. Antoinette's husband is first portrayed as highly prejudiced and later as on the verge of breakdown himself. Daniel Cosway, the author of the letter that helps break up their marriage, may be lying.

The effect of all this is to make the novel, on one level, realistic. This is what we do in real life – we piece together facts and opinions that we learn at different times and from different sources, and then try to make sense of them. In *Wide Sargasso Sea*, however, bits of information about events and relationships between characters are missing. The narrative refers to them in passing or indirectly. Rhys seems to have decided to withhold some of the relevant details from the reader. We shall never know what Antoinette's relations with her cousin Sandi actually were, because the information is not in the novel. Some readers find this stimulating; others find it irritating.

Third person narrative

This is the style of writing that uses the pronouns 'he', 'she' and 'they'. The narrative voice may often be that of the author, expressing his or her own personal point of view, but this is not always the case. It is also

> ### ■ Think about it
>
> Using letters allows a writer to expand the information in a text by giving a different viewpoint. You might consider presenting your creative writing coursework in the form of a letter from one of the characters in the narrative you are studying.

possible to write a **third person narrative** that conveys the point of view of a character in the story. Most commonly this is through the use of **free indirect speech**.

The omniscient narrator

One of the advantages of third person narrative is that the author can see everything that is going on, including what goes on in the minds of different characters, and can describe scenes where they are not present. Because the author in this sense knows everything, he or she is often known as the **omniscient narrator**.

The text paired with *Frankenstein*, Truman Capote's *In Cold Blood*, uses the omniscient narrator method. The major events in this narrative really happened, so Capote must use the third person in order to appear detached, clear-sighted and balanced in judgement. He allows himself many of the freedoms of a novelist in telling the story, however.

Here he introduces Perry Smith, one of the two murderers in the case.

> Outside the drugstore, Perry stationed himself in the sun. It was a quarter to nine, and Dick was a half hour late; however, if Dick had not hammered home the every-minute importance of the next twenty-four hours, he would not have noticed it. Time rarely weighed upon him, for he had many methods of passing it – among them, mirror gazing. Dick had once observed, 'Every time you see a mirror you go into a trance, like. Like you was looking at some gorgeous piece of butt. I mean, my God, don't you ever get tired?' Far from it; his own face enthralled him. It was a changeling's face, and mirror-guided experiments had taught him how to ring the changes, how to look now ominous, now impish, now soulful.

You will see that Capote interprets Perry's thoughts for us, as well as describing his actions in detail. Capote wants to paint a portrait, from the beginning, of a deeply damaged man, odd in both appearance and psychology, so we learn things such as that 'his own face enthralled him', and that he had a tenuous grip on outside reality, making 'mirror-guided experiments' with his own expression rather than looking outward to the world around him.

Free indirect speech

The narrative voice does not have to be the author's, even when it uses third person pronouns. Sometimes we catch an echo of a character's distinctive style of speech or inner thoughts when these are reported by someone else or conveyed by the author in description. This is known as free indirect speech.

In the opening of *Nineteen Eighty-Four*, the narrator is presumably the author and Winston Smith is seen from the outside.

> It was a bright cold day in April, and the clocks were striking thirteen. Winston Smith, his chin nuzzled into his breast in an effort to escape the vile wind, slipped quickly through the doors of Victory mansions, though not quickly enough to prevent a swirl of gritty dust from entering along with him.

Here, however, is the cruelly **ironic** ending. The brainwashed and defeated Winston sits in the Chestnut Tree Café. His fight for independence is over; torture has crushed him into conformity with what the Party wants.

> O cruel, needless misunderstanding! O stubborn, self-willed exile
> from the loving breast! Two gin-scented tears trickled down the
> sides of his nose. But it was all right, everything was all right, the
> struggle was finished. He loved Big Brother.

This is partly seen from the outside; it is Orwell who observes the 'two
gin-scented tears', but it is also partly reflecting Winston's own broken
thoughts as he tells himself that his rebellion against the Party was 'cruel,
needless misunderstanding'. We know that it was no such thing. It was
a desperate and lonely stand against the forces of a totalitarian system.
However, the Party has now gained total control.

Orwell's use of free indirect speech here is serious and tragic, but this
narrative method can equally well have a comic effect. Bill Bryson, who is
fond of introducing a variety of voices in his narrative, sometimes uses a
similar technique in *The Lost Continent*.

 ## Critical response activity

Here Bryson is describing his arrival at a dinette in Georgia. What do you think
is his opinion of the people he sees there?

> Fourteen people just stopped eating, their food resting in their
> mouths, and stared at us. It was so quiet in there you could have
> heard a fly fart. A whole roomful of good ole boys with cherry-
> coloured cheeks and bib overalls watched us in silence and
> wondered whether their shotguns were loaded. It was disconcerting.
> To them, out here in the middle of nowhere, we were at once a
> curiosity – some of them had clearly never seen no long-haired,
> nigger-loving, Northern, college-edjucated, commie hippies in the
> flesh before – and yet unspeakably loathsome.

His description carries the echo of the crude speech of the people he
is describing, using their own **dialect**. He mocks their grammar in
the phrase 'never seen no' and their pronunciation in his spelling of
'edjucated', as well as their manners and appearance.

Dialogue

Dialogue between characters makes a narrative more dramatic and gives
it some of the features of a play because each speaker has a characteristic
voice.

You will find that even writers of non-fiction use a good deal of dialogue
because it makes the narrative livelier and more immediate. In fact, the
use of dialogue is one of the techniques that blurs the distinction between
fiction and non-fiction, because all written dialogue is shaped and edited
by the author. In real life people very rarely, if ever, talk as clearly and
succinctly as they do in books. Dialogue in books may look realistic, but
it does not contain the false starts, hesitations and repetitions of everyday
speech unless they are put there for a purpose.

 ## Critical response activity

Bryson uses direct speech much more frequently than indirect. What do you
think is his main purpose in using dialogue here? In the local tourist office he
asks for directions to William Faulkner's old home at Rowan Oak, and gets the
reply:

 ### Key terms

Dialect: a variety of a particular
language, characterised by
distinctive features of accent,
grammar and vocabulary, used
by people from a particular
geographical area or social group.

Dialogue: direct speech between two
or more characters in a narrative.

Occasionally characters have no names. The husband in *Wide Sargasso Sea* is never named and this creates an awkwardness. We do not know quite how to refer to him and end up giving him a name – Rochester – to avoid having to call him 'the husband' all the time. The effect of this difficulty is to alienate the reader from the character.

The other character who has no name is Frankenstein's creature, who is not human, and whom Victor Frankenstein rejects. Giving the creature a name would imply accepting a relationship with him, which is precisely what Victor refuses to do, even though he has given the creature life. Later, as the murders mount up, all Victor wants to do is destroy his own creation. Interestingly, the creature (especially as portrayed by Boris Karloff in the 1931 film) has become a modern icon and many people think that the name 'Frankenstein' belongs to him and not to Victor, his maker.

Descriptions of appearance

The third person narrative has an advantage in the matter of description. It can tell us what the main character looks like from the outside. First person narratives can easily enough describe other characters when the main protagonist meets them, but have more difficulty in presenting actual portraits of the hero or heroine. It can be done, however. Do you remember Philip Marlowe's first entrance? He says, humorously:

> I was wearing my powder-blue suit, with dark blue shirt, tie and display handkerchief, black brogues, black wool socks with dark blue clocks on them. I was neat, clean, shaved and sober, and I didn't care who knew it. I was everything the well-dressed private detective ought to be.

In fiction, there is a tendency to draw comparisons between the physical appearance of characters and their psychology. Orwell chooses to describe Winston Smith as 'a smallish, frail figure'. Although he is technically the hero of *Nineteen Eighty-Four*, this description is one of the early signals that he will ultimately be defeated.

Here, from a first person narrative, is the portrait of Jane Eyre's old enemy, Aunt Reed. You will notice that there are a great many **qualitative adjectives** in the description. In a way, it is a portrait that says as much about the intelligent child, Jane, who is making these close observations as it does about the adult who is being observed, and it underlines the conflict between the two characters. Its detail is impressive, suggesting close study and objectivity.

Key terms

Qualitative adjectives: words that give information about the qualities of the noun they describe, e.g. a *frail* figure.

Critical response activity

How do you, as a reader, react to the following portrait of Mrs Reed?

> Mrs Reed might be at that time some six or seven and thirty; she was a woman of robust frame, square shouldered and strong limbed, not tall, and, though stout, not obese; she had a somewhat large face, the under-jaw being much developed and very solid; her brow was low, her chin large and prominent, mouth and nose sufficiently regular: under her light eye-brows glimmered an eye devoid of ruth; her skin was dark and opaque, her hair nearly flaxen; her constitution was sound as a bell – illness never came near her.

Commentary

This portrait conveys above all an impression of solidity. It uses adjectives such as 'robust', 'square', 'strong', 'large', 'solid', 'prominent'. Mrs Reed seems to resemble a fighter. The rather fragile child sitting opposite her never stands a chance. The description also includes a moral judgement, where it mentions her 'eye devoid of ruth' (pity). The action follows this up, since Mrs Reed's treatment of Jane amounts to severe cruelty.

The detective Philip Marlowe is attractive to women. Victor Frankenstein's fiancée, Elizabeth, is remarkably pretty: 'her hair was the brightest living gold' and 'her blue eyes cloudless'. In fairy tales, it is normal for the prince to be handsome and the witch to be ugly. We have a strong tendency to make a connection between beauty and goodness in our daily lives, and writers are well aware of this even when they deliberately reverse the reader's expectations. Few physical descriptions are without some sort of bias.

In their different ways, *Frankenstein* and *In Cold Blood* both follow this convention but also make protests against it. The creature Victor Frankenstein has brought to life is rejected because he is ugly. The scene with the De Lacey family drives home this point. The creature helps the family throughout the winter, and while he keeps out of sight they refer to him as a 'good spirit'. He approaches the father, who is blind, hoping to plead his case for tolerance with someone who will not be prejudiced against his appearance. As soon as the sighted members of the family lay eyes on him, they recoil in horror and reject him without allowing any chance for explanation. It is one of the most moving moments of the novel.

Perry Smith, the subject of *In Cold Blood*, was, of course, a real person, not a fictional creation, and Capote stresses his physical appearance as part of the case for special consideration. On Perry's first appearance at the beginning of the book, Capote tells us that while sitting down he seems to be 'a more than normal-sized man', but when he stands up his oddity is immediately apparent.

> His tiny feet, encased in short black boots with steel buckles, would have fitted into a delicate lady's dancing slippers; when he stood up, he was no taller than a twelve-year-old child.

The comparisons here, with a woman and a child, deliberately stress Perry's vulnerability as well as his strangeness.

Capote wants to tell us throughout his narrative that, unlike the other murderer in the case, Perry is not normal. It is this feature of Perry that haunts the detective, Alvin Dewey, throughout the case, so that as Perry finally hangs, the image remains of 'the same childish feet, tilted, dangling'.

Spoken words

In the section on dialogue you looked at two contrasting speeches – one from Philip Marlowe, and one from Auguste Dupin – and noted that their contrasting linguistic styles are a feature of the presentation of character. Chandler gives his hero naturalistic speech, and this is one of the ways in which he makes the character credible to the reader.

> 'Take it easy now,' I said. 'It's loaded in all five. I'll go over and set this can in that square opening in the middle of that big wooden wheel. See?' I pointed. She ducked her head, delighted. 'That's about thirty feet. Don't start shooting until I get back beside you. Okey?'
>
> 'Okey,' she giggled.

 Practical activity

Make two lists of characters in fiction – one list of heroes and the other of villains – not necessarily in novels but in films or television series too. Put a tick by all the ones who are good-looking and a cross by all the ones who are physically unattractive. Does this show you anything?

 Practical activity

Select passages from your set texts where characters are introduced for the first time and underline the adjectives the writers use. Are several of these from the same **semantic field**? If so, what are the implications for the role of that character within the plot structure?

Key terms

Semantic field: a group of words within a text relating to the same topic; for example, tyre, brake, pedal, starter motor and exhaust are all from the semantic field of cars.

Let us look at Carmen's contribution to this dialogue. Even very short utterances may be significant in building character. Dialogue does not have to be extensive to be effective and Carmen's speeches in this scene are even more terse than Marlowe's. If you read the extended version of this extract on pp132–3, you will see that she hardly says anything until she has him at close range, and then says, 'Stand there, you son of a bitch', and starts firing a gun at him. Chandler conveys Carmen's corrupt character with complete economy. The word 'giggled' shows she regards attempted murder as merely amusing, and the expression 'you son of a bitch' sums up her contempt for him and his life.

Marlowe's final 'My, but you're cute' is deeply ironic. It takes us back to the first chapter of the novel, where Carmen said this as she threw herself into Marlowe's arms (and it rounds off one element of the plot, again with great economy). Marlowe is the opposite of Carmen; he is unshakeably honest. When he found her naked in his bed, he threw her out. Right at the end of the novel, when Vivian in turn calls him 'son of a bitch' and offers him money (which he refuses), he defends himself in a long speech, but his extended explanation actually adds little to what is implied here already.

Dupin's way of speaking is the complete opposite of Marlowe's, partly because Poe wants to stress his intellectual, rather than his moral, qualities. Even at the time when it was written, it was not meant to sound like the stuff of ordinary speech but rather the language of an extraordinary character. Dupin is the earliest in a long line of eccentric literary detectives that later includes Hercule Poirot and Miss Marple.

The three Dupin stories are first person narratives told by Dupin's friend, but the detective himself is allowed to explain his thought processes at great length. (A very similar thing happens with Legrand in *The Gold Bug*.) Here is a short extract from a long account in 'The Purloined Letter'.

> I dispute the availability, and thus the value, of that reason which is cultivated in any especial form other than the abstractly logical. I dispute in particular, the reason educed by mathematical study. The mathematics are the science of form and quantity; mathematical reasoning is merely logic applied to observation upon form and quantity. The great error lies in supposing that even the truths of what is called pure algebra, are abstract or general truths. And this error is so egregious that I am confounded at the universality with which it has been received …

Poe is elaborating on the context here, drawing out the explanation to maintain suspense in the structure of his tale. When Dupin finally gets down to showing just how he finds the stolen letter, it is on the basis that a clever man will hide something by making it 'excessively obvious', and the narrative then speeds up. In the meantime, however, Dupin's speech, with its references to logic and mathematics and its unusual vocabulary (with many words having Latin roots, such as 'educed' and 'egregious'), has established him as outstandingly learned and quite fiendishly clever, able to defeat any opponent by sheer brain power.

Because speech is such a powerful way of creating and dramatising character, it often blurs the distinction between fact and fiction. The dialogue in literary prose has always been edited and tidied up to represent actual speech. In reality most people's spontaneous speech is a great deal more untidy than the dialogue between characters in novels or other texts.

Here is a little scene from *In Cold Blood*, when the news of the Clutter murders is spreading around the town. Mother Truitt and Myrtle Clare are only very minor figures in the action as a whole. They are waiting for a train to come through and drop off the mail.

Think about it

When you come to work on the creative writing part of your coursework, you will be limited as to space, but you may still want to use dialogue for its dramatic effect and because it gives variety to the narrative. If you plan carefully, just a few words of direct speech can carry a lot of information.

AQA Examiner's tip

The characters in fiction are not real people and have no life outside what the author chooses to describe. It is important to remember this in your analysis. For example, it is irrelevant to speculate about details of personal relationships between Poe's narrator and Dupin, or Dupin and the writer of the stolen letter, beyond what is given or strongly implied within the story itself.

In your creative writing, however, you are the author and can invent as much as you like, provided that your invention is reasonably convincing.

On that Sunday morning Mrs Clare had just poured herself a cup of coffee from a freshly brewed pot when Mother Truitt returned.

'Myrt!' she said, but could say no more until she had caught her breath. 'Myrt, there's two ambulances gone to the Clutters'.'

Her daughter said, 'Where's the ten thirty-two?'

'Ambulances. Gone to the Clutters' – '

'Well, what about it? It's only Bonnie. Having one of her spells. Where's the ten thirty-two?'

Mother Truitt subsided; as usual Myrt knew the answer, was enjoying the last word. Then a thought occurred to her. 'But, Myrt, if it's only Bonnie, why would there be two ambulances?'

This conversation perfectly portrays the relationship between mother and daughter, with one not listening to the other. The phrase 'as usual' suggests that this happens often; 'It's only Bonnie. Having one of her spells' also suggests a routine happening. The exchange between mother and daughter appears to be entirely natural, but if you look closely you will see that it is carefully controlled to lead up to the dramatic question 'why would there be two ambulances?' The irrelevant question about 'the ten thirty-two' actually helps to create suspense, which builds up to the later and even more dramatic revelation that the Clutters have been murdered. All of this conversation could have happened and something very similar probably did; but the narrative has been artistically and consciously shaped by Capote's use of dialogue.

Making your own judgement

Of course, we do not simply have to take what all the characters say at face value. We are often conscious of the narrator's voice, too. This voice may convey implied judgements as well as explicit ones.

 ## Critical response activity

Here is the voice of Blanche Ingram in *Jane Eyre*, talking about the governesses she has had in the past. Jane, who is employed as a governess, is in the room. How does Charlotte Brontë make us dislike Blanche?

I have just one word to say of the whole tribe; they are a nuisance. Not that I ever suffered much from them; I took care to turn the tables. What tricks Theodore and I used to play on our Miss Wilsons, and Mrs Greys and Madame Jouberts! Mary was always too sleepy to join in a plot with spirit. The best fun was with Madame Joubert: Miss Wilson was a poor sickly thing, lachrymose and low spirited: not worth the trouble of vanquishing in short; and Mrs Grey was coarse and insensible: no blow took effect on her. But poor Madame Joubert! I see her yet in her raging passions, when we had driven her to extremities – spilt our tea, crumbled our bread and butter, tossed our books up to the ceiling, and played a charivari with the ruler and the desk, the fender and fire irons.

Commentary

Brontë shows us that Blanche Ingram is not in the least ashamed of her behaviour here and uses Blanche's own words to condemn her. The speech shows that she has deliberately tormented the governesses employed to teach her and she refers to being obnoxious as 'fun'. She regards it as a triumph that the governesses were reduced to tears or to 'raging passions'.

Practical activity

At some point in your course you might like to organise a quiz based on the texts you are working with. One type of question that is very effective is 'Who says this?' followed by a short quotation.

At this stage in the novel, Blanche and Jane appear to be rivals. The point Charlotte Brontë is making is how much more worthwhile Jane is as a character than Blanche. However, while Jane is a mere governess (a position little higher than that of a servant), Blanche has social position; she also has the advantages of conventional beauty. By her use of speech, Brontë makes Blanche expose her own worst characteristics with unconscious irony.

The relationship of action and character development

When you first looked at plot, as distinct from story, you were actually also starting to think about character because the two are so closely connected. If 'the queen died of grief' is a plot, then we already have some idea of the kind of person the queen was. She must have been capable of deep emotion. Action both develops and reflects character; it operates on both the large scale and the small.

Some kinds of novel are full of murders and interrogations, seductions and desertions. This is the stuff that makes an exciting plot, and plot and character are closely intertwined. However, sometimes small actions, with little relevance to the main thrust of the plot, can be equally revealing of character.

On the large scale, it is possible to see the whole of Jane Eyre's life as a series of battles. Her first conflict is with her Aunt Reed; at school she has to control her own rebellious spirit; later, there is conflict between her love for Rochester and her determination not to be his mistress; and there is another conflict with St John Rivers. She comes through all these trials with her spirit unbroken and receives her reward in the end, having proved herself both intelligent and courageous.

On a different scale, here is a memorable moment from *Travels with a Donkey in the Cévennes* (not a novel, of course, but an account of a real journey) that shows both Stevenson's love of nature and his imaginative qualities. It comes from the chapter called 'A Night Among the Pines', when he has been camping out in the open, under the stars. What is it about this passage that is so revealing?

> I hastened to prepare my pack, and tackle the steep ascent that lay before me; but I had something on my mind. It was only a fancy; yet a fancy will sometimes be importunate. I had been most hospitably received and punctually served in my green caravanserai. The room was airy, the water excellent, and the dawn had called me to a moment. I say nothing of the tapestries or the inimitable ceiling, nor yet of the view which I commanded from the windows; but I felt I was in someone's debt for all this liberal entertainment. And so it pleased me, in a half-laughing way, to leave pieces of money on the turf as I went along, until I had left enough for my night's lodging. I trust they did not fall to some rich and churlish drover.

Much of Stevenson's story is involved with the practical difficulties of finding his way and getting the donkey up steep hills. However, here is a moment of pure fantasy as he compares his sleeping place in the pine wood with a 'room' and the sky with a 'ceiling'. There is a slightly apologetic note as he describes himself scattering coins on the ground in a 'half-laughing' way, but there is also a sense that this 'importunate' fancy reveals a deeply romantic vein in his character.

Characters who change

In *Aspects of the Novel*, E. M. Forster makes a useful distinction between 'flat' and 'round' characters. 'Flat' ones can often be summed up in a single phrase or are seen purely from the outside. 'Round' characters have an inner life; because of this, they are capable of change, for better or worse. In *Frankenstein*, the way the creature changes in response to society's treatment of him is one of the main concerns of the novel.

One of the most noticeable differences between *Jane Eyre* and *Wide Sargasso Sea* is that Jane is strengthened by the conflicts she experiences and overcomes, whereas Antoinette is weakened by conflict and becomes more and more trapped. In *Wide Sargasso Sea*, the Rochester figure also changes under pressure. 'The man not a bad man, even if he love money,' Christophine says of him at one point, but the language choices of the novel trace his degeneration from weak to cruel.

From the beginning he feels uncomfortable. Here is part of his narrative as he follows Antoinette to her home at Granbois. The basic information in this extract is taken directly from *Jane Eyre* but is already adapted to create a weaker character than Charlotte Brontë's Rochester.

Critical response activity

What methods does Rhys use to make us judge this character? Do we see him in the same way in which he sees himself?

> Everything is too much, I felt as I rode wearily after her. Too much blue, too much purple, too much green. The flowers too red, the mountains too high, the hills too near. And the woman is a stranger. Her pleading expression annoys me. I have not bought her, she has bought me, or so she thinks. I looked down at the coarse mane of the horse … Dear Father. The thirty thousand pounds have been paid to me without question or condition. No provision made for her (that must be seen to). I have a modest competence now. I will never be a disgrace to you or to my dear brother the son you love. No begging letters, no mean requests. None of the furtive shabby manoeuvres of a younger son. I have sold my soul or you have sold it, and after all is it such a bad bargain? The girl is thought to be beautiful, she is beautiful. And yet …

The weary repetition of 'too much' conveys his discomfort and alienation in Antoinette's world. There is bitterness and **sarcasm** in the phrase 'my dear brother the son you love', but the rhythms are dreary rather than aggressive. There are hesitations in 'The girl is thought to be beautiful, she is beautiful.'

Later he is convinced that Antoinette has betrayed him and the language becomes demented.

> If I was bound for hell let it be hell. No more false heavens. No more damned magic. You hate me and I hate you. We'll see who hates best. But first, first I will destroy your hatred. Now. My hate is colder, stronger, and you'll have no hate to warm yourself. You will have nothing. I did it too. I saw the hate go out of her eyes. I forced it out. And with the hate her beauty. She was only a ghost. A ghost in the grey daylight. Nothing left but hopelessness.

Note the very short sentences here and the frantic repetitions of 'hell' and 'hate'. The verbs are strong and energetic: 'hate', 'destroy' and 'forced'. The vague irritation has been replaced by pitiless, destructive energy.

Because of their conflicts, neither Antoinette nor her husband is the same at the end of the novel as at the beginning. Unlike the heroine of *Jane Eyre*, they have deteriorated psychologically.

Think about it

How many of the characters in the texts you are studying actually change and develop during the course of the book?

 Key terms

Sarcasm: use of ironic language with an intention to hurt or mock.

16   How does setting contribute to the writer's themes?

Think about it

One of the ways in which you might approach the creative writing section of your coursework is by altering the setting in time and place of a story and moving it into a modern context. What kind of changes in the characters' general way of life would this involve?

One of the differences between *Cinderella* and *Jane Eyre* is that *Cinderella* takes place in Far, Far Away and *Jane Eyre* takes place in England. It is not quite the England we know from our own daily experience, however. Setting is concerned with time as well as with place. *Jane Eyre* takes place in an England where people have servants and travel on horseback or by stagecoach, where women have very limited prospects of employment and where people who are mentally ill are liable to be locked up in attics.

The appeal of setting can be strong. If readers want to hear more and more about a character they are familiar with, the same often applies to location too. There is also a particular pleasure in reading about life in places different from where we live ourselves; this is one of the ways in which literature can enlarge our experience. Such places do not always have to be agreeable. The mean streets of Philip Marlowe's world create as evocative a background as any other and are the appropriate setting for Chandler's characters.

Sometimes the setting of a literary work virtually *is* the theme. Narratives such as *Travels with a Donkey in the Cévennes* and *The Lost Continent* take the reader along with them. They can enlarge our world by showing us interesting aspects of travel without any of the actual hardships of making the journey ourselves, and they may even inspire us to want to imitate the journey in real life. They may stress the pleasures of the journey or the pains depending on the way in which the writer manages the descriptive detail of the narrative.

Time

Different worlds: themes in the context of history

L. P. Hartley begins his novel *The Go-Between* with this statement: 'The past is a foreign country; they do things differently there.' Sometimes we need to make an imaginative leap to understand why narratives develop in the way they do because of the gap between our experience and that of the characters in the story. Historical context is something that you need to be aware of in your study. You may need to consider how society has changed politically and economically. Let us take a very strange comment from *Utopia*:

> Your sheep that were wont to be so meek and tame and so small eaters, now, as I hear say, be become so great devourers and so wild, that they eat up and swallow down the very men themselves. They consume, destroy and devour whole fields, houses and cities.

Was there a strange breed of cannibal sheep roaming the country in the reign of Henry VIII, that was only put down by vigilant groups armed with muskets? No, of course there wasn't. During this period much of what had previously been common land, open to everybody to cultivate, was enclosed with fences for the first time. The farmers who enclosed the land made a huge profit out of rearing sheep (primarily for their wool), but the previous users of the land often suffered hardship. More has put this in a striking way to emphasise it, but the modern reader needs a little background information to get the full sense.

Sometimes texts are partly taken out of time, such as when writers portray imaginary worlds. Neither Utopia nor Airstrip One, which is what *Nineteen Eighty-Four* calls Britain, has ever existed in the literal sense. However, each of them is an imaginative extension from reality, and as such reflects the world in which the author lives. *Harry Potter and the Philosopher's Stone* creates in Hogwarts a fantasy world that could not really exist, because of the magic element; that is part of its point. At the same time, it reflects our own society and its values in many ways.

One of the influences on J. K. Rowling's story is *Tom Brown's Schooldays*, a story of public school life in the 19th century (based on a real school, not a magic one). Both novels stress the importance of games; both condemn bullying; both show pupils breaking the rules occasionally. However, whereas Tom Brown's world is completely male-dominated, in Harry Potter's we have the strong female characters of Hermione and Professor McGonagall.

The representation of women in literature is one of the things that has changed a great deal over the centuries, especially in the last 40 years or so. Because of this, some actions in the literature of the past need to be seen in context before we can fully understand them. In *Frankenstein* and in Poe's stories, women tend to take only minor and passive roles. *Jane Eyre* famously makes a plea for women's independence, but the prize it looks forward to, as the ultimate happy ending, is still marriage.

When it is apparent that Rochester has attempted a bigamous marriage to her, Jane immediately runs away. She understands that he is married to the mad woman in the attic in name only. She clearly loves him desperately – she says so: 'Not a human being that ever lived could wish to be loved better than I was loved; and him who thus loved me I absolutely worshipped.' Students who are used to women having much more independence than was common in the 19th century and a much freer sexual morality often ask at this point why she leaves if she loves him so much. Are we meant to find the overwhelming passion she talks about convincing?

Jane answers the question of motivation herself later (in Chapter 31), after she has suffered considerable hardship and built a new life. She refers to Rochester's offer to live with her unmarried as a 'silken snare' and a 'fool's paradise'. She imagines 'living in France, Mr Rochester's mistress; delirious with his love half my time – for he would – oh, yes, he would have loved me well for a while. He did love me – no one will ever love me so again.' However, in leaving him she has 'adhered to principle and law, and scorned and crushed the insane promptings of a frenzied moment'. Charlotte Brontë makes her heroine take the only reasonable course of action in the moral climate of the time.

Time and genre: the historical novel

The historical novel is a sub-genre on its own, largely invented by Sir Walter Scott in the 19th century. Its aim is to recreate imaginatively events from a previous period of time, but inevitably it does this from the perspective of the time in which it is written. *Wide Sargasso Sea* was published in 1966, long after the period in which it is set. Although it borrows some characters and part of its plot from *Jane Eyre*, there are some important contrasts between the two novels.

- Although *Jane Eyre* is not precisely dated, Jane says she has been married for 10 years at the time she writes her story. This would mean that Antoinette could not have been born after about 1805.

Think about it

One of the things that has changed a lot over the centuries is law enforcement and who is responsible for policing. Is law and order important in the plot development and characterisation of the texts you have been reading? Would things be the same today?

Practical activity

List the female characters in the two texts you have been studying and consider how much they initiate action and how much they are passive or minor characters. Is there a significant difference between the older and the more modern text?

However, Rhys shifts the historical date of the action to include references to the Emancipation Act of 1833, which freed the slaves. It is a post-colonial novel with a theme of race, something that would not necessarily have occurred to Charlotte Brontë.

■ Rhys's novel explores attitudes to women and their sexuality in a way that would have been most unlikely in 19th-century literature.

■ *Wide Sargasso Sea* uses the language of the 1960s.

Charlotte Brontë's novel provides a starting point, but Jean Rhys has the conscious intention of challenging its assumptions. David Lodge discusses this point in *The Art of Fiction*, where he suggests that what the historical novel can do is 'bring a twentieth-century perspective to bear upon nineteenth-century behaviour, perhaps revealing things about the Victorians that they did not know themselves, or preferred to suppress, or simply took for granted'.

In *Wide Sargasso Sea*, Rhys raises the issue of slavery and the hatred that exists between the former colonists and the freed slaves. In doing so, she invites us to draw some parallels between the position of slaves and that of women. There is a sense in which Antoinette is colonised and exploited by her husband, just as the whole territory of the West Indies had been colonised by the white planters.

Her husband, of course, does not see it like this. You may remember the passage we looked at earlier, which gives his thoughts as he writes an imaginary letter, on the ride up to Granbois.

> Dear Father. The thirty thousand pounds have been paid to me without question or condition. No provision made for her (that must be seen to). I have a modest competence now. I will never be a disgrace to you or to my dear brother the son you love. No begging letters, no mean requests. None of the furtive shabby manoeuvres of a younger son. I have sold my soul or you have sold it, and after all is it such a bad bargain? The girl is thought to be beautiful, she is beautiful. And yet …

Representation of women is one of the aspects of literature that has changed significantly over time. Jane Eyre, although highly independent in many ways, was quite content to regard her Rochester as 'Master'. Here, Jean Rhys is bringing out another historical aspect of her theme of marital conflict. A married woman in the early 19th century could not hold property in her own right. It was regarded as belonging to her husband unconditionally, unless there was a specific legal 'settlement'. This is one of the reasons that Antoinette is trapped in her marriage: she literally has no money and no means of getting a living.

Although the voices in the novel vary, the text is all firmly written in 20th-century English. Something Rhys wisely does not attempt in *Wide Sargasso Sea* is a **pastiche** of Victorian style.

Narrative time: keeping to the real point

Novice writers often have trouble managing time in their narratives. They characteristically begin with waking up, washing, having breakfast … and only then get down to the real point of the story. Few professional writers do this. They telescope time. Even when they are writing what amount to daily diaries, as Stevenson and Bryson are, they leave out the duller bits.

Stevenson consistently gives you the date when he has reached a particular point in his journey and he often implies that he spent part

Key terms

Pastiche: a work that imitates the style of another work.

■ Think about it

What difference have the following inventions made to the plots that are possible in literature?

■ The electric light

■ The motor car

■ The mobile phone

of the day writing up his experiences, but there are obvious gaps in the account. He does not tell you every time he bought supplies, though he must have done so regularly; he skips over these details except in the beginning. The narrative then picks up speed, slowing down only when he has an adventure of some kind.

Most books vary the narrative pace in a similar way. *Jane Eyre* covers the whole period of the heroine's life from her childhood to her marriage, but with different levels of detail. Charlotte Brontë is quite conscious of the way her narrative is paced, and discusses it with the reader. At the beginning of Chapter 10, she says:

> Hitherto I have recorded in detail the events of my insignificant existence; to the first ten years of my life, I have given almost as many chapters. But this is not to be a regular autobiography: I am only bound to invoke memory where I know her responses will possess some degree of interest; therefore I now pass a space of eight years almost in silence.

After Jane leaves Rochester, we follow her sufferings day by day for two chapters, until she is rescued by the Rivers family. Then weeks or months pass until Chapter 31 begins: 'My home, then, when I find a home, is a cottage.' In the 'gap' between Chapter 30 and Chapter 31 she has become the teacher in the village school and the narrative moves on to the next crisis, her relationship with St John Rivers.

A book in which something very odd obviously happens to time is *Alice's Adventures in Wonderland*. The story starts with the White Rabbit looking at his watch and saying, 'Oh dear! Oh dear! I shall be too late!' As with everything in the book, there is a simple, surface meaning for the child reader that conceals deeper layers for the adult who thinks further and really questions meanings. In one way, the time sequence is clear – it takes place in real time while Alice is sitting in the field, dozing – but is it really?

Critical response activity

Lewis Carroll plays with the idea of time. The episode of the Mad Hatter's tea party discusses different concepts of time, including subjective time. The topic begins with the March Hare's unusual watch, which tells the day of the month but not the hour. How many different senses of the word 'time' can you find in this extract?

> Alice sighed wearily. 'I think you might do something better with the time,' she said, 'than wasting it in riddles that have no answers.'
>
> 'If you knew time as well as I do,' said the Hatter, 'you wouldn't talk about wasting it. It's him.'
>
> 'I don't know what you mean,' said Alice.
>
> 'Of course you don't,' the Hatter said, tossing his head contemptuously. 'I dare say you never even spoke to Time!'
>
> 'Perhaps not,' Alice cautiously replied; 'but I know I have to beat time when I learn music.'
>
> 'Ah! That accounts for it,' said the Hatter. 'He won't stand beating. Now, if you only kept on good terms with him, he'd do almost anything you liked with the clock. For instance, suppose it were nine o'clock in the morning, just time to begin lessons: you'd only have to whisper a hint to Time, and round goes the clock in a twinkling! Half-past one, time for dinner!'

Practical activity

Make a chronology of events in the texts you are studying, to see how the author focuses on important sections and links them together. Is it possible to make a list of the main events and work out their dates? Doing this can make the difference between real time and narrative time very obvious.

Link

To read the rest of Chandler's 'ten commandments', see p92.

This is ridiculous, of course, but why? The watch is absurd because it does not tell the hour, but many of us have watches that tell the day as well as the hour. Talking about Time as 'him' is absurd, and so is the pun on beating time, but we are all familiar with the personification of Father Time in literature. All these ideas about time work on different levels. Being on 'good terms' with time is rather like what happens in fiction. Time can take on different meanings and we are allowed to skip the dull bits. Like the White Rabbit, events can also pop up in all sorts of unexpected places.

Stories do not have to begin at the beginning; they can start in the middle or, as *Frankenstein* does, at the end. That novel starts with the creature leading Victor Frankenstein across the arctic ice, goes back to the beginning with Victor's narrative, back to the beginning again with the creature's narrative and then fills in the gap up to the point at which it started.

Place

There are only a limited number of story patterns, but an infinite number of possible settings. David Lodge points out that the sense of place 'was a fairly late development in the history of prose fiction', but in modern narratives setting plays an important part in distinguishing one story from another. Detectives, for example, usually have a clear territory in which they operate. Do you remember Raymond Chandler's 'ten commandments' for the detective story? Here is number 3:

> It must be realistic in character, setting and atmosphere. It must be about real people in a real world.

Poe's stories are very different from Chandler's and he deliberately brings in the unusual. He is still careful about setting, however, introducing French names and places that create an exotic background for the enjoyment of his original American readers.

Many kinds of books give detailed and realistic descriptions of the places in which their narratives are set. Readers will often accept strange plots and characters more readily in a believable setting. Mary Shelley creates, as a main character, an eight-foot vegetarian creature who teaches himself to read *Paradise Lost* from a copy that he finds in the forest. However, she uses passages of realistic description to make the story credible to the reader. When Victor Frankenstein heads for the Orkneys to start work on a new creature, we know exactly how he will get there.

> We had arrived in England at the beginning of October, and it was now February. We accordingly determined to commence our journey towards the north at the expiration of another month. In this expedition we did not intend to follow the great road to Edinburgh, but to visit Windsor, Oxford, Matlock, and the Cumberland lakes, resolving to arrive at the completion of this tour about the end of July. I packed up my chemical instruments and the materials I had collected, resolving to finish my labours in some obscure nook in the northern highlands of Scotland.

In contrast, both *Alice's Adventures in Wonderland* and *Harry Potter and the Philosopher's Stone* have fantasy settings in worlds where material objects do not behave in the usual ways. In the world of Harry Potter there is a railway station, but it has a platform called nine and three-quarters that is reached by crashing into the barrier between platforms nine and ten. There is a school, with lessons, games and a library, but the staircases move and the buildings are liable to be invaded by monsters at any time. These features may seem to contradict the idea that the world of Harry Potter reflects our own social and moral values. However, it is often just the surface details of Hogwarts that create an impression of difference. Pupils still wait anxiously for the post from home, even if owls deliver it.

Place as a major theme: travel writing

Travel writing is again a sub-genre on its own. By its nature it is largely concerned with the description of place, although not always description of scenery. It goes a very long way back in the history of literature; *Utopia* mentions the popularity of Amerigo Vespucci's 'Travels', referring to the 'three last voyages of those four that be now in print' as being 'in every man's hands'. To some extent *Utopia* itself is an imitation of a popular form, developed to present an imaginary world.

Curiously enough, although there is plenty of writing about exploration in earlier literature, it is not until the Romantics at the end of the 18th century that we get a great deal of description of nature and what real, individual places look, sound and smell like. Such description then becomes very important.

Descriptions that appeal to the senses

Both *Frankenstein* (1818) and *Travels with a Donkey in the Cévennes* (1879) show this Romantic influence clearly. Here is an extract from *Frankenstein*.

 Critical response activity

Mary Shelley was living in Switzerland when she began to write the novel. How many ways can you see in which this description of a place in the Alps appeals to the reader's senses?

> It is a scene terrifically desolate. In a thousand spots the traces of the winter avalanche may be perceived, where trees lie broken and strewed on the ground; some entirely destroyed, others bent, leaning across the jutting rocks of the mountain or transversely upon other trees. The path, as you ascend higher, is intersected by ravines of snow, down which stones continually roll from above; one of them is particularly dangerous, as the slightest sound, such as even speaking in a loud voice, produces a concussion of air sufficient to draw destruction upon the head of the speaker. The pines are not tall or luxuriant, but they are sombre and add an air of severity to the scene. I looked on the valley beneath; vast mists were rising from the rivers which ran through it and curling in thick wreaths around the opposite mountains, whose summits were hid in the uniform clouds, while rain poured from the dark sky …

We can see the trees, ravines and mists, and feel the rain. Sound becomes threatening because even 'speaking in a loud voice' may start an avalanche.

This kind of writing may have begun with the Romantics, but a similar taste is evident in many modern contexts. You will remember the beginning and ending of *In Cold Blood*, with their descriptions of the open landscape. In the following extract from *The Lost Continent*, Bill Bryson is touring Illinois. He hates the tourists and the shops selling souvenirs, but values the beauty of the wild landscape highly.

 **Examiner's tip**

Like historical detail, the geographical setting of a story needs to be accurate. This involves either local knowledge or careful research. When you write a story of your own, you will have an advantage if you have actually visited the settings you describe.

Link

Travel writing is discussed in detail in Unit 1, Chapter 8.

The Smoky Mountains themselves were a joy. It was a perfect October morning. The road led steeply through broad-leaved forests of dappled sunshine, full of paths and streams, and then, higher up, opened out to airy vistas. All along the road through the park there were look-out points where you could pull the car over and go 'Ooh!' and 'Wow!' at the views.

Unifying the narrative structure

One difficulty with travel writing for its own sake, as distinct from the use of landscape as a background for a story as in Mary Shelley's *Frankenstein*, is finding a unifying structure to prevent the whole narrative from becoming just a series of disconnected **episodes**. As you will remember, Stevenson uses his donkey, Modestine, as a linking device, to give shape to the whole narrative.

Bryson has a more complicated task and solves the problem in a different way. First, his journey is an attempt to recall his own youth; second, it is a quest to discover America. He says, 'One of the things I was looking for on this trip was the perfect town. I've always felt certain that somewhere out there in America it must exist.'

This imaginary place he jokingly calls Amalgam, and he refers to it repeatedly when a place pleases him. This ideal town becomes the standard by which he judges the real towns he passes through.

🔍 Place and atmosphere

Let us go back to Winston Smith again, as the opening of *Nineteen Eighty-Four* is quite rightly famous. Every detail counts here.

It was a bright cold day in April, and the clocks were striking thirteen. Winston Smith, his chin nuzzled into his breast in an effort to escape the vile wind, slipped quickly through the doors of Victory Mansions, though not quickly enough to prevent a swirl of gritty dust from entering along with him.

The first sentence sounds thoroughly normal until we reach the word 'thirteen'. Even now, the digital clocks with 24-hour cycles that we are used to do not strike 13. It is the first sign that this is a strange world, and of course 13 is an 'unlucky' number. 'Victory Mansions' suggests a world conscious of war. The 'gritty dust' sets the mood. This is a world of grime and austerity (Orwell was writing in 1948 and knew all about the effects of war at first hand). The plot of the novel goes on to explore the nature of life under a grim political regime.

Weather and landscape play a part in setting the mood in many novels, sometimes even seeming to be an integral part of the action. The Victorian critic John Ruskin, who disliked this literary effect, coined a special term for it. In *Modern Painters* he wrote 'All violent feelings … produce … a falseness in impressions of external things which I would generally characterise as the "**pathetic fallacy**".'

The strange name has stuck, although its common use has now broadened. The word 'pathetic' implies something that arouses sympathy in the reader. However, because nature cannot really reflect human feelings, it is a 'fallacy' to suggest that it does.

Mary Shelley does not just use landscape to create a realistic or impressive background. She often uses a change in the weather to introduce one of the appearances of the creature. The 'dreary' November night when he is first given life is by no means the only example. In

---

▪ Key terms

Episode: an isolated event, separated from the main series of events.

Pathetic fallacy: the literary technique of representing internal human states and emotions through the description of external details such as landscape and weather. In this sense 'pathetic' means arousing sympathy: in other words, the term 'pathetic' suggests that the landscape is in *sympathy* with a character's feelings. The word 'fallacy' reminds us that this supposed relationship is a deception: inanimate landscapes and weather systems cannot truly echo the feelings and emotion of people, even though writers might have us believe otherwise.

Book II, just before the creature's narrative, Victor has been admiring the landscape around Chamounix, where, he tells us:

> The unstained snowy mountain-top, the glittering pinnacle, the pine woods, and ragged bare ravine, the eagle, soaring amidst the clouds – they all gathered round me and bade me be at peace.

The next day, when he is about to meet the creature on the mer de glace, everything has changed:

> the rain was pouring down in torrents, and thick mists hid the summits of the mountains, so that I even saw not the faces of those mighty friends.

In spite of the grimy realism of his settings, Raymond Chandler, too, is conspicuously fond of similar effects. As Marlowe sits outside Geiger's store, waiting to follow him home (in Chapter 6 of *The Big Sleep*), 'Rain filled the gutters and splashed knee-high off the pavements.' Later, while Marlowe is still watching, 'It got dark and the rain-clouded lights of the stores were soaked up by the black street. Street-car bells jangled crossly.' It is a wait, of course, that ends in the discovery of Geiger's corpse, and the dreariness of the weather both corresponds to Marlowe's mood and provides an appropriate background for a sordid event.

 ## Critical response activity

The ending of the novel portrays an equally grim industrial scene, the complete opposite of the luxurious mansion in which Carmen Sternwood lives and which was described in the opening chapter. What kind of mood is Chandler setting here?

> There was a pile of rusted pipe, a loading platform that sagged at one end, half a dozen empty oil drums lying in a ragged pile. There was the stagnant, oil-scummed water of an old sump iridescent in the sunlight.

Commentary

At first sight, this may seem to be just a description of a suitably lonely spot in which to practise shooting that lists the features in a matter-of-fact way. The place is also, however, a good spot for Carmen to attempt another murder, because it is not only secluded but corrupted too. The decayed and disgusting industrial scene is symbolic of moral decay and the language used makes sure that we have noticed the corruption: 'The smell of that sump would poison a herd of goats.'

What do we mean by style?

▨ Key terms

Rhetoric: the technique of using language persuasively in order to influence the opinions and behaviour of an audience.

Complex sentence: a sentence with two or more clauses linked by subordinating conjunctions.

AQA Examiner's tip

It is particularly important to avoid feature-spotting when you are discussing style (for example, naming a phrase as a metaphor then just moving on to discuss something else). There is not much point in merely recognising an adjective or a metaphor. What you have to think about all the time is the effect of this choice of language on the meaning of the text.

Style is both highly personal and infinitely variable. This topic considers a few of the more detailed aspects of language use, but there is no simple formula for analysing style. All we can say in general terms is that there are a number of language features that will affect meaning.

Fashions in style change over time, like everything else. Going right back to the Middle Ages, well before *Utopia* was written, there were whole books that gave advice about features of **rhetoric**, for example, and how writers should pattern their language for maximum effect.

🔍 Features of language

Sentences

The most obvious thing about sentences is that they can be either long or short. It is more common to find large numbers of long sentences in texts dating from before the 20th century. Poe's first sentence in 'The Purloined Letter' continues for five lines of text and you can find many examples that are even longer. These are also ten **complex sentences**. Because such sentence structures are less common in popular fiction now, students sometimes assume that the audience for this kind of writing in the 19th century would have been a very limited one, but this is not the case. Many readers in the past liked, and expected, a more elevated style.

It is true that authors hoping for a mass audience nowadays tend to write more simply. Bill Bryson, whose *The Lost Continent* was published in 1989, has a liking for short sentences to create a chatty style. Chapter 6 begins typically:

> Just south of Grand Junction, Tennessee, I passed over the state line into Mississippi. A sign beside the highway said WELCOME TO MISSISSIPPI. WE SHOOT TO KILL. It didn't really. I just made that up.

Short sentences can be highly effective in creating tension. Raymond Chandler uses this technique frequently; it is particularly appropriate to his subject, as his hero often deals with violence or potential violence. Take the moment when Marlowe is warned off by the gangster Eddie Mars.

> There was hate in his eyes. I went out and through the hedge and into my car and got into it. I turned it around and drove over the crest. Nobody shot at me. After a few blocks I turned off, cut the motor and sat for a few moments. Nobody followed me either. I drove back into Hollywood.

Nothing actually happens except that Marlowe gets into his car and drives off, but the writing is full of suspense, created by the tense pauses.

Sometimes sentence structures break down to indicate agitation of thought. You will remember *Wide Sargasso Sea*, where Rochester is wild with hate: 'I did it too. I saw the hate go out of her eyes. I forced it out. And with the hate her beauty. She was only a ghost.' Or there is the moment of Winston Smith's defeat, with its anguished exclamations: 'O cruel needless misunderstanding! O stubborn, self-willed exile from the loving breast!'

Good writers vary their sentence structures to create a variety of effects. In particular, it is always worth looking out for exclamations and questions. Like Jane Eyre's 'Reader, I married him!', they often mark significant moments. What you, as a critic, have to remember is that it is not the length or shortness of the sentence that matters, or whether it is **declarative** or **interrogative**, but what its effect is.

Vocabulary

George Orwell had strong views on vocabulary. In an influential essay called 'Politics and the English Language', he gives a list of rules for good style. Two of them are:

- Never use a long word where a short one will do.
- Never use a foreign phrase, a scientific word or a jargon word if you can think of an everyday English equivalent.

This is sound advice for anyone designing a form or writing instructions, and Orwell's own prose is clear, stylish and elegant. However, literary prose is often a little more complicated. Just as they may expect and enjoy long sentences, some audiences actually *like* impressive words, even if they would not necessarily use such language themselves.

Poe's narrator in *The Murders in the Rue Morgue* and the other stories frequently uses foreign words and phrases such as '*par excellence*' and '*charlatanerie*' – mostly French, because the setting is Paris, but some Latin, too. For a reader who does not understand these expressions, they will probably appear as dead spots, though the intention is obviously to create character and atmosphere. Stevenson uses French phrases *Travels with a Donkey* for exactly the same reason. Their meaning is usually clear from the context, as in this dialogue with a peasant he meets on the road.

> 'Your donkey,' says he, 'is very old?'
>
> I told him I believed not.
>
> Then, he supposed, we had come far.
>
> I told him we had but newly left Monastier.
>
> 'Et vous marchez comme ça!' cried he; and throwing back his head, he laughed long and heartily.

Even if you cannot read the French phrase here (which means 'And you are going along like that!'), you will get the idea of ridicule from the context.

Words tend to belong in families and to reinforce one another when they come from the same semantic field. Here is a passage from *Nineteen Eighty-Four* describing the interrogation of Winston Smith.

> Sometimes it was fists, sometimes it was truncheons, sometimes it was steel rods, sometimes it was boots. There were times when he rolled about the floor, as shameless as an animal, writhing his body this way and that in an endless, hopeless effort to dodge the kicks, and simply inviting more and yet more kicks, in his ribs, in his belly, on his elbows, on his shins, in his groin, in his testicles, on the bone at the base of his spine. There were times when it went on and on until the cruel, wicked, unforgivable thing seemed to him not that the guards continued to beat him but that he could not force himself into losing consciousness.

The emotional effect of this extract arises from the repetition of 'kicks' and from the whole group of words describing parts of the body, all being assaulted: 'ribs', 'belly', 'elbows', 'shins', 'groin', 'testicles', 'bone'.

Key terms

Declarative sentence: one that makes a statement.

Interrogative sentence: one that asks a question.

Practical activity

Take a place you know well, not necessarily an attractive one, and compile a list of adjectives to describe it. Include details of smell and touch, if possible. Doing this may give you some ideas for an approach to your creative writing coursework.

 Key terms

Figurative language: language that draws an imaginative comparison between what is described and something else, resulting in an image that cannot literally be true, but may enable us to perceive something more vividly or allow us greater insight into the story or character.

Simile: an imaginative comparison drawn between two different things, linked with the words 'like' or 'as': for example, 'her hands were as cold as ice' or 'the man was like a bear'.

Metaphor: a direct comparison drawn between two different things as if the subject really is the thing it is being compared to: for example, 'her hands were ice-blocks' or 'he was a bear of a man'.

Personification: a form of metaphor in which human qualities are attributed to things that are non-human: for example, 'the windows stared blankly'.

 Examiner's tip

It is always safest to make positive comments about style and to discuss what is there rather than what is not. Very few texts contain no figures of speech, but many include language choices that are not immediately obvious as metaphors.

Descriptive detail

You have already considered one use of descriptive detail in Charlotte Brontë's account of Aunt Reed, with all its adjectives. Adjectives can be particularly evocative in describing places as well as people.

 Critical response activity

Bryson composes his descriptions, both favourable and unfavourable, with great care in *The Lost Continent*. Where are the adjectives here, for example, and what are their effects?

> I drove on through the low, marshy flatlands, much taken with the simple beauty of the Chesapeake peninsula, with its high skies and scattered farms and forgotten little towns.

It is the combination of adjectives such as 'low, marshy', 'simple', 'high', 'scattered' and 'forgotten' that makes this description so precise.

Here is a moment from *Wide Sargasso Sea*.

> One morning soon after we arrived, the row of tall trees outside my window was covered with small pale flowers too fragile to resist the wind. They fell in a day, and looked like snow on the rough grass – snow with a faint sweet scent.

There is nothing here that is remarkable in itself; it is the cumulative effect that matters. We have 'tall', 'small', 'pale', 'fragile', 'rough', 'faint', and 'sweet': all these add another detail to the description and between them they appeal to all the senses.

Figurative language

Figurative language includes **simile**, **metaphor** and **personification**. You may have considered their use when working on the Anthology because they are common in poetry, but it may not have occurred to you how common they are in prose too. You will notice the simile 'looked like snow' in the extract above.

When Orwell wants to describe how sinister the guards look outside the Ministry of Love (where prisoners are tortured), he simply calls them 'gorilla-faced', using a metaphor. This works in exactly the same way that figurative language does in poetry, by forming an association of ideas. Orwell means that the guards look fierce and beastly. Chandler uses a similar metaphor when he describes how Carmen has 'become animal, and not a nice animal' as she tries to kill Marlowe.

Not all metaphors are significant; many of them we hardly notice. The last sentence of *Wide Sargasso Sea* reads, 'But I shielded it with my hand and it burned up again to light me along the dark passage.' Here 'shielded' is in fact a metaphor, if you think about it, but it is such a common expression for that particular action of the hand that it will probably not stand out as such in context.

Other figures of speech may stand out only too sharply, causing a brief stylistic shock. Chandler often uses witty and unexpected figurative language for humorous effect in *The Big Sleep*, as in 'she approached me with enough sex appeal to stampede a business men's lunch', 'she was sore as an alderman with the mumps' and 'she knew as much about rare books as I knew about handling a flea circus'.

Symbols

Symbols are details that resonate beyond the immediate context and have a wider significance to the theme. An obvious example is the chestnut tree in *Jane Eyre*. In Chapter 23, Jane and Rochester are walking in the garden where there is 'a giant horse chestnut, circled at the base by a seat' on the evening when Rochester makes his (bigamous) proposal of marriage. That night, after a storm when 'the thunder crashed, fierce and frequent' the chestnut tree is struck by lightning and half of it split away. Jane does not realise it yet, but the reader does: the marriage is clearly doomed.

 Critical response activity

Not all symbols are as obviously constructed as this. They often grow naturally out of relatively small details in the text. Here is the moment in *Wide Sargasso Sea*, in many ways a deliberate parallel, when Antoinette and her own Rochester arrive in their bedroom at Granbois. Can you see how these actions have wider implications for the development of the novel?

> There were two doors, one leading to the veranda, the other very slightly open into a small room. A big bed, a round table by its side, two chairs, a surprising dressing-table with a marble top and a large looking-glass. Two wreaths of frangipani on the bed.
>
> 'Am I expected to wear one of these? And when?'
>
> I crowned myself with one of the wreaths and made a face in the glass. 'I hardly think it suits my handsome face, do you?'
>
> 'You look like a king, an emperor.'
>
> 'God forbid,' I said and took the wreath off. It fell on the floor and as I went towards the window I stepped on it. The room was full of the scent of crushed flowers.

The fragile, scented wreath of flowers is placed on the bed as a gesture of welcome. First of all the husband uses it as a crown, thinking of his own importance, then he steps on it – just as much of an ill omen as the chestnut tree struck by lightning.

Punctuation

In modern times as well as historical ones, whole books have been written about such matters as punctuation. You might enjoy *Eats, Shoots and Leaves* by Lynne Truss because it is amusing as well as helpful. It deals with the correct use of punctuation and how this affects meaning. (If you do nothing else, read the panda story on the back cover, which shows how a comma can transform the whole sense of a sentence.)

The purpose of punctuation is to show us how to read a text. It replaces things such as pauses that in oral communication help to give meaning but cannot be conveyed in any other way on the printed page. Remember these two important points about punctuation:

- In older texts, including 19th-century ones, the punctuation is often not that of the original author but that of a later editor.
- Punctuation is not so much a stylistic feature in itself as a way of marking how the text should be read. It is more helpful to look at the rhythms of the writing than to comment on the number of commas or semi-colons used.

Key terms

Symbol: an object or action that, beyond its basic meaning, represents an idea or concept.

Further reading

Truss, Lynne, *Eats, Shoots and Leaves*, Profile Books, 2003

When you are reading an older text you will often notice that the punctuation is much heavier than it would be in a more modern one. Consider this single sentence from the opening of *Alice's Adventures in Wonderland*, at the moment when Alice is sitting making a daisy chain and sees the White Rabbit run past her.

> There was nothing so *very* remarkable in that: nor did Alice think it so *very* much out of the way to hear the rabbit say to itself, 'Oh dear! Oh dear! I shall be too late!' (when she thought it over afterwards, it occurred to her that she ought to have wondered at this, but at the time it all seemed quite natural); but when the Rabbit actually *took a watch out of its waistcoat-pocket*, and looked at it, and then hurried on, Alice started to her feet, for it flashed across her mind that she had never before seen a rabbit with either a waistcoat-pocket or a watch to take out of it, and burning with curiosity, she ran across the field after it, and was just in time to see it pop down a large rabbit-hole under the hedge.

In your own writing, you would be most unlikely to use one colon, one set of brackets and one semi-colon in the same sentence. You would probably replace the colon and semi-colon with full stops, but what would be the actual effect of this? The punctuation is not of any very great interest in itself and does not cause much, if any, actual difficulty for the reader, but there would be a marginal difference in style. The long sentence hurries on its way without full stops and this is the real point: the rhythm. A naive comment would be to say something like 'there is a lot of punctuation here'. It is much more useful to say that the punctuation of the sentence produces a hurrying effect, like the movement of the rabbit.

Another feature you might notice here is that Lewis Carroll uses a different type style (italics) for the emphasis of 'very' and 'took a watch out of its waistcoat-pocket'. A modern writer might also do this, to draw attention to something extraordinary – and indeed it is extraordinary that a rabbit should have a waistcoat pocket.

Register

Register is the quality of language that is determined by its social context. There is an infinite variety of registers, but studies have shown that even tiny children can recognise some of their variations, enough to talk to their toys in a 'mummy' voice, for example. When the register is wrong the effect can be bizarre. For example, imagine Poe's rather pompous detective Auguste Dupin saying 'Okey dokey', or Harry Potter calling one of his friends 'old boy'. When you are working on your creative writing coursework, you need to keep this in mind.

The degree of formality or informality in a text and the extent to which it uses technical language help to create a particular register. Context, purpose and audience all have a bearing on it.

Formality

Edgar Allan Poe and Raymond Chandler clearly write in different ways as far as formality is concerned. You will remember that we discussed the different lengths of their sentences on p114 and their typical vocabulary choices. These features, together with some other stylistic choices such as forms of address used, determine register.

Another obvious example of an older text being more formal than a later one can be seen by comparing *Travels with a Donkey in the Cévennes*

Key terms

Register: a type of language defined in terms of its appropriateness for the type of activity or context in which the language is used, including the purpose, audience and situation of a piece of speech or writing.

and The Lost Continent. Stevenson uses **syntax** that is not quite natural to us now when he writes, 'It was already hard upon October before I was ready to set forth, and at the high altitudes over which my road lay there was no Indian summer to be looked for.' A modern writer would probably avoid the construction 'over which my road lay' and the passive 'to be looked for'. Bryson writes less formally, with one of his customary jokes: 'At the edge of town I joined Iowa Highway 163 and with a light heart headed towards Missouri. And it isn't often you hear anyone say that.'

Technical language

 Critical response activity

Writers often use technical language of various kinds. They obviously do so more often in non-fiction, but why do you think Chandler might be going into technical detail in this extract from *The Big Sleep*?

> I went over to the folded-back French window and looked at the small broken pane in the upper part of it. The bullet from Carmen's gun had smashed the glass like a blow. It had not made a hole. There was a small hole in the plaster which a keen eye would find quickly enough. I pulled the drapes over the broken pane and took Carmen's gun out of my pocket. It was a Banker's Special, .22 calibre, hollow point cartridges. It had a pearl grip, and a small round silver plate set into the butt was engraved: 'Carmen from Owen'.

Commentary

The technical language here is important to the realism of the novel. Every detail is relevant to the plot: either to Carmen's involvement with the underworld and the violence of the preceding scene or to her nymphomaniac tendencies. In particular, the exact technical description of the gun is important because she tries to kill Marlowe with it at the end of the novel.

Capote's *In Cold Blood* is a narrative that includes a great deal of technical detail. It is natural that it should, as the author is reporting fact even though he is using it to argue a case against the death penalty for Perry Smith.

 Critical response activity

Capote's description of Death Row from *In Cold Blood* is given below. Can you spot the point at which the deadpan technical description takes on a more emotional tone?

> The cells are identical. They measure seven by ten feet, and are unfurnished except for a cot, a toilet, a basin, and an overhead light bulb that is never extinguished night or day. The cell windows are very narrow, and not only barred but covered with wire mesh black as a widow's veil; thus the faces of those sentenced to hang can be but hazily discerned by passers-by.

Commentary

The precise technical information at the beginning is absolutely convincing and gives Capote the status of an expert. He has been there and seen this for himself. The simile 'black as a widow's veil' brings in a note of deeper gloom.

 Key terms

Syntax: the structure of sentences.

Research point

You may find it useful to research the passive voice on the internet. There are various websites that explain the term clearly using examples. Try:

www.usingenglish.com

www.ego4u.com

www.learnenglish.org.uk

Type 'passive' into the search box in each case.

This chapter covers:

- different kinds of humour: situation, character, verbal humour and moral viewpoint.

Students often find it difficult to comment on humour, but it is an important aspect of tone and can arise out of situation, character, language – or any other aspect of writing. Successful literary analysis often depends on the ability to distinguish between humour of different types, for example between slapstick and wit.

Situations

 ### Critical response activity

Even very serious narratives can contain humour. You may remember the extract from *In Cold Blood* that we discussed on pp103–4 when we were talking about dialogue. In it Mother Truitt and Mrs Clare are having a conversation. Mrs Clare telephones a neighbour and the account continues as in the extract below. Why might this be considered comic?

> The conversation with Mrs Helm lasted several minutes, and was most distressing to Mother Truitt, who could hear nothing of it except the non-committal monosyllabic responses of her daughter. Worse, when the daughter hung up, she did not quench the old woman's curiosity; instead, she placidly drank her coffee, went to her desk, and began to postmark a pile of letters.
>
> 'Myrt,' Mother Truitt said. 'For heaven's sake. What did Mabel say?'
>
> 'I'm not surprised,' Mrs Clare said. 'When you think how Herb Clutter spent his whole life in a hurry, rushing in here to get his mail with never a minute to say good-morning-and-thank-you-dog, rushing around like a chicken with its head off – joining clubs, running everything, getting jobs other people wanted. And now look – it's all caught up with him. Well, he won't be rushing any more.'
>
> 'Why, Myrt? Why won't he?'
>
> Mrs Clare raised her voice. 'BECAUSE HE'S DEAD. And Bonnie too. And Nancy. And the boy. Somebody shot them.'

Commentary

Mrs Clare's reaction is so inappropriate that it's funny. Instead of telling her mother what has happened, she at first keeps calm and silent. Then she launches into a stream of irrelevant personal grievances before she eventually gets to the point. Even though the context is deeply serious, the way Capote describes these two women learning the news has elements of absurdity.

Both *Alice's Adventures in Wonderland* and *Harry Potter and the Philosopher's Stone* rely a great deal on humour for their effect, such as fantastic, bizarre situations such as the baby that turns into a pig or the fire-breathing dragon being hatched in a wooden hut. J. K. Rowling often creates humour by exaggeration. Harry is not merely treated unkindly by the Dursleys, but kept in a cupboard. When letters start to arrive for him, there are twelve on Friday, twenty-four on Saturday and on Sunday, when there should be no post, 'thirty or forty letters came pelting out of the fireplace like bullets'.

Comic characters

Both *Alice's Adventures in Wonderland* and *Harry Potter and the Philosopher's Stone* have richly humorous characters with inventive names, such as the Mock Turtle or the fierce three-headed dog on guard in *Harry Potter* whose name is Fluffy.

Another of these characters is Hagrid in *Harry Potter*. His appearance is comic: he is a giant of a man with a face 'almost completely hidden by a long, shaggy mane of hair and a wild tangled beard'. So is the contrast between his huge size and his soppiness over animals. The fact that one of his pet animals is a dangerous and forbidden dragon is particularly ludicrous. He also speaks dialect, often a comic device in literature. For much of the story, Hagrid occupies a place somewhere between the world of the children and that of the adults; he is large, but not quite grown up.

Language

Chandler and Bryson both have distinctive styles of verbal humour. Chandler partly uses wit to make Philip Marlowe, who might otherwise appear too good to be true, into a more likeable character. On their first meeting, when Carmen Sternwood says 'Tall, aren't you?' he replies, 'I didn't mean to be.' She then sucks her thumb and falls into his arms, so he tells the butler, 'You ought to wean her. She looks old enough.'

Bryson continually makes jokes. The first two paragraphs of his narrative, just explaining that he originally came from Des Moines, are typical; so is his transition to the anecdote that follows. Having claimed ironically that 'Everybody in Des Moines is strangely serene', he immediately undermines this by describing a neighbour who was 'the nearest possible human equivalent to Fred Flintstone, but less charming'. Characteristically, he makes some fantastic statement and then explains, in case you have mistaken his intention, 'I just made that up.' His comedy, too, often turns upon exaggeration.

Alice's Adventures in Wonderland uses a great deal of verbal humour of a different sort, with wordplay and parodies. Here is the Mock Turtle explaining about his education.

> 'When we were little … we went to school in the sea. The master was an old Turtle – we used to call him Tortoise –'
>
> 'Why did you call him Tortoise, if he wasn't one?' Alice asked.
>
> 'We called him Tortoise because he taught us,' said the mock Turtle angrily. 'Really you are very dull!'

The whole Mock Turtle episode is full of puns. Ordinary lessons in the sea include 'Reeling and Writhing', while the Drawling-master taught 'Drawling, Stretching, and Fainting in Coils'.

Moral viewpoint

Although the main narrative is prose, *Alice's Adventures in Wonderland* is full of comic verses, most of which turn the conventional world upside down. Here Lewis Carroll takes a very moral tale, written by Isaac Watts (1674–1748). The poem, which aimed at giving children conventional moral values about work, was extremely well known in its day and you still see the line 'Satan finds some mischief still/For idle hands to do' quoted occasionally. It goes like this.

> How doth the little busy bee
> Improve each shining hour,
> And gather honey all the day
> From every opening flower!

As Alice recites the verse, which she has been made to learn by heart, it turns into this. What are the similarities and the differences?

> How doth the little crocodile
> Improve his shining tail,
> And pour the waters of the Nile
> On every golden scale!
>
> How cheerfully he seems to grin,
> How neatly spreads his claws,
> And welcomes little fishes in,
> With gently smiling jaws!

The form of the poem is the same but the sense is completely altered. Instead of the uplifting moral example of the bee, we have a quite different kind of animal, lurking and waiting for its innocent prey. Although the characters in *Harry Potter and the Philosopher's Stone* break the school rules, sometimes to comic effect, we know that good behaviour is going to triumph over bad in the end, but much of the humour of *Alice's Adventures in Wonderland* is subversive.

19 Stylistic changes over time

This chapter covers:

- observing changes in grammar over time
- distinguishing between archaisms and other unusual words
- noting the invention of new words.

Key terms

Diachronic variation: the changes in language over time.

Students are usually very sensitive to changes over time and quick to spot cultural references in a book that would be unusual in daily life now. With other kinds of **diachronic variation**, especially of vocabulary, there is a further complication because you have to judge whether a word really has fallen out of use or whether it is just unfamiliar to you. The best help with this is wide general reading.

 Practical activity

Even if you have not read the books they come from, you can probably have a good guess at which of the following quotations go furthest back in time, just based on your general experience. Put them in chronological order, with the oldest first.

a 'You will rejoice to hear that no disaster has accompanied the commencement of an enterprise which you have regarded with such evil forebodings.'

b 'You could have heard a fly fart.'

c 'She enjoyed her work, which consisted chiefly in running and servicing a tricky electric motor.'

d 'Master Raphael, quoth he, I wonder greatly why you get you not into some king's court.'

Commentary

Answer: (d), (a), (c), (b).

The following features of language and context enable us to place these short texts in this order:

d *Utopia*, by Thomas More: has archaic grammar and vocabulary.

a *Frankenstein*, by Mary Shelley: has unfamiliar rhythms, vocabulary and sentence structure.

c *Nineteen Eighty-Four*, by George Orwell: represents women in a modern way.

b *The Lost Continent*, by Bill Bryson: very colloquial, using an expression that might have been considered taboo before about 1960.

Diachronic change

Grammar

There is something about the word 'grammar' that frightens students, but grammar is actually something we all understand from the time that we first begin to speak. Young children work out for themselves that to add -s to a word makes a plural. Lewis Carroll's 'Jabberwocky', in *Through the Looking Glass*, is a well-known example of how a reader can easily guess the meanings of vocabulary as long as the grammar is familiar.

In the line 'All mimsy were the borogoves' it is obvious that 'borogoves' is a plural noun and that 'mimsy' describes the borogoves, even before Humpty Dumpty translates it for us. (We learn from him that a 'borogove' is a thin shabby-looking bird with its feathers 'sticking out all round' and that 'mimsy' is 'flimsy and miserable'.) This is obvious because we know without thinking about it that the definite article 'the' precedes a noun.

We mostly take the structures of grammar for granted, which is why they can cause us difficulty when they have changed over time. The older a text, the more likely it is that the grammar will be different from that of standard modern English. Sir Thomas More wrote *Utopia* in Latin, which was the international language of its day – not quite in the way that English is now, but it was certainly understood by scholars and was used by the Catholic Church for ordinary communication. It would be surprising if the original language had not left its traces in the translation's grammar and vocabulary. The literary English of the time was also influenced by Latin models because Latin was taught extensively in schools. For this reason, word order is often slightly different from that found in modern English. The edition you are reading is Robinson's translation of 1551, made so that the book would be available to a wider audience.

Critical response activity

Here is a short extract from Robinson's own introduction, in the letter to William Cecil. Can you spot the verb forms and the connective that are different from those of modern usage?

> I return again to Utopia. Which (as I said before) is a work not only for the matter that it containeth fruitful and profitable, but also for the writer's eloquent Latin style pleasant and delectable. Which he that readeth Latin, as the author himself wrote it, perfectly understanding the same, doubtless he shall take great pleasure and delight both in the sweet eloquence of the writer and also in the witty invention and fine conveyance or disposition of the matter, but most of all in the good and wholesome lessons which be there in great plenty and abundance.

Commentary

There are at least three grammatical features here that are now completely **archaic**:

- the suffix -eth on 'containeth' and 'readeth', which would now be 'contains' and 'reads'
- the form of the verb 'to be' in 'which be there in great plenty'; this would now be 'are'
- the use of 'Which' at the beginning of a sentence; in the second sentence above we would probably write 'This book' or 'It'; the third sentence would be something like 'Anyone who reads Latin …'.

Robinson also uses a number of **doublets** in the structure of his sentences: 'pleasant and delectable', 'pleasure and delight', 'good and wholesome', 'plenty and abundance'. To a modern ear these sound redundant, and if you wrote like this in your essays you would probably be criticised. But we have to realise that they were considered ornamental at the time and are intended to be impressive.

To understand this text you have to be aware of the changes in normal grammar that have taken place over time. Some of the vocabulary also appears unusual – we would be unlikely now to use words such as 'conveyance' or 'delectable' when referring to a style of writing (although 'delectable' is not entirely impossible) – but it is the grammatical structures that have changed most strikingly.

The influence of Classical models of writing lasted a long time. Until the end of the 19th century, it was common for writers to use considerably longer sentences than they do today, with a much higher incidence of dependent clauses. Here is a single sentence from 'The Purloined Letter'.

Key terms

Archaic: language that is characteristic of an earlier period or has fallen into disuse.

Doublets: pairs of words with the same or similar meaning, used for effect.

But then the *radicalness* of these differences, which was excessive;
the dirt, the soiled and torn condition of the paper, so inconsistent
with the *true* methodical habits of D—, and so suggestive of a
design to delude the beholder into an idea of the worthlessness
of the document; these things, together with the hyperobtrusive
situation of this document, full in the view of every visiter, and
thus exactly in accordance with the conclusions to which I had
previously arrived; these things, I say, were strongly corroborative of
suspicion, in one who came with the intention to suspect.

This kind of writing has a tremendous forward momentum. There is
nowhere to stop. Dupin carries us on relentlessly towards his conclusion.
It is also a very formal and dignified kind of writing, which demands
serious attention throughout. The reader cannot hurry through this, but
has to savour it.

The word order of 19th-century prose is often different from that of
modern usage. Look again at the quotation on p115 from *Travels with a
Donkey*.

The order 'says he' is not common now; we usually put the pronoun
first. The construction 'but newly left' is also more characteristic of older
prose. Features like this affect the rhythms of a text but do not generally
create many difficulties over meaning.

Modern writers such as Bill Bryson and J. K. Rowling use a higher
proportion of simple sentences or compound sentences. It is a mistake,
however, to think that they do not vary the structural patterns of their
sentences considerably. Their writing would otherwise seem very
monotonous.

Vocabulary

Some words are actually archaic; some, such as 'quoth' for 'said', even
obsolete. Some may be merely surprising. You need to discriminate
between these possibilities with the help of a good dictionary.

Dictionaries have different purposes. The little ones you can carry around
are excellent for checking spelling. For historical meanings, you need to
consult a larger one that deals with **etymology**.

The *Shorter Oxford English Dictionary* (which is a lot bigger than it sounds
from its title) is a good place to look up the history of words. You will
probably find it in the reference section of your school or college library.
You can also find the full 20-volume *Oxford English Dictionary* online. The
Collins English Dictionary, a single-volume desk dictionary, is an excellent
choice that is both comprehensive in its coverage and easy to use.

There is some unusual vocabulary in this list of things that Stevenson
loaded up for his trip in the Cévennes.

> The main cargo consisted of two entire changes of warm clothing
> – besides my travelling wear of country velveteen, pilot coat, and
> knitted spencer – some books and my railway rug, which being also
> in the form of a bag, made me a double castle for cold nights.

The words that you would probably have to look up here are 'pilot coat',
which is a type of short overcoat of coarse woollen cloth, and 'spencer',
which is another type of short jacket.

In the quotation, 'railway rug' is old-fashioned but we can understand
it, and Stevenson generally writes 'sleeping sack' where we would say
'sleeping bag' – again, a use that would be unusual in modern English but
is not strictly archaic.

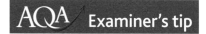

AQA Examiner's tip

When commenting on sentence
length and structures, you will need
to give examples to back up your
points, but you will probably not
want to use up your word allowance
by simply copying out something
like this. One way out of the
difficulty is to write 'The sentence
beginning "But then the radicalness
of these differences ..." shows
[whatever you want to say]'. The
three-dot ellipsis indicate that there
is text missing.

 Key terms

Etymology: the study of the origin
and development of words.

It is important to distinguish between vocabulary that has become obscure and the ideas behind it. The really strange thing about Stevenson's equipment is that he takes an egg beater with him, or at least he starts out with one and later throws it away. The phrase is not at all archaic, but the idea of taking an egg beater on a camping trip seems extraordinary.

Some of the specialised vocabulary in his narrative is technical. Apparently, to get a donkey to go forward you tell it 'Proot!'

Let us go back to that extract from Poe at the top of p125 and look at the vocabulary there. Do any of the words used contribute to the formality of the language?

A number of the words here have Latin roots: 'radicalness', 'hyperobtrusive' and 'corroborative', among others. The English language has a particularly large and rich vocabulary because, although it was originally a Germanic language, it has adopted a huge number of words from Norman French, Latin and all over the world. There is a tendency for the words with Latin origins to be **polysyllabic** and to be used in formal contexts.

Coinages

Sometimes literature uses words that are entirely new. The word 'Utopia' was unknown until More invented it, but it has become a standard way of referring to an imaginary ideal world. We even have an opposite for it in 'dystopia', meaning an invented world that is disagreeable.

Some texts invent a vocabulary, and even a grammar, that is all their own. *Nineteen Eighty-Four* is one of these and some of its **coinages** have passed into the language. Almost everyone will have heard of Big Brother and Room 101, even if they do not know where these phrases originally came from. Besides these terms, Orwell invents a whole language – Newspeak – as an essential part of the world of *Nineteen Eighty-Four*.

The language of Newspeak in Orwell's novel has been reduced so that it is impossible to express some ideas – ones that the Party finds unacceptable or inconvenient. Winston Smith's job is to alter records of the past when they contain facts and phrases that the ruling Party no longer approves of. We see him working on examples such as the order:

> times 3.12.83 reporting bb dayorder doubleplusungood refs unpersons rewrite fullwise upsub antefiling.

Orwell translates:

> In Oldspeak (or Standard English) this might be rendered:

> The reporting of Big Brother's Order for the Day in the 'Times' of December 3rd 1983 is extremely unsatisfactory and makes references to non-existent persons. Rewrite it in full and submit your draft to higher authority before filing.

We might now use 'unpersons' or another of Orwell's coinages, 'doublethink', in common speech.

The coinages in *Harry Potter and the Philosopher's Stone* are well known and contribute a great deal to atmosphere and humour in the book. The division of the world into wizards and 'muggles' has become familiar to a wide audience, as has the invented game of 'quidditch'. Lessons at Hogwarts have appropriate names such as 'herbology', while Neville's 'Remembrall' is something we could probably all do with.

Key terms

Polysyllabic words: words with more than one syllable.

Coinages: newly invented words.

Cultural change: themes in their context

This chapter covers:

This chapter covers:

- researching into the background to your texts using reference sources
- being aware of readership.

AQA Examiner's tip

When you look things up, keep a careful note of exactly where you find information, including the addresses of websites and the titles, authors and page numbers of books. You will then be able to check it without going to a lot of extra trouble later on and to include a bibliography in your coursework submissions.

AQA Examiner's tip

Some information about the writer and the date of publication is essential if you are going to understand a text in depth. However, although this information will help your understanding considerably, it really is background. Most of it will stay in your notes rather than appearing in the finished coursework.

Further reading

Boxall, Peter (ed.) *1001 Books You Must Read Before You Die*, Cassell, 2006

Drabble, Margaret (ed.) *The Oxford Companion to English Literature*, Oxford University Press, 2000

Head, Dominic (ed.) *The Cambridge Guide to Literature in English*, Cambridge University Press, 2006

Thorne, J. O. and Collocott, T. C. (eds) *Chambers Biographical Dictionary*, Chambers, 2002

Texts do not exist in isolation. They are products of the period in which they were written and we interpret them according to our own experience.

You will find it helpful to have some background information about the texts you are studying and the circumstances in which they were produced before you begin to write your coursework. This may involve a little basic research.

How to find out about background

Your first thought will probably be to head for the nearest computer and use the huge variety of resources on the internet. This requires a little planning, however. If you find the search engine Google and type in 'Jane Eyre', you will get approximately 2,600,000 hits. The most useful are likely to be those towards the top of the list, but not necessarily. The different articles available may range from scholarly studies to complete rubbish.

In order to get the best out of search engines, you have to think first what kind of information you really want and make the key words of your search as precise as possible. It might be:

- background about the author's life
- works used or referred to in the set text
- other works by the same author, for comparison
- historical details concerning the narrative's setting.

At some point you are probably going to use Wikipedia, which is one of the most exciting research tools available – but be careful. Anyone can write articles for Wikipedia, and although many of them are excellent, they may contain mistakes and idiosyncratic opinions. You need to evaluate and check information that you find in this way.

Do not neglect books. It may seem obvious, but it is easy to overlook what is right in front of you. When using books for research, remember:

- the text you are studying will usually tell you when it was first published, on the back of the title page
- to read the introduction, if there is one. Sometimes it will contain useful material such as a chronology of the author's life or historical background; this will have been checked by the editor and is likely to be reliable. Often several editions of classic texts are available at the same time in a good bookshop. If the first edition you see does not have notes and an introduction, check whether there are others.

Your school or college library will almost certainly have a reference section that will help you locate basic facts.

Historical audiences

It is important to consider what the original audience of a text was like and what its expectations were. You need to avoid some common over-simplifications here. If you go back to the 16th century when *Utopia* was published, books were a rarity and educated audiences relatively small. Each book was printed one page at a time and the pages were hung up to dry before being sewn together by hand. Even so, the Church had huge numbers of employees (relative to the size of the population as a whole) who could read. There were grammar schools and universities and a number of authors came from poor backgrounds.

By the 19th century things had changed. Cheap machine-printing began in about 1840. During the rest of the century literacy increased and so did the appetite for fiction as a form of entertainment. There were many schools, even for the poor, although these were of variable quality. The Sunday Schools, among others, made a great contribution to literacy. There were still people who were illiterate, but by the middle of the 19th century about three-quarters of the population probably had some reading ability. If you think about it, there are many trades in which literacy is essential and, in an age when all business documents were written out by hand, huge numbers of people were employed as clerks.

Circulation figures could be large, even by modern standards. In 1850 (one year before the UK census recorded a population of approximately 18 million) the first number of Dickens's weekly periodical *Household Words* cost two pence and sold 100,000 copies. (A large number of Victorian novels were published for the first time as serials in this periodical.) After a time, *Household Words* settled down to a rather lower circulation figure of 38,500 a week, but a less literary penny weekly, the *Family Herald*, was selling 300,000 copies a week in 1854. In America, *Uncle Tom's Cabin* by Harriet Beecher Stowe, published in 1852, is often credited with being the first novel to sell a million copies.

One common mistake is to think of reading as an 'upper-class' activity in the 19th century. This is to misunderstand the nature of Victorian society. In 1844 Lord Jeffrey wrote an essay on the poet Crabbe (published in *Contributions to the Edinburgh Review*). He said, 'in this country there probably are not less than three hundred thousand persons who read for instruction and amusement among the middling classes of society. In the higher classes there are not as many as thirty thousand.'

All this is relevant to your understanding of those set texts that were written in the 19th century and the audience they expected. Students often think that because Poe has a complex style with long sentences and a liking for foreign words he must have had a small, elite audience. This is not so. He was a journalist and, although he never made very much money, he raised the regular circulation of the *Southern Literary Messenger* from fewer than 1,000 copies to more than 5,000 when he worked on it in about 1835.

It may also be helpful for you to know what other books or literary traditions the text's original audience is likely to have been familiar with. **Intertextuality** is important for some narratives. *Frankenstein* contains many references to *Paradise Lost*, starting with a quotation on its title page. It is helpful to have at least a general idea why, because this gives a clue to the presentation of the creature. The last chapter of *Travels with a Donkey in the Cévennes* quotes some lines from Wordsworth, which suggests that the Romantic poets had an influence on Stevenson's thinking. His liking for wild places in the mountains reflects values that became common from the time of the Romantics and can help to explain his motivation in setting out on such a journey. Lewis Carroll, on the other hand, often mocks his sources and produces nonsensical parodies of familiar rhymes such as 'Twinkle, twinkle, little bat', knowing that his audience will laugh because they recognise the original.

■ Key terms

Intertextuality: the way one text partly depends on reference to another text for its meaning.

The relevance of the author's life and times

It is important to be discriminating and to realise the ways in which different types of background information can be useful. Biographical information about the author of your text is likely to be one of the first things you look for, if only out of curiosity. Some of the things you find out may be interesting, but not actually relevant to your coursework. Robert Louis Stevenson's father, Thomas, was famous for building lighthouses and Edgar Allan Poe had a long history of gambling and alcohol problems, but neither of these facts will actually help you much with your coursework.

Personal involvement

Authenticity of experience, however, is highly relevant. Some writers use their own experience of life directly in their fiction. The appalling picture of Lowood School in *Jane Eyre* was based on Charlotte Brontë's own unhappy experiences at Cowan Bridge, and this fact gives greater depth and credibility to the scenes at the school. Charlotte Brontë's friend and biographer Elizabeth Gaskell affirms that 'there was not a word in her account of the institution but what was true at the time when she knew it', although she also says that Brontë would not have written quite as she does if she had realised that the original of the place would immediately have been recognised.

Sometimes an author becomes personally involved with his narrative and this is obviously true in the case of the travel writing. Truman Capote's personal involvement with *In Cold Blood* is slightly less obvious but no less important. He was originally interested in the way a mass murder would affect a small community, which is why the book begins and ends with Holcomb itself. As a fascinating biography of Capote by Gerald Clarke describes, he soon became a party to the actual investigation of the murders and personally involved with Perry Smith.

Dates

Knowing something of the author's dates may also help you appreciate the authenticity of descriptions. Orwell, writing in 1948, used the experiences of the Second World War to set the tone of his novel and his original readership would have recognised this clearly. He reversed the last two figures of the date to set the novel in the future, but it is well known that he intended it, like his *Animal Farm*, to be a warning against the dangers of Communism in the post-war period.

Historical dates like this can help us to judge the likely effect of a work on its first audience. To take another example, Sir Thomas More is well known for his dispute with Henry VIII over the King's marriages. The disagreement eventually led to More's indictment for treason in 1534 and his execution the following year. That More was a courtier, a successful lawyer and a member of the Privy Council is certainly relevant because it shows that he had first-hand experience of the business of government. However, *Utopia* was written in 1516, when More was in high favour with the young king. These facts may well affect the way you look at some passages in *Utopia*, particularly those concerned with marriage.

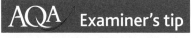

AQA Examiner's tip

Background information is important because it affects your understanding and attitude, but you will not have space for much of it within the coursework itself. Record it as evidence of planning. When you come to write, concentrate on the text above all. Your knowledge of the context will be apparent in your depth of understanding.

Planning the first coursework piece

This chapter covers:

drawing on insights from literary and linguistic studies in:

- long-term planning
- choosing suitable text extracts
- understanding assessment criteria.

AQA Examiner's tip

Allow yourself plenty of time to work on your coursework, especially as the deadline approaches. It is a good idea to leave longer than you believe you will actually need to allow for accidents such as being ill or your printer breaking down. Coursework that is rushed for submission at the last minute is unlikely to do you justice.

How should this coursework assignment be planned and completed? Careful planning right from the beginning will save you a lot of trouble later on. You need to keep a record in your notes of everything you do and when, so that you can provide evidence of planning when you submit the final coursework.

Choosing the extracts for your analysis

- First of all, read the whole of both books through quickly, before you start studying them in depth. This will give you an idea of the plot and the characteristics of each book as a whole.
- Read both books again in the light of your given theme.
- Choose extracts of 500 to 800 words that are reasonably self-contained to work on. Do not exceed the word limit. You are allowed to edit the texts slightly: that is, you can leave out a sentence or two of less relevant material to shorten the extract you are working on. You should show this in the text by an ellipsis.

Writing your coursework

When you do the actual writing:

- There is no need to compare the texts in every paragraph of your written work. It is often more helpful to explain the links between them at the beginning and then work on the texts separately.
- You are not required to submit drafts, but you will need to re-draft your work as a normal part of the process of preparing the final version that you submit for assessment.
- Leave some time between writing the first draft and correcting it. It is much easier to see mistakes and potential improvements after an interval of rest. Do not forget to use the spell check, but do not assume that it is infallible. For example, it will not draw your attention to the fact that you wrote 'there' instead of the intended 'their'.
- Choose passages that will give you an opportunity to discuss in detail some of the features of writing we have discussed so far in this unit, such as methods of characterisation, setting or imagery.

Let us see how this works out in practice. Suppose the set texts you are studying are *Jane Eyre* and *Wide Sargasso Sea*, and your theme is conflict. There are a variety of possibilities that you could choose. Among them might be:

- conflicts in childhood: Jane Eyre's problems with the Reed children and Antoinette's with Tia
- psychological conflicts as each heroine considers her relationship with her husband
- conflicts between Bertha and Rochester and Antoinette and her husband
- the scenes where Bertha and Antoinette, respectively, attack Richard Mason.

An example of full-length analytical coursework

Let us put all the ideas about theme, style and change over time together in a single example. Suppose your set texts are Edgar Allen Poe's *Selected Tales* and *The Big Sleep* by Raymond Chandler. Your theme (one that is very common in literature) is the deceiving appearance.

A number of passages would do very well to illustrate this. The following two come from similar moments at the end of the story when the plot unravels and the deception is exposed. In 'The Purloined Letter' Dupin explains how he recovered the letter; in *The Big Sleep* Marlowe solves the mystery of how Rusty Regan disappeared – killed by Carmen Sternwood.

Extract A: 'The Purloined Letter'

No sooner had I glanced at this letter, than I concluded it to be that of which I was in search. To be sure, it was, to all appearance, radically different from the one of which the Prefect had read us so minute a description. Here the seal was large and black, with the D— cipher; there it was small and red, with the ducal arms of the S— family. Here, the address, to the Minister, was diminutive and feminine; there the superscription, to a certain royal personage, was markedly bold and decided; the size alone formed a point of correspondence. But, then, the *radicalness* of these differences, which was excessive; the dirt; the soiled and torn condition of the paper, so inconsistent with the *true* methodical habits of D—, and so suggestive of a design to delude the beholder into an idea of the worthlessness of the document; these things, together with the hyperobtrusive situation of this document, full in the view of every visiter, and thus exactly in accordance with the conclusions to which I had previously arrived; these things, I say, were strongly corroborative of suspicion, in one who came with the intention to suspect.

I protracted my visit as long as possible, and, while I maintained a most animated discussion which the Minister, on a topic which I knew well had never failed to interest and excite him, I kept my attention really riveted upon the letter. In this examination, I committed to memory its external appearance and arrangement in the rack; and also fell, at length, upon a discovery which set at rest whatever trivial doubt I might have entertained. In scrutinizing the edges of the paper, I observed them to be more *chafed* than seemed necessary. They presented the *broken* appearance which is manifested when a stiff paper, having been once folded and pressed with a folder, is refolded in a reversed direction, in the same creases or edges which had formed the original fold. This discovery was sufficient. It was clear to me that the letter had been turned, as a glove, inside out, re-directed, and re-sealed. I bade the Minister good morning, and took my departure at once, leaving a gold snuff-box upon the table.

The next morning I called for the snuff-box, when we resumed, quite eagerly, the conversation of the preceding day. While thus engaged, however, a loud report, as if of a pistol, was heard immediately beneath the windows of the hotel, and was succeeded by a series of fearful screams, and the shoutings of a mob. D— rushed to a casement, threw it open, and looked out. In the meantime, I stepped to the card-rack, took the letter, put it in my pocket, and replaced it by a *facsimilie*, (so far as regards to externals,) which I had carefully prepared at my lodgings; imitating the D— cipher, very readily, by means of a seal formed of bread.

The disturbance in the street had been occasioned by the frantic behaviour of a man with a musket. He had fired it among a crowd of women and children. It proved, however, to have been without ball, and the fellow was suffered to go his way as a lunatic or a drunkard. When he had gone, D— came from the window, whither I had followed him immediately upon securing the object in view. Soon afterwards I bade him farewell. The pretended lunatic was a man in my own pay.

'But what purpose had you,' I asked, 'in replacing the letter by a *facsimilie*? Would it not have been better, at the first visit, to have seized it openly, and departed?'

'D—,' replied Dupin, 'is a desperate man, and a man of nerve. His hotel, too, is not without attendants devoted to his interests. Had I made the wild attempt you suggest, I might never have left the Ministerial presence alive. The good people of Paris might have heard of me no more. But I had an object apart from these considerations. You know my political prepossessions. In this matter, I act as a partisan of the lady concerned.

Extract B: *The Big Sleep*

I followed the ruts along and the noise of the city traffic grew curiously and quickly faint, as if this were not in the city at all, but far away in a daydream land. Then the oil-stained, motionless walking-beam of a squat wooden derrick stuck up over a branch. I could see the rusty old steel cable that connected this walking-beam with half a dozen others. The beams didn't move, probably hadn't moved for a year. The wells were no longer pumping. There was a pile of rusted pipe, a loading platform that sagged at one end, half a dozen empty oil drums lying in a ragged pile. There was the stagnant, oil-scummed water of an old sump iridescent in the sunlight.

'Are they going to make a park of all this?' I asked.

She dipped her chin down and gleamed at me.

'It's about time. The smell of that sump would poison a herd of goats. This the place you had in mind?'

'Uh-huh. Like it?'

'It's beautiful.' I pulled up beside the loading platform. We got out. I listened. The hum of the traffic was a distant web of sound, like the buzzing of bees. The place was as lonely as a churchyard. Even after the rain the tall eucalyptus trees still looked dusty. They always look dusty. A branch broken off by the wind had fallen over the edge of the sump and the flat leathery leaves dangled in the water.

I walked around the sump and looked into the pump-house. There was some junk in it, nothing that looked like recent activity. Outside a big wooden bull wheel was tilted against the wall. It looked like a good place all right.

I went back to the car. The girl stood beside it preening her hair and holding it out in the sun. 'Gimmie,' she said, and held her hand out.

I took the gun and put it in her palm. I bent down and picked up a rusty can.

'Take it easy now,' I said. 'It's loaded in all five. I'll go over and set this can in that square opening in the middle of that big wooden wheel. See?' I pointed. She ducked her head, delighted. 'That's about thirty feet. Don't start shooting until I get back beside you. Okey?'

'Okey,' she giggled.

I went back around the sump and set the can up in the middle of the bull wheel. It made a swell target. If she missed the can, which she was certain to do, she would probably hit the wheel. That would stop a small slug completely. However, she wasn't going to hit even that.

I went back towards her around the sump. When I was about ten feet from her, at the edge of the sump, she showed me all her sharp little teeth and brought the gun up and started to hiss.

I stopped dead, the sump water stagnant and stinking at my back.

'Stand there, you son of a bitch,' she said.

The gun pointed at my chest. Her hand seemed to be quite steady. The hissing sound grew louder and her face had the scraped bone look. Aged, deteriorated, become animal, and not a nice animal.

I laughed at her. I started to walk towards her. I saw her small finger tighten on the trigger and grow white at the tip.

I was about six feet away from her when she started to shoot.

The sound of the gun made a sharp slap, without body, a brittle crack in the sunlight. I didn't see any smoke. I stopped again and grinned at her.

She fired twice more, very quickly. I don't think any of the shots would have missed. There were five in the little gun. She had fired four. I rushed her.

I didn't want the last one in my face, so I swerved to one side. She gave it to me quite carefully, not worried at all. I think I felt the hot breath of the powder blast a little.

I straightened up. 'My, but you're cute,' I said.

Her hand holding the empty gun began to shake violently. The gun fell out of it. Her mouth began to shake. Her whole face went to pieces. Then her head screwed up towards her left ear and froth showed on her lips. Her breath made a whining sound. She swayed.

Sample response

Both these extracts relate in a similar way to the idea of deceiving appearances. Both come at the moment when the mystery is solved and both reveal how the detective discovered the truth by the use of a potentially dangerous plan that deceives the deceiver. Dupin goes to the blackmailer's apartment twice. He succeeds in an elaborate ruse to identify the missing letter, create another with an identical appearance and return the next day to substitute it for the original. Marlowe takes Carmen to a lonely spot because he has guessed that she killed Rusty Regan. On the pretence of teaching her to shoot, he deceives her, at some risk to himself, into giving herself away.

Starts with an overview comparing both texts, with focus on the given theme – in this case the deceiving appearance

A further link between the extracts

Both detectives are motivated here by the desire to help others: Dupin being a 'partisan' of the lady whose letter was stolen and Marlowe wishing to help his client, General Sternwood. Both are highly skilled in detection and proud of their achievements, although this is perhaps more obvious in the case of Dupin. Poe gives the framework narrative of 'The Purloined Letter' to Dupin's unnamed friend, but at this point Dupin is allowed to speak for himself to show off his methods.

Begins to discuss the extracts separately, bringing out the characterisation of Dupin. The sharp intelligence of the detective is important to the genre

Dupin has succeeded where all others have failed because of his powers of close observation, combined with his awareness of his enemy's character. It is a kind of game he is playing in order to bring the deception to light, games being a recurring theme throughout the Dupin stories. He is aware that D— is an unusually clever man and that his hiding place for the letter will not conform to normal expectations. When he sees a letter in full view in D—'s apartment it is the 'radicalness' of the apparent differences from the letter that he is looking for that strikes him. He notes its 'large and black' seal in contrast to the 'small and red' one he is supposed to be looking for.

Dupin's sharp intelligence finds this extreme contrast suspicious, leading him to conclude, in the light of his knowledge of the Minister's cleverness, that the letter left in full view must be the one he is looking for. His acute observation then allows him to memorise the appearance of the letter so closely that he can go away and produce an exact copy, imitating the size and folding of the letter and forging the seal with a piece of bread.

The scheme to substitute one letter for another calls for both ingenuity and courage. Dupin points out that if he had taken the letter openly, he 'might never have left the Ministerial presence alive'. His timing is impeccable. During both visits to the apartment he is never left alone and he substitutes the false letter in the brief moments when D— turns towards the window to investigate a violent disturbance in the street that Dupin, who thinks of everything, has previously arranged. Far from being daunted by his enemy's subtlety, Dupin is stimulated by it. He seems to show a certain admiration for D— as 'a man of nerve' like himself. Dupin also appears gallant in his support for the lady.

Discusses the function of the other character in this dialogue

Dupin's friend respectfully listens to the whole account without interruption, until he asks, 'But what purpose had you … in replacing the letter by a facsimile? Would it not have been better at the first visit, to have seized it openly and departed?' The function of this question, when it comes, is once more to show off Dupin's superiority. He replies that such a 'wild attempt' would have been impossibly dangerous in a place full of the Minister's supporters.

Linking paragraph, making a transition between one text and another

While Dupin's world has romantic elements and he helps a royal personage, Marlowe's is grimy and more democratic, reflecting a change in audience tastes for fiction over the years. While Dupin is rescuing one woman, Marlowe is exposing the crime of another.

Moves on to discuss the second extract in detail

Marlowe has a respect for General Sternwood, who first employed him to solve the mystery of Rusty Regan's disappearance, but he has suspected Carmen of corruption from the beginning. The account of the incident where Carmen tries to shoot him is again a first person narrative where, like Dupin, Marlowe shows evidence of both intelligence and courage. Both these stories use the past tense, but Chandler's account is much more immediate in the way it builds suspense.

Background is important in *The Big Sleep*, and is more fully realised than the rather general background of Paris in Poe's detective stories. The deserted spot where Marlowe is supposed to teach Carmen to shoot is a scene of decay and corruption. Everything is 'rusty', 'stagnant', 'ragged'. Marlowe makes a characteristic wisecrack that draws attention to the setting when he says, 'The smell of that sump would poison a herd of goats.' It is an outstandingly suitable spot for a murder or the concealment of a body.

Brings out the importance of setting the narrative

Like Dupin, Marlowe is in some physical danger. Short sentences build the tension and emphasise this: 'I laughed at her. I started to walk towards her. I saw her small finger tighten on the trigger and grow white at the tip.' The reader does not know at first that the gun is not loaded and only finds out at the same moment as Carmen that it is firing blanks. Even so, Marlowe is in some danger of injury as he approaches her. He says, 'I didn't want the last one in my face, so I swerved to one side.'

Notes the way language features contribute to the writer's effects

Chandler creates an extremely dramatic situation through the use of naturalistic dialogue here. We follow the action with the gun as it happens. Marlowe explains to Carmen, 'Take it easy now … It's loaded in all five. I'll go over and set this can in that square opening in the middle of that big wooden wheel. See?' Carmen herself says little, but her words are extremely revealing. She giggles as Marlowe tells her, apparently humorously, not to start shooting until he is back at her side, then she reveals her true character. All through the novel she has been attempting to seduce Marlowe. Now she turns the gun on him with the words: 'Stand there, you son of a bitch.' Marlowe's 'My, but you're cute' is an ironic echo of words at their first meeting when she threw herself into his arms. It briefly expresses his disgust.

Discusses the use of dialogue

Chandler creates Carmen's character not only through her actions and words but also through figurative language. She is associated with animal imagery, being 'not a nice animal', who makes a 'hissing' and 'whining' sound. (In fact Carmen is having a fit here, something that Chandler associates with her general degeneracy. This image may make a more sensitive modern audience uncomfortable.) She also has 'sharp little teeth'; underneath the surface appearance of the rich, privileged blonde is a much more primitive creature.

Comments on the significance of figurative language

Because the two narratives were written at different times, there are some differences in detail and cultural reference. These help to date them as a century apart. The letter Dupin rescues has been folded and sealed with wax rather than put into an envelope. Both stories mention guns, but while the one in 'The Purloined Letter' is a 'musket', normally loaded with 'ball', Carmen's little revolver is a more modern weapon.

Focus on change over time in the form of cultural references

The passage of time has also led to great differences in language. Poe's vocabulary is intended to be impressive: Dupin's visit is 'protracted', his talk 'animated discussion'. Many of the words Poe uses, like these and like 'diminutive', 'superscription' and 'preposessions', are polysyllabic and have Latin roots. The use of this kind of vocabulary is much more common in 19th-century texts than later ones and only the spelling of 'visiter' is actually obsolete. The use of an initial letter for a name, such as 'D—', is also uncommon in modern fiction. Chandler, on the other hand, creates a naturalistic effect through slang such as 'Okey' and ellipsis such as 'See?' His speakers sometimes make inarticulate noises like 'Uh-huh', and 'it is' is normally elided to 'it's'.

Focus on linguistic change over time. Clear sense of how contexts have shaped language

While Chandler's short sentences and short paragraphs build tension, Poe's are leisurely, often with numerous dependent clauses. The sentence beginning 'But then, the radicalness of the differences …' goes on for six lines. There are occasional syntactic features, such as the inversion 'what purpose had you', that also contribute to the formality of Poe's prose.

Summing up of the relationship of the two texts and the development of the genre

Poe's short stories of Dupin helped to create the taste for detective fiction that Chandler exploits at greater length in his novels. The plots of the texts have much in common: deep mysteries and layers of deceit that the detective must unravel through the use of his intelligence. However, Marlowe is much tougher than Dupin and by his time the reading public has become interested in a world of sordid crime, gangsters and industrial dereliction.

Commentary

This answer is not perfect, but it fulfils most of the assessment criteria, uses brief illustrative quotation and keeps within the word limit.

The coursework script has to compare the two extracts chosen to illustrate the theme, but that does not mean that every paragraph in the script has to refer to both texts. This response links the two together by themes, then mostly deals with them one at a time, before linking them together at the end. It would be possible to separate the texts even more than this without losing marks, as long as the script deals with the contrasting approaches of the two within the answer as a whole.

A good script will show knowledge of the theme and be able to set the chosen extracts in the context of the whole work. The answer below draws attention to the stage reached in the plot and to the way in which the idea of deception is central to both texts.

The coursework should show understanding of genre (in this case the detective story), characterisation and tone. Here there is comment on Dupin's pride in his achievement and on the courage of both detectives, as well as on some character features of both the Minister and Carmen.

Responses to literary texts should show understanding of narrative methods such as point of view. The script should bring out the attitudes and values of the characters, and discuss the writer's intentions. The answer above mentions the narrative voice of each extract and the attitudes of the detectives. It examines the use of figurative language in the description of Carmen.

Linguistic features are important, and the script should show understanding of how form, style and vocabulary shape meaning. Here there is a contrast between the formality of Poe's style and the more colloquial tone of Chandler, with the latter's greater emphasis on language that creates tension. A good script should use the technical vocabulary of criticism not just to identify features but to examine how they help to bring out the meaning of the text.

The script must also find room to consider diachronic change, context and genre development and include a brief reference to readership.

The creative task

■ the requirements for creative writing coursework

■ considering how your study of English Language and Literature up to this point will help you with your coursework.

This part of your coursework asks you to undertake a realistic exercise. All successful writers learn from one another and this applies to professional writers just as much as to A-level students. Throughout Section A of this unit you have been thinking about writing techniques as you studied the set texts. Now it is time for you to put some of your ideas into practice with a short piece of creative writing of your own. The limit for this is 500 to 850 words. Your first thought may be that this is quite a lot, but it represents only about two sides of typed A4 paper, depending on point size and layout. You will find that you soon use up the word limit and you may want to write more. You must resist that temptation and concentrate instead on producing focused and controlled writing that displays your skills within this 500 to 850 word frame.

■ Approaching creative writing

This section on creative writing concentrates on choices of point of view, genre and audience, which are all features you have already considered in relation to other authors' work. The study you have made throughout this book will inform you as you develop your own ideas and style.

You are likely to compose your creative writing coursework at a fairly late stage, when you have a thorough knowledge of the set texts. By that time you may well have discarded most of your early ideas in favour of others, but it is always better to have something to reject or adapt than to face a completely blank page.

Your aim is to surprise and delight your reader by original work that somehow enriches his or her idea of the original text. You do not have to agree with the ideas put forward or implied in the set texts themselves. Indeed, you may challenge them if you wish. As you have already learned, context is important and attitudes that seem obvious to one group of readers may seem very strange to another. You have only to think of how the last century changed attitudes to war, to the position of women, and even to something as commonplace as smoking, and the extent to which restrictions on individual behaviour are considered acceptable.

This creative writing coursework is a test of your:

■ understanding of one or both of the texts
■ understanding of the theme you have been studying
■ knowledge of different genres and their conventions
■ ability to interest an audience
■ own command of English
■ ability to control your writing to meet a specific word limit, which will be strictly enforced.

The basic information in this part of your coursework *must* come from the set books. You might, for example, choose to adopt a point of view contrary to one expressed or implied in the text you have studied, or you might write for a different audience or in a different genre. You could even combine the two set texts by creating an imaginary situation where a character from one book meets a character from another.

Let us begin in the next topic with an example of intertextuality from a published novel, *Wide Sargasso Sea*.

23 What do we mean by challenging the writer's point of view?

As it happens, two of the set books give a perfect example of how one text may challenge the point of view of another. Let us look at those first, before moving on to some examples written by students.

🔍 *Wide Sargasso Sea*, which was published in 1966, takes some of the characters from *Jane Eyre* and presents their story in a different light. It is able to do this because some attitudes have changed in the meantime. In the 19th century gentlemen expected to inherit land and enjoy an income from farming it or renting it to others; women were not expected to be independent, divorce was difficult and attitudes to mental illness were very different from those of today.

Edward Rochester, who appears as a character in both novels, is the younger son of a rich man, but does not originally expect to inherit money of his own. In order to get an income, he marries an heiress in the West Indies, a creole woman whose name is Bertha Antoinetta Mason in *Jane Eyre* and Antoinette in *Wide Sargasso Sea*. The marriage is a failure. Rochester's elder brother dies and he inherits Thornfield Hall, a large country house in England. He returns there with his wife, who is now mad, and secretly keeps her locked in rooms at the top of the house, guarded by a woman called Grace Poole.

In *Jane Eyre* Rochester gives his version of the whole affair in Chapter 27. His purpose in that novel is to excuse his own behaviour: he has attempted to contract a bigamous marriage to Jane Eyre while Bertha Mason is still alive. *Wide Sargasso Sea* either echoes or briefly quotes from this account at several points, but in order to establish an obvious connection between the two novels before the tragic ending when Antoinette dies in a fire, Rhys has to make some of the details more explicit. She does this in Grace Poole's narrative, a short self-contained section that comes towards the end of the novel and explains that Antoinette is now shut away.

▇ Critical response activity

This short account is more subtle than you might think on first reading. Consider the following questions as you read:

1 What specific links does it make with the text of *Jane Eyre*?

2 Where are there possible differences?

3 How does Rhys establish a personal voice for the narrator?

Grace Poole's narrative from *Wide Sargasso Sea*

'They knew that he was in Jamaica when his father and brother died,' Grace Poole said. 'He inherited everything, but he was a wealthy man before that. Some people are fortunate, they said, and there were hints about the woman he brought back to England with him. Next day Mrs Eff wanted to see me and she complained about gossip. I don't allow gossip. I told you that when you came. Servants will talk and you can't stop them, I said. And I am not certain that the situation will suit me, madam. First when I answered your advertisement you said that the person I had to look after was not a young girl. I asked if she was an old woman and you said no. Now that I see her I don't know what to think. She sits shivering and she is so thin. If she dies on my hands who will get the blame? Wait, Grace, she said. She was holding a letter. Before you decide will you listen to what the master of the house has to say about this matter. "If Mrs Poole is satisfactory why not give her double, treble the money," she read, and folded the letter away but not before I had seen the words on the next page, "but for God's sake let me hear no more of it." There was a foreign stamp on the envelope. "I don't serve the devil for no money," I said. She said, "If you imagine that when you serve this gentleman you are serving the devil you never made a greater mistake in your life. I knew him as a boy. I knew him as a young man. He was gentle, generous, brave. His stay in the West Indies has changed him out of all knowledge. He has grey in his hair and misery in his eyes. Don't ask me to pity anyone who had a hand in that. I've said enough and too much. I am not prepared to treble your money, Grace, but I am prepared to double it. But there must be no more gossip. If there is I will dismiss you at once. I do not think it will be impossible to fill your place. I'm sure you understand." Yes, I understand, I said.

'Then all the servants were sent away and she engaged a cook, one maid and you, Leah. They were sent away but how could she stop them talking? If you ask me the whole country knows. The rumours I've heard – very far from the truth. But I don't contradict, I know better than to say a word. After all the house is big and safe, a shelter from the world outside which, say what you like, can be a black and cruel world to a woman. Maybe that's why I stayed on.'

The thick walls, she thought. Past the lodge gate a long avenue of trees and inside the house blazing fires and the crimson and white rooms. But above all the thick walls, keeping away all the things that you have fought till you can fight no more. Yes, maybe that's why we all stay – Mrs Eff and Leah and me. All of us except that girl who lives in her own darkness. I'll say one thing for her, she hasn't lost her spirit. She's still fierce. I don't turn my back on her when her eyes have that look. I know it.

Commentary

In her other novels, all Rhys's heroines are victims: partly of exploitation by men, partly of their own sexuality. This is the fundamental idea behind *Wide Sargasso Sea*. Rhys wants to shift at least some of the sympathy in her version of events from Rochester to his unfortunate wife. However, Rochester is not simply a villain. The whole novel is much more ambiguous and much more even-handed than that. Let us think about some of the connections between the two texts and some of the differences.

Names are obviously one of the things that connect the texts and in Grace Poole's narrative some of the characters from *Jane Eyre* are explicitly named: Mrs Eff here is Mrs Fairfax, the housekeeper at Thornfield Hall, and Leah is the maid. 'He' is Rochester, never specifically named in *Wide Sargasso Sea* but recognisable from having been in the West Indies, from having inherited the estate from his father and brother, and from having brought back, in mysterious circumstances, a woman who is kept locked away. The refusal to give him a name is partly an indicator of Antoinette's failed relationship with him, but it is also a subtle acknowledgement by Rhys that her character is not actually the same as Charlotte Brontë's.

This section of the novel economically picks up on the fact that Rochester has lived away from England for some time by mentioning the small descriptive detail of the 'foreign stamp' on the letter. It gives a partial defence of him, as Mrs Fairfax explains that he is not 'the devil' but someone who was 'gentle, generous, brave' as a young man and has been changed by recent experiences. In this way Rhys maintains the ambiguity of the first person accounts earlier in the novel, where Rochester behaves cruelly but there are possibly some extenuating circumstances. Mrs Fairfax remarks on the present 'misery in his eyes'.

Through the use of dialogue, Rhys gives Grace Poole a voice of her own appropriate to her social situation. She addresses Mrs Fairfax as 'madam' but is clearly on terms of equality with Leah, the servant. Her language does not imitate the Victorian speech of *Jane Eyre*. It uses modern standard English grammar and vocabulary but at the same time is moderately colloquial, with phrases such as 'I don't serve the devil for no money' and 'If you ask me …', to make it sound like natural speech.

Apart from telling us that she has now become violent, this narrative gives some ambiguous information about Antoinette. It brings out one of the discrepancies between *Wide Sargasso Sea* and *Jane Eyre* concerning Antoinette's age. Charlotte Brontë's Bertha Mason is five years older than Rochester, as he tells us in his own defence, so she would have been aged 31 at this stage. Antoinette is about 10 years younger. The phrase 'you said that the person I had to look after was not a young girl', indicating Grace's surprise at Antoinette's youthfulness, can be taken as Rhys's subtle acknowledgement of this discrepancy. Because she is younger, Antoinette is more obviously a victim than Rochester's wife in *Jane Eyre* ever was.

The last paragraph of Grace Poole's narrative switches from dialogue to internal monologue, and it uses Thornfield Hall symbolically. The 'thick walls' appear to provide a refuge, 'keeping away all the things that you have fought till you can fight no more'. There is an implied suggestion here that Mrs Poole has considerable problems of her own to shelter from. The walls are not a refuge for Antoinette, however. She is still fighting.

To sum up, this narrative is linked to *Jane Eyre* by names and details of action and description. It is different from *Jane Eyre* because it has introduced a new narrator, a new point of view and language of its own time.

You might equally well think about other narratives from a different perspective. Some ways in which a piece of coursework might challenge the point of view of the set text could be:

- a political attack on Utopia as a society that holds slaves
- the 'animal rights' view of *Travels with a Donkey in the Cévennes*
- one of the characters Bill Bryson makes fun of answering back with an account of Bill's strange behaviour when they met.

24 Finding opportunities for creative work in different genres

This chapter covers:

- the advantages and disadvantages of various genres for creative writing coursework.

🔊 Every text displays genre characteristics and implies a particular sense of audience in the mind of the writer.

As well as changing the point of view, there are various other lines of approach that you might find helpful in planning your creative writing coursework:

- you can expand on the original text by introducing relevant extra material
- you can re-work the text in a different genre or for a different audience
- you can use a combination of these.

Your new text can be written for a reading audience or it can be in the form of a script for spoken delivery. Remember that it must reflect the set theme.

You will find many examples in creative literature of texts that have been adapted from one genre to another. Often when people think of *Frankenstein*, the first idea that often comes into their heads is not Mary Shelley's novel but James Whale's moving film, with Boris Karloff as the creature. This film itself was made not directly from the novel but from a stage adaptation.

Monologues, letters, diaries, speeches, newspaper reports, play scripts – all of these can give you an opportunity to show your understanding of the set texts in a creative way. Because this is an integrated course, you will find material you studied in Unit 1 and the Anthology highly relevant here. You might want to use the formats of other types of non-fictional document to present adaptations of literary material, for example those of accident reports or guide books.

🔊 **Your choice of genre for creative writing has to be compatible with the theme you are studying.** If you are looking for ways of writing about conflict in *Jane Eyre* and *Wide Sargasso Sea*, you might try writing one of the following:

- a letter from Jane Eyre to the former Miss Temple commenting on Mrs Reed's death
- papers left by Rochester to be given to his children after his death
- a section from Adele's autobiography, as she reveals the secrets of Thornfield Hall
- a dramatic monologue from Christophine on hearing of Antoinette's death
- a speech from Richard Mason at the memorial service for his half-sister
- a newspaper article reporting Bertha's or Antoinette's death
- research into the family history published by a descendant of Jane and Rochester.

AQA Examiner's tip

You need to be think carefully about your choice of genre. While there are many genres that you can choose for the presentation of your material, there are also some that you cannot use. For example, it is not possible to script a live interview with one of the characters. Sometimes students waste a lot of effort in writing things that look like transcripts, complete with hesitations and false starts. There is no point in doing this.

Monologues

A monologue, by definition, is the voice of one speaker. However, it may contain reports of conversations with others, as the example from *Wide Sargasso Sea* in Topic 23 does. It has to create the character of the speaker as it goes along as well as give information, so it has to imply his or her attitudes to events. A monologue from Mrs Reed in *Jane Eyre* would have

■ **Think about it**

If you decide to write something from the point of view of a minor character, skim-read through the text and make notes before you start planning your writing. You can put sticky notes in the relevant pages of the book or keep a list of references, but do not forget to write the page number of each reference so that you can find it again easily.

to convey her hatred of the child, but still show some underlying sense of guilt at the way Jane has been treated. A monologue from the nursemaid Bessie Leaven could be much more sympathetic, seeing both points of view in the conflict.

The main challenge is finding a suitable voice for the speaker because you have to create the character through the medium of speech. It is a mistake to try to write in a mock historical style or in any non-standard form of language that does not come naturally to you. For example, Christophine in *Wide Sargasso Sea* is a dialect speaker; Jean Rhys, who was brought up in Dominica, knew the dialect of that area well and was able to imitate it convincingly. Dialects are *never* just standard English with a few mistakes thrown in. They are rule-governed systems, and you have to know the rules in fine detail if you are going to produce authentic dialect forms in your writing.

■ **Critical response activity**

Here is the mystery of *The Big Sleep* retold from the point of view of a minor character: Vincent Norris, the Sternwoods' butler.

■ What particular aspects of the narrative has the writer of this piece concentrated on?

■ How has he tried to give Norris a distinctive voice?

Example of a first-person narrative: What the butler saw

He's been good to me, the General, General Sternwood. The family made their money from oil. Sad to see him now, sleeping in that orchid hothouse. He doesn't even like orchids. Can't be too long now before the big sleep takes him over.

Not that his two daughters help any: Vivian, Mrs Regan now, with her gambling, and Carmen with her fits and strange ways. I owe it to the General to keep their problems away from him in his last days. Some blame the old man for letting them run loose. They are bound to hook up with something that can't be hushed up.

Norris is the name, Vincent Norris, General Sternwood's butler. In my sixties, back as straight as an ironing board, solemn tones for the visitors. I look after him along with Mathilda, the maid, and the chauffeur, Owen Taylor. That is until Owen took the car over the pier. Bad business that, never did get cleared up. They said it was suicide. Tried to run off with Carmen at one time. Why we kept him on after that, I don't know.

Why did the General ask to see this smart guy Marlowe? It's just about Carmen's debts, I hope. Was there more she's been up to than that? But Vivian's seen him. She thinks it's about the disappearance of her husband Rusty Regan. I make many mistakes. Getting Marlowe in to see her wasn't one of them. He made some crack about having fun guessing what my duties are. More than meets the eye.

The General misses Rusty. Thinks he walked out on his daughter. Rusty chatted to him in the hothouse. Kept a lonely man company. He's supposed to have run off with a gangster's wife.

Afterwards, Marlowe comes back, this time with Miss Carmen in the back of his car. He wasn't here and I didn't see him. Maybe he was the right choice after all.

Next I hear from him is a message for Mrs Regan that he'd got the pictures and everything was all right. At the start, it was just three demand notes.

The General asked me to ring Marlowe after the newspapers got hold of the murder details. There was nothing about the Sternwoods in them. The General instructed me to send him a cheque for five hundred dollars. Marlowe said the incident was closed. I promised him some brandy and champagne when the General was well enough to thank him in person …

Not closed at all. Soon after, he brought Mrs Regan home, who pushed past me without speaking. He's gone in deep now, deeper than we want. I phoned him to come and see the General. This time I showed him up to his bedroom. Marlowe came out asking me about Regan. I guess the General had asked him to find him.

He went away with Carmen – was it down to the oil sump? But when he came back it was to see Vivian.

I can only guess what happened. But Miss Carmen was taken away soon after. Hopefully to somewhere she'd be looked after.

Did I know that she'd shot Rusty Regan? I guess Marlowe thought I did. But he knows that I'll never tell. And I don't think he will either.

The old man can lie quietly until the big sleep comes.

Commentary

This piece concentrates mainly on plot and summarises the whole novel. Its strength is the thorough way the writer has made use of little bits of information from throughout the novel and combined them into a single narrative.

The writer has given Norris a distinctive voice through the use of short sentences, often elliptical. Notice the way he refers to the characters formally in the way he would address them in the course of his job.

Letters and diaries

These are often good forms to choose because they give you a definite point in time to work from and this focus helps you sort out the relevant information. You have an upper limit of 850 words, but this could be divided into several short letters or diary entries if you write economically.

Layout is relatively simple to manage. Letters need no more than an address and date at the top and an appropriate **salutation** and signature, although you might have to give some thought to the way characters would address each other in the period context. The use of surnames was much more common in the past than it is now and letters were more formal. Diary entries usually just start with the date.

Like monologues, both these genres are first person narratives and need to convey the character of the writer, implying his or her attitudes and values as the writing unfolds.

Critical response activity

Here is an example of a series of short letters written by a student. How does this creative piece try to create two different voices?

Practical activity

Make a list of minor characters in the texts you have been studying and see how many of them might have a distinctive point of view about the events they witness. You might also suggest what attitudes and judgements would be most likely to be revealed by some or all of these minor characters.

Key terms

Salutation: the opening of a letter that says 'Dear —'.

Examples of informal letters

Letter 1

Hello Mum,

I was wrong to be nervous – Hogwarts is great. Love the place.

Remember we met the world famous Harry Potter at platform nine and three quarters? What am I saying? I bet you've not stopped talking about it! Well, we've become friends. We got chatting on the train. He might be famous, but he's not at all stuck up. Unlike that Malfoy – the guy's a nightmare.

I miss home. I even miss your cooking. This school's more than a little bit draughty as well. It's been nice to finally make some friends though! My brothers drive me nuts sometimes.

I'm in all the same classes as Harry. I can't believe my luck. I think I'm as good at magic as him as well. Or at least I would be if I had a better wand. I can't believe you've sent me off to school with my brother's chipped old one. It's embarrassing Mum! Harry's got a much better wand than me. I know you talked to Dad about it, but they don't cost that much. Please can I have a new one?

I need a dictionary too. Magic spells are hard with a broken wand – but I don't have to be bad at spelling words too (I crack myself up sometimes). Please can I have a new one as well?

The talking hat picked me out as Gryffindor. That's hardly a surprise is it? Just like the rest of the family. Harry's in with us too! The talking hat's not perfect though, it also picked out an annoying girl called Hermione. Can't stand her. All she ever does is whinge.

It'll be nice to get the dictionary and wand by the next owl.

Lots of love,

Ron.

Letter 2

Dear Ron,

I've told you a hundred times – and I will tell you once more. We simply do not have enough money to buy you things every time something new takes your fancy. Even if we could buy them, we wouldn't – you'd end up like that Malfoy. I've never liked him, he's spoilt rotten.

I am so very pleased that you are friends with Harry Potter. Your dad was extremely fond of his mother and father! Now you're friends with him, I'm sure you could ask to borrow his wand and dictionary. He looks like the sort of boy that shares things.

I don't like your tone about my cooking. At all.

There was never any question that you'd be anything other than in Gryffindor. Your father and I are delighted. If we had the money, we'd have opened a bottle of wine to celebrate.

When people are whingeing Ron, it's often because they're down in the dumps. I'm glad you've settled in, but I'm sure it's not been so easy for everyone else. Be nice to Hermione.

I don't like to nag you, Ron, but make sure you work hard, eat properly, clean properly (behind your ears too), treat the teachers with respect, do your homework, earn some house points, make your bed, don't make any inappropriate spells and be nice to your brothers.

Miss you terribly,

Lots of love,

Molly.

Letter 3

Hello Mum,

I'm still looking forward to getting a new wand and dictionary.

I never would have thought it – but I like Hermione after all. I'm not going to tell you all the details, because I'm sure you'd get cross, but she basically saved me and Harry from a spot of bother after a Mountain Troll was running loose in the school! More lively than home, eh?

I've not had any house points yet Mum. I'm gutted. I'm working hard as well. Hermione gets loads and loads. Personally I think it's because she's a girl. I joined the chess club, though, and won all my matches so far.

What do you think of Professor Severus Snape Mum? I can't stand him – and I'm sure he doesn't like me either. I think he's a bit creepy. I don't know how you get to work here, but I think they should be a bit more careful in employing some of the teachers.

You know you're a good cook Mum! You're famous for it.

Lots of love,

Ron.

Commentary

This is a lively piece. You will see that the writer has tried to create two different voices by using different language features. The young Ron Weasley and his mother are both rather stereotyped, but they are differentiated. Ron makes a joke, with the pun on 'spell', and his language is much more colloquial than his mother's. He talks about getting 'loads' of house points and Professor Snape being 'creepy'. He uses ellipses, such as 'Can't stand her!'

Mum is slightly more formal, affectionate but rather bossy. She says she doesn't 'like to nag' but gives a list of proper behaviour.

 ## Practical activity

You probably know the Harry Potter books, even if you are not studying *Harry Potter and the Philosopher's Stone*. As an exercise in style, see whether you can improve on or add to this series of letters from Hogwarts, keeping different voices for different characters. You might imagine Hermione writing home or Hagrid sending for information about dragons. They would use language in very different ways.

Speeches

Speeches for formal occasions are often written out as texts, although they are delivered orally. We are all familiar with the idea that public figures have speech writers who provide the actual text for them to read off a paper or an autocue.

You may already be aware of some of the common techniques of rhetorical speech and the features it tends to use, such as repetition, patterns of three, striking imagery and so on. George Orwell was particularly interested in persuasive language and its effects. Here is a brief and ironic description of a political speech from *Nineteen Eighty-Four*. Orwell makes the speech sound very exaggerated. This is to emphasise the point that the listener, Winston Smith, is sceptical about the Party but at the same time is not able to make a judgement about the nature of the opposition, represented by Goldstein.

Critical response activity

How convincingly does Orwell create the impression of a real speech in this extract from *Nineteen Eighty-Four*?

> Goldstein was delivering his usual venomous attack upon the doctrines of the Party – an attack so exaggerated and perverse that a child should have been able to see through it, and yet just plausible enough to fill one with an alarmed feeling that other people less level-headed than oneself might be taken in by it. He was abusing Big Brother, he was denouncing the dictatorship of the party, he was demanding the immediate conclusion of peace with Eurasia, he was advocating freedom of speech, freedom of the press, freedom of assembly, freedom of thought, he was crying hysterically that the evolution had been betrayed – and all this in rapid polysyllabic speech which was a sort of parody of the habitual style of the orators of the Party.

Commentary

Although they are described rather than presented directly, some of the features of the language of the speech itself are evident. There is the use of emotional language in the terms 'venomous', 'exaggerated', 'perverse' and 'hysterically', and the repetition of the word 'freedom' in a series of parallel phrases with an insistent rhythm.

Utopia, with its fundamental concern for good government, would present a number of opportunities for speech-making, either within the framework of the story itself or on the traveller's return home. Obviously, it would be even less sensible for you to try to imitate the English of the 16th century than that of the 19th.

Newspaper and magazine articles

Newspaper and magazine articles are something you will be familiar with from Unit 1 as well as from daily life. They are third person accounts and they need headlines, sometimes sub-headings, and quotations. It is important to envisage the kind of readership you are writing for because local papers are different from national ones and different publications have very different levels of formality.

Let's think about a literary example from a set text and the changes you would have to make to put it in a modern context.

Like many other writers, Edgar Allan Poe uses imaginary newspaper reports. Poe is actually using the report to introduce all the elements of the puzzle that his detective Dupin will then solve by sheer brain power, so every detail counts. A very brief look at its style will show you that the presentation is different from anything a modern newspaper would use: among other things, it has much more solid unbroken text. The language is, of course, characteristic of its period. No one would now explain that the police had to break in after some 'fruitless attempts to procure admission in the usual manner' and if you tried to write like this it would probably not be effective.

 ## Critical response activity

This extract shows the way Poe introduces the facts of the murder in the Rue Morgue. How similar is this to a modern newspaper account?

> EXTRAORDINARY MURDERS – This morning, about three o'clock, the inhabitants of the Quartier St Roch were aroused from sleep by a succession of terrific shrieks, issuing, apparently, from the fourth story of a house in the Rue Morgue, known to be in the sole occupancy of one Madame L'Espanaye and her daughter, Mademoiselle Camille L'Esplanaye. After some delay, occasioned by fruitless attempts to procure admission in the usual manner, the gateway was broken in with a crowbar, and eight or ten of the neighbors entered, accompanied by two gendarmes. By this time the cries had ceased; but as the party rushed up the first flight of stairs, two or more rough voices, in angry contention, were distinguished, and seemed to proceed from the upper part of the house. As the second landing was reached, these sounds, also, had ceased, and everything remained perfectly quiet. The party spread themselves, and hurried from room to room. Upon arriving at a large back chamber in the fourth story (the door of which being found locked, with the key inside, was forced open), a spectacle presented itself which struck everyone present not less with horror than with astonishment.

Commentary

The corpse of the daughter has been violently forced up the chimney, while the mother's body is found, with its head nearly severed, in a paved yard at the back of the building.

Poe has a sort of headline here, with 'EXTRAORDINARY MURDERS'. Newspapers today might be more sensational, or more informative, with 'Rue Morgue Mayhem' or 'Mother and daughter found dead'. Writing headlines, which often show a highly creative use of language, is an art in itself.

Few modern papers would run a paragraph quite this long and the most popular ones often have very short paragraphs, designed for liveliness and easy reading. The text is normally broken up by quotations. You might have something like 'The cries were terrible', a neighbour said. 'You could hear rough voices shouting, then scream after scream.'

Novels that deal with sensational events may provide good material for newspaper reports. There are a number of points in *Frankenstein* and *The Big Sleep* that could be treated in this way, **but remember that you also have to keep the report relevant to the theme you have been given**. A local newspaper's account of the outbreak of typhus fever at Lowood School might provide a useful insight into *Jane Eyre* but might also be difficult, though not impossible, to fit into the theme of conflict.

 ## Practical activity

Write headlines and quotations for this story to be printed in different newspapers, for example *The Times*, the *Sun* and the *City Express*. It does not have to be set in Paris, although the tall building with only one way in is essential.

147

Scripts

One way in which you might choose to adapt the material of your text into a different genre is by presenting it as a script. If you happen to also be studying media studies or you belong to a theatre group, you might want to use that experience to enrich your study of prose literature. Remember, though, that what is being assessed in your coursework here is your sustained use of the English language in the particular genre you have chosen. Storyboards would not be appropriate.

There are three common kinds of script, offering different problems and opportunities, and each with its own conventions. These are for:

- film or television
- radio
- stage plays.

If you look at a film script, you will probably notice the high number of short scenes and the high ratio of description to dialogue. Film is a very flexible medium and offers great opportunities for conveying information in visual form, but each shot has to be planned. There will usually be less speech than in a stage play. In the example below there is no speech in the first scene. The number of characters and locations used is limited only by the budget.

Radio scripts can also use a large number of characters; actors will often double different parts in different voices. You can use a narrator, but this is often a clumsy device in a play. If you want to avoid using a narrator, everything that the listener needs to understand has to be conveyed through the medium of sound. At the simplest level, to indicate that a character has entered you need another character to greet him or her, or you might use sound patterns such as footsteps. The script has to indicate the use of fades, sound effects, music, etc.

Writing for the stage presents different challenges again. There will be much more dialogue in a play script than in one written for film or television, but the way in which plays are written has to take into consideration the theatrical space available and how many different scenes will be required. Even if elaborate scenery is not used, there have to be far fewer different sets than in a film. This means contriving the way the actors are to be drawn in to the location where the scene is set. Actors need realistic cues and opportunities to come in and go out.

Critical response activity

Because of its strong storyline and dramatic events, there have been a number of professional films made of *Jane Eyre*. Here is the way one student visualised the opening as a film script. What features of **graphology** and language strike you here?

Jane Eyre

Scene 1. Exterior

(Late afternoon on a winter's day, wind blowing squalls of rain through the branches of trees. An establishing shot of a large country house in its own grounds. We move closer to the windows, then in through one of them, where Jane, a small girl of ten, is sitting on the window seat, behind the curtain, holding a book up to catch the last of the fading light. She shivers a little, being obviously cold, but carries on reading.)

Key terms

Graphology: the layout of a text, with use of such features as typeface.

Scene 2. Interior

(Cut to the interior of a large fire-lit room with a group of three children playing a card game round the sofa where their mother is sitting dozing. A servant brings in candles.)

John Reed: Where's Jane?

Georgiana: Oh never mind about her, we don't want her anyway.

John: Where's she gone? I bet she's run off into the rain.

Eliza: She's in the room next door, John. I saw her sneak in there earlier.

John: I'll get her, the little beast.

Scene 3. Interior

(He picks up one of the candles and we follow him through the doorway to a smaller room furnished with bookshelves, a table and some chairs. Eliza follows too. John looks round, puzzled.)

Eliza: Look, she's there in the window seat, reading.

(Jane comes out slowly from behind the curtain.)

Jane: What do you want?

John: Say, 'What do you want, Master Reed?' I want you to come here.

(He sits on the table and roughly pushes Jane in front of him, putting out his tongue as he does so.)

John: What were you doing behind the curtain?

Jane: Reading.

John: *(Snatches book)* Give me that. You've no business to take our books. You're nobody. You're not even a servant. You ought to go out and beg, not live here with gentlemen's children like us. Take that for your cheek!

(He hits her across the head with the book. She falls.)

Jane: I hate you! I hate you! You're wicked and cruel!

John: What! Did you dare say that to me?

(He grabs her by the hair and they struggle. She hits out wildly, catching him in the face.)

John: Mamma! Mamma! Jane's hurting me. Let go!

Eliza: *(Watches from a distance)* Georgiana, go and fetch someone.

(As the scuffle subsides Mrs Reed and a servant come rushing in.)

Servant: Dear! dear! what a fury to fly at Master John!

Mrs Reed: Take her to the red room and lock her in.

Commentary

There are more elaborate descriptions of the scene in this text than you would expect in a play script: these are set in italics. The actual dialogue is set out as it would be in a stage play, with the name of the speaker at the side and then the words spoken next to it.

If you compare this with the novel itself, you will see that the dialogue has been simplified.

25 Writing for a different audience

💡 Different kinds of audience

Audiences may be specialist in a number of ways. They can be defined by readership, such as age or gender, or by special interests, such as music, geography or criminology. To take a rather extreme case, you might imagine General Sternwood, the old man in *The Big Sleep*, writing to *Saga Magazine* (for the over-50s) about his orchids and how he lives in the conservatory with them to keep warm.

A text often has more than one audience, and this is particularly true of anything you write that will be formally assessed. Apart from the primary audience, you are also writing for your teacher, who will be looking out for your ability to be creative and accurate in your use of written English and for suitably chosen material. Students who are writing about gangsters or similar characters sometimes ask whether it is acceptable to use swear words for realism. The answer is that you should write what is appropriate for the subject, genre and audience you have selected, but there is no point in giving unnecessary offence. Always check with your teacher if you are unsure about the suitability of what you have in mind.

One way that you might adapt material for a different audience is by writing a text for children. This is never a soft option, however, and to do it well involves a very skilled use of language. The first problem is that the very term 'children' covers such a wide range of different people, with different abilities and interests at different ages. You have to define an age group specifically and do some basic research in the kind of literature that age group usually reads. Even this does not entirely solve the problem because of the huge variation between individuals. (Jane Eyre, aged ten, had been reading the 18th-century political satire *Gulliver's Travels*.) Some children are capable of reading Victorian novels quite early in junior school, while others will need texts written in relatively simple language several years later. On the other hand, children do not like being patronised any more than anyone else, so the subject matter has to be appropriate for their experience and interests.

The best texts for children, like *Alice's Adventures in Wonderland*, are often inventive and witty. They work on a variety of levels and have something to offer adults, too. It was written by an Oxford lecturer in mathematics and contains a number of puzzles about logic and jokes about death (for example, the Mock Turtle is going to end up literally in the soup). Wider references and double meanings are more likely to be appreciated and understood by the secondary, adult, audience.

Adaptations

Changing the genre by adapting a novel into the format of a play is a common way of making texts accessible to children, as a play can be used with a group and will usually have parts to suit different abilities. There is a potential problem here: while some novels are written in such a way that it is easy to take the dialogue and adapt it, others will need very substantial alteration.

If you look at the confrontation between Jane Eyre and Mrs Reed that follows soon after the short scene we considered above, you will see that using the dialogue without alteration would simply not work as a play, especially a play for children. It goes like this.

> 'I am glad you are no relative of mine: I will never call you aunt again as long as I live. I will never come to see you when I am grown up; and if anyone asks me how I liked you, and how you treated me, I will say the very thought of you makes me sick, and that you treated me with miserable cruelty.'
>
> 'How dare you affirm that, Jane Eyre?'
>
> 'How dare I, Mrs Reed? How dare I? Because it is the *truth*. You think I have no feelings, and that I can do without one bit of love or kindness; but I cannot live so: and you have no pity. I shall remember how you thrust me back – roughly and violently thrust me back – into the red-room, and locked me up there to my dying day; though I was in agony; though I cried out, while suffocating with distress, "Have mercy! Have mercy, aunt Reed!" And that punishment you made me suffer because your wicked boy struck me – knocked me down for nothing. I will tell anybody who asks me questions, this exact tale. People think you are a good woman, but you are bad; hard hearted. *You* are deceitful!'

There is a real sense of the child speaking here, when she says things like 'I will never come to see you when I am grown up.' The language is moving to read, but even so it is too complex to work as a play script, especially for a young audience, and would have to be much simplified, to something more like the version below.

Sample response

 Critical response activity

How has the language of the previous extract been adapted in the following sample response?

Jane:	I'm glad you're not my real aunt. I'll never call you aunt again as long as I live. I won't come and see you when I'm grown up, and if anyone asks me how I liked you, and how you treated me, I'll say the very thought of you makes me sick. You were cruel to me.
Mrs Reed:	How dare you say that, Jane Eyre?
Jane:	How dare I? Because it's the *truth*. You shut me in the red room and you punished me just because John knocked me down. It's you that tells lies.

Commentary

This adapted version uses elisions, such as 'I'm' and 'you're', because this sounds more natural to a modern ear. The unusual word 'affirm' has been changed to the much less colourful 'say'. The sentences are shorter because they are designed not just for a listening audience but for one that is younger too.

The overall effect is that Jane's speech, with its repetitions and emotive language, has been reduced to its core meaning. At the same time some of the historical and social detail of the world of *Jane Eyre* has been diluted.

This script is in no way 'better' English than the original. The adapted version is only a pale shadow of Charlotte Brontë's novel. It has lost the

Practical activity

Read the script aloud, as this is the best test of whether it works or not. If you are able to record a reading of it, that would be even better.

strong, active verbs such as 'thrust' and 'suffocating', and the powerful adverbs 'roughly' and 'violently', as well as the pulsing rhythms that show the child's distress. However, the text is fitted for its new purpose because it has become something that a particular listening audience can grasp easily and this is the main criterion by which will it be judged.

Planning

As part of your coursework you have to show evidence of planning. You should briefly discuss what audience your creative writing coursework is intended for as part of this and note in general terms the kind of changes you have had to make.

- Although you are not expected to produce a detailed commentary on your new text, you might note whether you have been able to try it out on an appropriate audience.
- If you have used existing works as a model, you should give a reference to these.

26 How will the creative writing coursework be assessed?

This chapter covers:

- understanding assessment criteria

- seeing how coursework can be improved on re-drafting.

Criteria for assessment

Here is a brief reminder of the qualities on which creative writing coursework will be judged:

- interest and originality
- relevance to the set theme
- appropriate use of genre
- quality of written English.

Sample response A: *Jane Eyre*

> **Theme: conflict**
>
> Gateshead
>
> 15 May 183–
>
> My dear Mrs Nasmyth,
>
> So much has happened since the day of your marriage when we last met, that neither of us is quite the same person any more. You have your husband and your parishioners to care for, and all the various tasks of managing a house as well as raising poultry and visiting the poor, while the last half year has brought tremendous changes in my own life.
>
> Since, until recently, I had never stirred from Lowood for eight years, you may be surprised to see that this letter is written from Gateshead, and not from Thornfield Hall. I have not deserted my new master nor my little pupil Adele, but I have taken leave of absence from them to pay my last respects to my aunt, Mrs Reed, who died this week.
>
> One should not speak ill of the dead, and I no longer feel that angry hatred towards her that I did as a child, only pity, but I have to admit that I came to Gateshead, when I was summoned here, out of Christian duty rather than out of any love for my aunt. As the coach brought me along the lanes I could not help feeling some natural delight in seeing the white of the mayflower in the hedges and the lambs in the fields, rather than any deep grief, and I was hoping that I would not be delayed too long from returning to my master and to the comfort and security of Thornfield, which has now become my home.
>
> Aunt Reed was not old. Her untimely death was brought about by grief for the death of her own son, John, my former enemy (though enemy no more, since all such conflicts are resolved by death). He bullied me and domineered over me as a child, and as he grew older neither his habits nor his temper improved. He became a lawyer in London, but was much given to wild ways, harassing his mother for money, getting into debt and into prison, and it is thought he may have taken his own life in the end. Still, he was his mother's darling, and the news of his death brought on a stroke, from which she never recovered.
>
> As a lonely little child of ten, I defied Aunt Reed. We confronted one another more like two equals than adult and child, and in bitterness

I told her then that I would never come to see her when I was grown up. Since those days I have been more fortunate in life. I had your protection, and then friendship, at Lowood and in these last months a pleasant home with people that have become dear to me. I offered Aunt Reed my hand in friendship and forgiveness, although she refused it, rambling in her rage, and speaking of guilt and fear. It seems her conscience troubled her violently about her behaviour towards me and the promise she once gave to her husband to look after me when he died.

My old nurse Bessie told me last year that after I was sent away to school a Mr Eyre, my father's brother, came looking for me. Bessie thought he might have been a wine merchant or some such line of business as he was on his way to Madeira in a hurry to look after his affairs. Three years ago he wrote to Gateshead, saying he wished to make me his heir, but Aunt Reed told him I was dead. This is the lie that was troubling her conscience. Is it not strange, that she could hate me so much as to do this?

I have stayed on after her funeral a little to help my cousins Georgiana and Eliza to settle their affairs, then Gateshead will be shut up until it can be sold or a tenant can be found for it. I have also occupied such leisure as I had by drawing. I was so pleased to hear that the little picture I gave you hangs in your parlour and gives you pleasure. One day I hope to see you again, in spite of the distance.

Yours affectionately

Jane Eyre

(701 words)

Commentary

Although almost the whole of its material is taken from the novel and re-phrased, this letter gives a careful account of Jane Eyre's movements. It summarises the facts of this part of the narrative, putting together details from different chapters of the text. The timing is carefully worked out from evidence in Brontë's novel, and brief touches of historical background are provided where the letter refers to Mrs Nasmyth's likely occupations. It is original in its exploration of Jane's feelings on the journey and its use of setting.

The letter attempts to convey Jane's essential honesty, to give a faint hint of her growing feelings for Rochester in the way she mentions Thornfield Hall and to suggest a relationship with the former Miss Temple. It deals with the set theme of conflict by references to John Reed as well as to Jane's aunt.

Standard English is used, although the language is sometimes a little more formal than most modern writing. This is so that the letter will not appear anachronistic. For example, the word 'parlour' for a sitting room is no longer common and Jane does not use elisions. She addresses her friend relatively formally as 'Mrs Nasmyth' and signs 'Yours affectionately', reflecting the manners of the time.

It is likely that this coursework would achieve a grade in the top band because of its relevance to the set theme, its appropriate use of genre and its controlled use of written English.

AQA Examiner's tip

When you use information from the set texts to create a new document, do not lift whole phrases and sentences from the original unless you have a special reason for doing so. When you put these into the new text, the seams will show. Make notes from the original text and then put these into your own words.

Sample response B: 'The Purloined Letter'

Theme: the deceiving appearance

I must retrieve the letter.

An incident has occurred with a certain Minister D— that may leave me in <u>an uncompromising</u> position. A while ago a certain letter was taken in plain view <u>from my person</u> and kept out of reach. So I employed a Monsieur G a prefect of the Parisian Police <u>into</u> my services to retrieve the purloined letter, for all the good it was worth.

Upon meeting this prefect he seemed very eager and willing to take on the task, for a fee of course. But as time went by he seemed more and more unfit for the task than I had ever <u>regarded</u>. So, desperate to get the letter back, I raised his fee with the hope that this would encourage his search for the letter to become more <u>expedient</u>, but still no such luck, when all of a sudden fortune, <u>shined</u> down on me.

A man named Dupin took pity on me, and in his suspicions <u>under went</u> a mission to retrieve the letter. Dupin had reasons of his own for helping me. He had said 'D—, at Vienna once, did me an evil turn, which I had told him quite good-humouredly, that I should remember'. But D— was not just holding a grudge, he was also a clever man. These are dangerous but useful qualities to have on my side.

So due to the lack of success from Monsieur G, although Dupin had <u>gave</u> sound advice on his behalf about the letter, Dupin <u>continued ahead</u> with the task. He visited the despicable Minister D— under false pretences that he was socially calling on his old friend. In <u>perusing</u> the apartment Dupin found my letter upon a card rack hanging from a brass knob; it would be too daring a move to snatch it at once. So he left a snuff box in the hope that he would return with the intention to this time definitely take the letter. Upon calling on Minister D— he <u>acted deceivingly to reminisce on the day before conversation</u> they discussed.

Much to Minister D—'s dismay outside Dupin had paid a 'drunkard' to cause a scene distracting Minister D—'s attention <u>to</u> the matter at hand. Swiftly Dupin switched my letter for a false copy and placed it in his pocket. Ignorant <u>to</u> the fact, Dupin's last action would be Minister D—'s downfall.

A second time Monsieur G visited Dupin with the news of still having not found the letter but gaining a raise in his fee. Monsieur G said to Dupin, 'a very liberal reward – I don't like to say how much, precisely; but one thing I will say, is that I wouldn't mind giving my individual cheque for fifty thousand francs to anyone who could obtain me the letter.' Willing to give up his money for the sake of his reputation, which could be questionable in the incompetence of missing a letter that stands right in front of his nose.

With regard to the comment <u>of</u> payment, my friend Dupin asked Monsieur G to write him a cheque, and in return he would give him the letter that he had unsuspectingly apprehended from Minister D—. In doing so Dupin gave Monsieur G the purloined letter and Monsieur G raced off <u>out the door</u>. At the time of Monsieur G's absence the only people present <u>where </u>Dupin and his friend. When <u>Dupin's</u> friend quizzed him on the full facts, Dupin proceeded to converse with him, explaining in detail the full story.

I fortunately got the purloined letter back and I will now see to it that Minister D—'s reputation is destroyed.

(603 words)

Commentary

This draft example of coursework is more ambitious in its choice of subject. It tells the story of Poe's 'The Purloined Letter' from the point of view of the woman from whom it was stolen, which is a perfectly valid approach. It uses the theme of the deceiving appearance and it shows understanding of Poe's text.

However, although the account of Dupin's retrieving the letter is coherent, it does not actually add very much to the original story. It substitutes the woman's first person narrative for Dupin's, but mostly summarises the account of the actual retrieval of the letter given by Dupin himself.

The draft attempts to recreate 19th-century English – something that it is exceptionally difficult to do successfully. It would probably be better to alter the key word 'purloined', which is an uncommon usage in modern standard English, to 'stolen' from the start. The practice of giving names by initials, as if to protect the anonymity of real characters, is also now very old-fashioned. Credible French names would immediately have the effect of making the story more plausible to a modern reader.

The weakest point of the draft is its misuse of language. Some of the mistakes or inelegancies of grammar and vocabulary have been underlined. As it stands, this coursework would not score high marks and needs re-drafting.

Some suggestions for further development of this piece could include:

- The woman must be of high rank, as the letter was stolen 'from the royal apartments'. The writer could give some hints as to who she actually is – a princess or even a queen, perhaps. This information does not necessarily have to be historically correct, but one possibility is to represent her as a real person, with a real historical background. This would need some research.

- The part of the story she has actually taken part in is the stealing of the letter, rather than its recovery. The writer could make more of the scene in the 'royal boudoir', when the letter actually disappears. There is scope to make something more of the appearance of the Minister, D—, and the way he behaves.

- The woman's character needs to be developed more fully. At the moment there is little said about her emotions, apart from irritation at G's incompetence and a very brief expression of her desire to take vengeance on D—. By the time the letter is recovered, she has been in the power of D— for 'eighteen months'. How has she reacted during this time?

- The writer could give some hints of what the letter contains. It seems to be a political plot, but it could be compromising in other ways.

Practical activity

Put this text into correct standard modern English, keeping the basic information the same.

Creative writing coursework

Your new coursework text has several possible audiences. When you have written your first draft, and put it through the spell check, wait a couple of days and then read it aloud to yourself. Does it sound right? You will probably find that you want to make small alterations and additions at this stage.

Next, ask other people to read it – particularly people from the kind of audience it is written for – and to give you their honest reactions. If you are writing for children, find a child of the right age. The best person to give you an opinion of your writing will be a critical friend – that is, someone who will offer an honest evaluation of both the strengths and the weaknesses of your work in a constructive way. You yourself need to evaluate the quality of the feedback that is offered: do not accept only what you want to hear and reject unwelcome comments.

Finally, imagine yourself reading it aloud to your teacher, whose responsibility it is to apply the assessment criteria and pass on your coursework marks to AQA. Would he or she be impressed? Be prepared to re-draft sections that do not work as well as they might. Take care to avoid careless technical errors such as misspellings and faulty punctuation. Remember that your work may be read by an external moderator appointed by AQA. It is this person's responsibility to approve or, if necessary, recommend adjustments to the marks awarded.

Present your work neatly, with a title page.

Further reading

Crystal, David, *The Story of English*, Penguin, 2005

Forster, E. M., *Aspects of the Novel*, Penguin Classics, 2005

Lodge, David, *The Art of Fiction: Illustrated from Classic and Modern Texts*, Penguin, 1992

Orwell, George, 'Politics and the English Language' in *Inside the Whale and Other Essays*, Penguin, 1991

Truss, Lynne, *Eats, Shoots and Leaves*, Profile Books, 2003

Revising for the examinations

The most important prerequisite for achieving the highest possible marks is to enter the examination room thoroughly well prepared for what you need to do. This includes knowing your set texts thoroughly, understanding which assessment objectives apply to each question and understanding how to apply relevant techniques so that you put all of your knowledge and skills to their most effective use. Revision for the examinations is important but must be seen as the culmination of many months of consistent hard work. A couple of weeks' intensive revision can never be an adequate substitute for consistent application throughout the whole course of study.

Re-reading the relevant sections of this book will highlight what you need to do in the examination for each unit but there is some general advice that can be applied to all of the examinations you will face in English subjects.

Know the rules

Make sure that you know the following:

- How long is the examination?
- How many sections does the examination contain?
- How many questions do you need to tackle and from which sections?
- How many marks are available for each question?
- How long should be spent on each question?
- Is it an open book or a closed book examination (meaning, are you allowed to refer to an unmarked copy of a set book during the examination or must you memorise quotations and rely only on memory for making references to the book during the examination)?
- Which Assessment Objectives apply to the examination?

Mind the GAP

Some examination papers require you to write in a creative/imaginative/transformative mode. For such questions you need to plan very carefully to ensure that the writing you produce is appropriate to the task which is presented to you. The three key considerations are:

Genre

Audience

Purpose

Genre

The task may require you to write a letter, a report, an extract from a novel or short story, a newspaper report or a magazine article, for example. Make sure that you produce writing that matches the specified genre. Your own reading should be sufficiently wide to enable you to be familiar with a wide range of genres and sub-genres so that you are able to make informed decisions in the examination about what genre conventions you need to incorporate into your writing to make it as authentic as possible.

Audience

The task will also specify (directly or by implication) the target readership for your answer. You may be required, for example, to write for a general adult audience if your task is to produce a serious report for a national daily newspaper such as *The Times* or the *Guardian*. Your approach would need to be modified if you were asked to write for the *Mirror* or the *Sun*, to reflect the different audiences and the distinctive approaches of tabloid newspapers.

Purpose

The task specified on the examination paper will also identify a purpose for your writing and you need to be quite sure that you reflect that purpose accurately in what you produce. You may, for example, be asked to analyse a problem; it would be a serious mistake to interpret that as a request for a persuasive piece which embraces a particular solution and tries to influence readers to accept that solution to the exclusion of all others.

As with your judgements about genre and audience, your interpretation of the purpose of the task should be firmly rooted in the wording of the task. Examination questions are worded carefully to make them as clear as possible, *not* to try to catch you out. Candidates' misjudgements about genre, audience and purpose invariably arise from a failure to read the question carefully or a wilful insistence on answering a different question from the one set.

The triple T test

For all questions it is helpful to apply the triple T test. Have you understood the following aspects, which are all required for success?

- task
- timing
- techniques.

Task

Any examination is a test of what you *know*, what you *understand* and what you *can do*. Knowing the texts you have studied is vital, but in itself is not enough to guarantee that you will do well in the examinations. On one level, knowing the text may simply mean that you know the plot well and can recount it faithfully in fine detail. However, your examination question will definitely *not* ask you simply to re-tell the story of a novel, a play or a poem. If that is what you do in your answer you will severely limit the credit which an examiner will be able to give your work. Knowing the text well at AS level means knowing the plot well and knowing about the writer's distinctive uses of language and structure in his or her exploration of themes and ideas.

Make sure that you understand exactly what the question or task requires you to do. The first and the most obvious step – but one that is often neglected by candidates – is to read the question closely and analyse it in terms of what you need to do in order to produce a relevant and effective response.

Timing

You need to know exactly how much time you can afford to spend planning and writing each answer. In examinations that consist of two or more sections, it is vital that you relate the time you devote to each question to the number of marks available. Depending on the nature of the question or task, you need to spend time planning your response. In the case of questions on unseen texts, it is vital that you allocate enough time to read and annotate the text thoroughly. Refer carefully to the advice given earlier in this book about the techniques that need to be applied to particular questions in the examination.

Technique

When you write about a set text or a text encountered for the first time in an examination paper, you need to demonstrate your understanding of those aspects of the text that are relevant to the question or task. The essential strategy is to be able to identify relevant aspects of the text, to select relevant evidence to illustrate those aspects and finally to write about your chosen evidence in such a way as to fulfil the requirements of the question. This process is shown in the diagram below.

Point   ⟶   Evidence   ⟶   Explanation

If you approach your examinations with a firm grasp of this approach, you will make the best possible use of your knowledge and understanding and have the confidence that you will achieve a grade that reflects your abilities.

Glossary

A

Adverbial phrase: a phrase containing information about how, where or when an action takes place.

Anecdotes: short accounts of an interesting or amusing incident or event.

Antithesis: the juxtaposition of contrasting words or phrases to create a sense of balance or opposition between conflicting ideas.

Archaic/archaism: marked by the characteristics of an earlier period, or fallen into disuse.

Argument: a connected series of ideas, backed up by relevant facts, which try to make a case, and convince us of its truth and validity.

Asyndetic list: a form of list, in which there is no conjunction (such as 'and' or 'but') separating the final two items. This can give an open-ended feel to the list, perhaps suggesting there is more that could be added. The opposite to this is a syndetic list, such as 'At the market I bought apples, oranges, pears *and* bananas'.

Audience: the readers of or listeners to a text.

C

Caesura: a pause in the middle of a line of verse, usually indicated by a punctuation mark.

Clause: a construction that contains, as a minimum, both a subject and a verb. It can stand alone as a sentence, as in 'I bought a book' (main or independent clause) but may be part or a larger construction, as in 'when I went out' (subordinate or dependent clause).

Closed book examination: an examination in which you are not allowed to take copies of the books you have studied into the examination room.

Coherence: the continuity of organisation and meaning that unifies a spoken or written text.

Coinages: newly invented words.

Collocation: an established phrase which places words in a fixed order.

Colloquialism: language that may be used in ordinary conversation but is not appropriate in formal or literary contexts.

Complex sentence: a sentence with two or more clauses linked by subordinating conjunctions.

Conditional: a clause which qualifies a statement, usually introduced by 'if', 'provided that' or similar conjunctions.

Conjunction: a word used to connect phrases and clauses within a sentence.

Connotations: the associations and feelings that words evoke in addition to their basic meanings, for example, although 'smile' and 'grin' refer to similar facial expressions, the word 'smile' has connotations of warmth and friendship, whereas the word 'grin' may have connotations of falseness, malice or stupidity about it.

Context: the social situation, including audience and purpose, in which language is used; this situation is an important influence of the language choices made by speakers and writers.

Context dependence: those aspects of a text whose meanings depend on an understanding of the circumstances in which it has been produced.

Coordinating conjunction: words such as 'and', 'but' and 'or', which are used to link together independent clauses; for example, in the sentence 'he likes swimming but he hates shopping' each clause could stand independently.

D

Declarative sentence: a sentence that makes a statement.

Denotation: the primary, literal meaning of a word or phrase.

Diachronic change/variation: the changes in language over time.

Dialect: a variety of a particular language, characterised by distinctive features of accent, grammar and vocabulary, used by people from a particular geographical area or social group.

Dialogue: direct speech between two or more characters in a narrative.

Discourse markers: words or phrases that give structure to speech or writing, enabling a writer or speaker to develop ideas, relate points to each other or move from one idea to the next, e.g. however, likewise, in addition, in contrast, nevertheless, furthermore, therefore.

Discourse analysis: systematic study of a text, often applied specifically to spoken language.

Discursive writing: exploring and discussion a topic or issue – usually non-fiction.

Doublets: pairs of words with the same or similar meaning, used for effect.

Dynamic verbs: verbs that describe physical actions, such as 'to jump'.

E

Elision: the running together of words or the omission of parts of words, such as 'gonna' for 'going to' or 'y'know' for 'you know'.

Ellipsis/elliptical: the omission of part of a sentence. 'Hope you get well soon' is an example of ellipsis, as the pronoun 'I' has been left out. Ellipsis can also be represented by three dots (…) to indicate the missing part of the sentence.

End-stopped line: a line of verse with a punctuation mark at the end of the line to indicate a pause.

Enjambement: continuity of the sense and rhythm from one line of verse to the next without end-stopping.

Episode: an isolated event, separated from the main series of events.

Etymology: the study of the origins and development of words.

Expletive: a swear word or phrase.

 F

Faction: works in which real events are used as a basis for fictional narrative.

Field-specific lexis: specialised vocabulary relating to a particular topic or subject.

Figurative: words or phrases whose meaning is different from their literal sense.

Figurative language: language that draws an imaginative comparison between what is described and something else, resulting in an image that cannot literally be true, but may enable us to perceive something more vividly or allow us greater insight into the story or character.

First-person narrative: a story that is narrated by a character from within the story itself, using the pronoun 'I'.

Free indirect speech: a form of indirect speech that reports the words of a character, but omits the reporting clauses such as 'he said that …'

 G

Genre: a class or category of text, with its particular conventions of language, form and structure; for example, short story, science fiction novel, Shakespearean comedy.

Genre conventions: the usual characteristics of a particular genre (or type) of text

Graphology: the layout of a text, with use of such features as typeface.

 H

Homophone: literally, sounding the same: words of similar pronunciation but different meaning/spelling.

Hyperbole: exaggeration used for impact and effect.

 I

Idiom: a commonly-used phrase whose meaning is not related to the literal sense of its words.

Imperative sentence: a sentence that gives a command.

Infinitive/infinitive clause: the part of a verb usually preceded by 'to'; a clause containing such a verb.

Intensifier: a word (like 'very' or 'much') that intensifies the meaning of the adjective or adverb to which it is attached.

Initialism: an abbreviation formed by a set of initials standing for a longer phrase.

Interrogative sentence: a sentence that asks a question.

Intertextuality: the way one text partly depends on reference to another text for its meaning.

Intransitive: a verb that does not need to be followed by an object.

Ironic: the adjective describing something that contains irony.

Irony: a mismatch or discrepancy between what is written and what is actually meant.

 L

Lexis: choice of vocabulary in text/'the total stock of words in a language' [COD].

Lexical field: a broad area of meaning that includes a number of different words or phrases.

Loan word: 'a word adopted from a foreign language with little or no modification' [COD].

Lyric poem: a short poem exploring a feeling or reflection (rather than telling a narrative).

 M

Metaphor: a direct comparison drawn between two different things as if the subject really is the thing it is being compared to: for example, 'her hands were ice-blocks' or 'he was a bear of a man'.

Modal verb: 'an auxiliary verb expressing necessity or possibility' [COD].

 N

Narrative: an account of connected events.

Non-fluency features: the natural 'mistakes' of speech, which include hesitations, self-corrections and repetition.

Noun phrase: a phrase consisting of a noun and any adjectives and articles attached to it.

O

Object: in grammar, the person or thing being directly affected by the action.

Objective: a view point which attempts to achieve neutrality (c.f. subjective).

Omniscient narrator: an omniscient narrator has a complete overview of the story, and can move freely between different characters and scenes, with full knowledge of everything that happens.

Open book examination: an examination in which you are allowed to take unmarked copies of the books you have studied into the examination room and refer to them if you wish as you write your answers.

P

Paralinguistic features: non-verbal aspects of communication such as intonation or pausing, which work alongside language to help speakers to convey meaning effectively.

Pastiche: a work that imitates the style of another work.

Pastoral: a list of words/phrases without the use of any conjunctions.

Pathetic fallacy: the literary technique of representing internal human states and emotions through the description of external details such as landscape and weather. In this sense 'pathetic' means arousing sympathy: in other words, the term 'pathetic' suggests that the landscape is in *sympathy* with a character's feelings. The word 'fallacy' reminds us that this supposed relationship is a deception: inanimate landscapes and weather systems cannot truly echo the feelings and emotion of people, even though writers might have us believe otherwise.

Pentameter: a line with five stressed syllables.

Personification: a form of metaphor in which human qualities are attributed to things that are non-human: for example, 'the windows stared blankly'.

Phonetic spelling: the spelling of words to represent how they are pronounced (e.g. '…'elp me orf this 'orse').

Phrasal verb: a phrase consisting of a verb and an adverb or preposition.

Plot: the main sequence of narrative events in a story, organised in such a way as to create links between them and maintain interest for the reader.

Politeness marker: a word or phrase which introduces politeness into discourse (please, thank you, etc.).

Polysyllabic words: words with more than one syllable.

Pragmatics: the study of what is implied and understood by language use in context.

Prefix: an element placed at the beginning of a word to adjust or qualify its meaning.

Premodification/premodifier: the placing of a modifying word or phrase before the subject of the modification.

Prosodic features: the vocal aspects of speech (volume, stress, intonation, speed) that contribute meaning.

Protagonist: the leading character, or one of the major characters, in a literary text.

Qualitative adjectives: words that give information about the qualities of the noun they describe, e.g. a *frail* figure.

Question tags: the short questions frequently 'tagged' on to the end of spoken utterances.

Register: a type of language defined in terms of its appropriateness for the type of activity or context in which the language is used, including the purpose, audience and situation of a piece of speech or writing.

Rhetoric: the technique of using language persuasively in order to influence the opinions and behaviour of an audience.

Salutation: the opening of a letter, such as Dear —.

Sarcasm: use of ironic language with an intention to hurt or mock.

Semantics: the study of the meanings of words.

Semantic change: the change in meaning of a particular word over time.

Semantic field: a group of words within a text relating to the same topic; for example, tyre, brake, pedal, starter motor and exhaust are all from the semantic field of cars.

Simile: an imaginative comparison drawn between two different things, linked with the words 'like' or 'as': for example, 'her hands were as cold as ice' or 'the man was like a bear'.

Stance: the point of view adopted by the narrator of a text

Standard English: the vocabulary and grammar of English generally regarded as 'correct'.

Subject: In grammar, the person or thing acting on the verb

Subjective: A personal, possibly biased point of view (c.f. objective).

Subordinate clause: words such as 'although', 'because' or 'unless', which are used to link a main clause to a subsidiary or dependent one.

Subordinating conjunction: words such as 'although', 'because' or 'unless', which are used to link a main clause to a subsidiary or dependent one: for example, in the sentence 'Although it was raining, the party was a success', the

phrase 'although it was raining' is secondary in importance to the main point of the sentence – 'the party was a success'.

Symbol: an object or action that, beyond its basic meaning, represents an idea or concept.

Syndetic list: a form of list in which a conjunction (such as 'and' or 'but') separates the final two items. For example, 'At the market I bought apples, oranges, pears *and* bananas.'

Syntax: the structure of sentences.

Synchronic variation: the variation in language use at any given point in time.

Synonym: a word that has the same or similar meaning to another word; for example, 'smile' and 'grin' are synonyms, as they mean more or less the same thing, but carry different **connotations**.

Synonymy: two or more words or phrases having very similar meanings.

Tetrameter: a line with four stressed syllables.

Theme: the subject of a piece of writing, often representing an idea that recurs during the narrative.

Third-person narrative: narrative using 'he', 'she' and 'they', as distinct from first-person narrative, which uses 'I' and 'we'. The story is told from a less personal point of view than a first-person narrative, such as from the author's own perspective.

Transcript: an exact written representation of speech.

Triplet: a pattern of three repeated words or phrases.

Voice: the distinctive manner of expression that is characteristic of a particular writer or speaker, or of a created literary character.

Index

Entries in **bold** are key terms